MAKING JUSTICE OUR PROJECT

.

Making Justice Our Project

Teachers Working toward Critical Whole Language Practice

Edited by

CAROLE EDELSKY
Arizona State University

National Council of Teachers of English
1111 W. Kenyon Road, Urbana, Illinois 61801-1096

Staff Editor: Tom Tiller
Prepress Services: Precision Graphics
Interior Design: Jenny Jensen Greenleaf
Cover Design: Carlton Bruett

NCTE Stock Number: 30445-3050

It is the policy of NCTE in its journals and other publications to provide a
forum for the open discussion of ideas concerning the content and the
teaching of English and the language arts. Publicity accorded to any particular point of view does not imply endorsement by the Executive
Committee, the Board of Directors, or the membership at large, except in
announcements of policy, where such endorsement is clearly specified.

Library of Congress Cataloging-in-Publication Data

Making justice our project : teachers working toward critical whole
    language practice / edited by Carole Edelsky.
        p.   cm.
    "NCTE stock number 30445"—T.p. verso.
    Includes bibliographical references and index.
    ISBN 0-8141-3044-5 (paper)
    1. Language experience approach in education. 2. Critical
pedagogy.   I. Edelsky, Carole.
LB1576.M3613   1994
370.11'5—dc21   99-41266
                                                            CIP

CONTENTS

FOREWORD

BESS ALTWERGER
Towson State University

ELIZABETH R. SAAVEDRA
University of New Mexico

The whole language movement is in crisis—not because of a
fatal flaw in its theoretical foundation or due to insurmount-
able weaknesses in its pedagogical framework. Even the vicious
conservative attacks on whole language, so vigorously promoted
by the mainstream media, are not fully responsible for this crisis.
Indeed, most of the criticisms and accusations behind these
attacks could easily be countered and discredited by knowledgeable whole language professionals. The crisis in whole language
is due in large part to the whole language movement itself—for
its failure to assert its own political identity, anticipate and prepare for the inevitable conservative backlash, and openly ally
itself with the larger progressive struggle for social and cultural
justice. Had the whole language movement taken a different
road, it might now be in a much stronger position to use the current attacks as opportunities for exposing the reactionary politics
of the opposition and for raising the demand for equitable and
democratic education for all students. This volume, however,
which is written by whole language teachers who boldly assert
the politics of their pedagogy, represents the hope for the future
of whole language. Within these pages we can find the ideas and
inspiration necessary for creating for students democratic and
critical spaces which foster meaningful and transformative learning. But to realize the hope embodied in this book, we must first
critically examine the history of the whole language movement
and begin to chart a new course for the future.

The whole language movement began as a grassroots effort by teachers and teacher educators to develop a pedagogical framework that would adequately reflect the enormous paradigmatic shifts occurring in the fields of literacy, linguistics, and language development. Together, they studied theory and interrogated classroom practice in a variety of scholarly contexts, including university seminars, school-based teacher study groups, and extended workshops. Classroom changes usually resulted from carefully examined knowledge and beliefs, and were accomplished at some professional risk by the teachers involved. Because whole language took an affirmative stance in asserting strong theoretical and practical principles for guiding literacy and learning, it was often viewed by those in positions of power and authority as being an oppositional pedagogy. Most whole language teachers quickly learned that creating more collaborative, inquiry-based, meaning-centered classrooms and valuing student experience and knowledge constituted an enormous threat to the existing power structure and hierarchy of schools. Meeting with resistance and opposition in their educational communities, whole language teachers formed local support networks, later known as TAWL (Teachers Applying Whole Language) groups, in order to continue learning and agitating for change.

Early whole language advocates could not afford the luxury of ignoring the political nature of their pedagogy, for professional survival depended on anticipating and preparing for the struggles they would face. Testing, tracking, standardization, and imposed curriculum—all of which were challenged by whole language principles—were fiercely defended by the school establishment and consequently exposed as tools of power and dominance. Particularly in poor and oppressed communities, the battle for whole language led to a clearer understanding of the role of traditional schools in maintaining race and class inequities. In short, an education in whole language meant an education in the politics of schooling in America. And it was at this early point in the movement that whole language had the greatest potential for identifying itself as a critical and liberatory pedagogy—a movement for educational and social justice.

What happened? Ironically, "whole language" became too popular. With increasing frequency, it became the topic of numerous articles and professional texts, with noted publishers devoting much of their education collections to the subject. Conference programs for organizations like NCTE and IRA offered an increasing number of sessions on topics related to whole language. Local TAWL groups planned regional conferences devoted entirely to sharing expertise among teachers. Gradually, whole language became a national phenomenon, the most intriguing and appealing new trend in education since open education. What began as a local, grassroots movement of knowledgeable and courageous educators—who were struggling for the rights of teachers and students to control learning and teaching—was becoming just another trendy, new approach to literacy instruction.

And everyone—including whole language's natural adversaries, such as state school systems and basal publishers—began to jump on the bandwagon, finding some set of associated methodological practices palatable, pliable, or profitable enough to swallow. In this way, they could maintain their control over the reproductive function of schools in our society and diffuse whole language as a pedagogy of resistance and transformation. By the early 1990s, whole language, as it was presented in district inservice workshops and basal texts, had become so diluted, so tame, that it became hard to distinguish it from previous traditional paradigms. Methods and materials (shared reading, trade books, big books, journals, authentic assessment) which once sprang from theoretical principles and progressive politics, were adapted to quasi-behaviorist theory and status quo politics, and became the "whole" of the whole language movement. School districts adopted the "whole language approach" as their official curriculum, mandating it and imposing it on teachers, regardless of theoretical orientation or understanding. While some rejoiced at this institutional acceptance, others mourned the loss of whole language as a pedagogy of resistance and struggle. Whole language had been appropriated by the very system of power and authority that it had originally opposed, now rendering it safe and impotent, and widely appealing to educators and institutions representing a broad, at best liberal, ideology. A pedagogy of power had become the pedagogy of the powerful.

A serious consequence of the appropriation and institutionalization of whole language was the shift in its cultural identity.

Early in the movement, whole language educators took clear positions on the rights of all students to their linguistic and cultural heritage and against any institutionalized systems, such as homogeneous reading tracks, basal hierarchies, and standardized testing, which served to sort students on the basis of race, class, or culture. Within local school communities in Michigan, Arizona, New Mexico, and the Navajo Nation, whole language teachers clearly stood with the poor and disenfranchised in the battle to democratize schools. Through writing workshops, literature studies, and inquiry projects, whole language classrooms gave voice to students who had traditionally been silenced in school. Sterile, culturally biased basals were replaced with multicultural literature that represented, extended, and even challenged the cultural experiences of students.

Gradually, however, as whole language gained institutional and commercial acceptance, and as greater numbers of less knowledgeable or committed educators jumped on the trendy whole language bandwagon, the movement came to be identified with the white, privileged, dominant culture. Though some whole language theorists and teachers continued to discuss issues of cultural and social justice in their writing and presentations, their politicized voices became less audible within the whole language community. Sessions at local and national whole language conferences which dealt with cultural topics such as bilingual literacy development were often ill attended by the increasingly white, middle-class attendees. Instead of building alliances with organizations such as the National Coalition of Educational Activists and other progressive groups to fight for educational equity, the now sizable whole language movement grew politically quiet, choosing to protect its fragile alliance with the educational establishment. Many educational activists and teachers of color grew increasingly alienated from whole language, viewing it as the new darling of the same oppressive system. Fueling the rejection of whole language were educators such as Lisa Delpit and Maria De La Luz Reyes, who criticized process-oriented, whole language practices as inappropriate and even harmful to children of color. Prominent whole language educators responded to these arguments, but it was too late to reverse the damage done to the credibility of whole language as a pedagogy in service of cultural justice and equity.

Such was the state of the whole language movement when the inevitable conservative backlash erupted. Having failed to build strong alliances with progressive and activist educational communities, and having cowered away from a strong social and political agenda, the whole language movement had only the educational establishment to protect it. Predictably, state and local school systems abandoned whole language with record speed, citing poor test scores as justification. They immediately offered whole language as the sacrificial lamb, diverting the blame for its failures away from the criminal inequities of the American educational system. Without official sanction, teachers have also abandoned whole language in droves. Those who only succumbed to the mandate of whole language, never accepting it is a paradigm, are understandably happy to be ending their charade, relieved to be returning to the easy life of skills and phonics programs. What seemed to be a strong and unified movement was in large part an illusion, created through mandate, coercion, and the simple allure of fashion. But for those educators who remain steadfast in their commitment to the theoretical principles and progressive potential underlying whole language, this crisis is a great opportunity to reclaim whole language as a pedagogy of resistance.

Whole language educators must once again acknowledge the political role that literacy plays in maintaining systems of power and domination in a class society. With the current return to homogeneous tracking, standardized testing, hierarchical basal schemes, and state-approved textbook adoption lists, this political role of literacy, which whole language threatened to disrupt, has been firmly reinstated. Those teachers who are struggling to maintain their whole language perspectives must understand that in doing so they are not only defending an instructional model for literacy, but a political stance toward education. Classroom literacy never be politically neutral. Literacy can be taught either as a tool of critical inquiry or of passive transmission. It can be a vehicle for posing and solving important social problems or for accepting official explanations and solutions. The organization of classroom life, the way learning is assessed, the materials and practices used for instruction may all either reinforce hierarchical systems of authority and power or demonstrate principles of critical democracy and justice. The conservative right understands the political nature of literacy only too well and, in collaboration with the American school establishment and the American media, will continue its efforts to destroy any educational movement, such as whole language, which threatens its political agenda.

Whole language must become part of a larger educational effort to transform education and society in the direction of equity and social justice. With renewed intellectual rigor, whole language educators must study critical theory, feminist theory, and anti-racist literature to broaden our knowledge base. We must begin to see ourselves not just as whole language educators, but as educational activists with clear pedagogical principles. Through coalitions with other progressive educational and community groups we must rededicate ourselves to restoring hope and promise to this country's children—of every color, class, culture, gender, language, and ability level. The teachers in this book have already begun their new journey. May their stories inspire us all to join them!

Introduction

CAROLE EDELSKY
Arizona State University

This book presents examples of educators who are bringing together perspectives that, as Shannon (1990) has documented, have a history of separation: whole language and critical pedagogy. The intent is to offer rich descriptions of practice, not as recipes for how to do it, but rather as a vision of what might be done. For whole language educators, that vision would be of holistic classrooms where students negotiate curricular issues and make significant choices about their learning *and also* where the teacher's side of the negotiations and the teacher's choices foreground systems of privilege and struggles for justice; where students learn written language through really using language *and also* where they study the political implications of *how* language is used. For critical pedagogues, the vision would be of classrooms where equity is on the front burner *and also* where curriculum is broadly open to students' choices; where the political meanings of language-in-use are examined *and also* where the teacher has socio-psycholinguistic–based theoretical reasons for making sure that literacy is developed through use rather than being objectified as something to be taught.

These possible visions point to gaps in each perspective. By and large, what whole language educators fail to reflect on sufficiently is the non-neutrality of curricular choices, the historical and cultured (media-sponsored, corporate interest–supporting) nature of individual interests. By and large, what critical educators fail to interrogate sufficiently is the dominant ideology of teaching as method (rather than, for example, teaching as material display of theoretical and philosophical—as well as ideological—orientations) and the origins and implications of the prevailing view of reading as word getting.

The teachers who have contributed to this volume are filling those gaps. They have reflected on and interrogated those notions. And they are continuing to do so because they aren't "finished." That is, no one who has written for this volume, certainly including myself, would say that he or she has completely figured out how to resolve the tensions involved in bringing these two perspectives together. In the best sense, this is a work in progress, one available for public view before the drywall has been put up. Some of the contributors have been particularly candid about what they are still working on; for example, avoiding assigning exercises, promoting more skillful language use, accommodating the outside community's desires, going beyond the surface in critique, and dealing with school bureaucracies. A careful reading will reveal other unresolved issues that are implied rather than foregrounded. Indeed, this volume *en toto* is an acknowledgment of some of what I am still working on (along with other critical whole language educators): the whiteness and middle classness of whole language's image.

That image is both correct and mistaken. What's wrong with the image is that whole language as theory-based practice *is* attractive to some minority educators and minority communities, and so it *does* offer a rich and valuable educational experience to many minority students; whole language as a theoretical perspective *does* incorporate minority and pro-minority scholars' views of the intersect of language, culture, and education into its basic premises, and so it *could* be a truly multicultural, multilingual movement. But it isn't. That is what's right about the image. That is what Bess Altwerger and Elizabeth Saavedra are talking about in the Preface. That is what is on view in this volume. Where are the African American whole language teachers who are also critical pedagogues who might write about their practice? The critical Asian American teachers who also work from holistic stances? The Native Americans with both perspectives? The lesbian and gay critical whole language contributors? The physically disabled critical whole language teachers? Their absence in this volume may well reflect the insularity of my (our) networks more than it does the actual existence of those teachers. I hope so. But whether or not that is the case, one of the many areas I am still working on is finding more ways to form coalitions with minority educators who might have both holistic and critical inclinations.

This must seem like a bad time to be looking for teachers with both whole language and critical inclinations; even worse, to be urging already whole language teachers and already critical teachers to take on yet one more (i.e., each other's) "stigma." It would be understandable, given the attacks on all but the most traditional, for nontraditional educators of any stripe to lie low. Current efforts by state and national legislators to mandate systematic phonics and to "outlaw" information supporting whole language, along with the media-reported/generated opposition to "multicultural" curricula and to what is deemed "politically correct" questioning, are intended to—and do—threaten progressives in education.[1] While these attacks also anger and energize those with politically progressive commitments, they are nevertheless reminders that being a critical whole language teacher does indeed entail risks. Some of the contributors to this volume refer to these risks. But what is remarkable is the relative absence of "trouble" resulting from the practice reported here. Certainly, these educators are fortunate (they work where there is at least some leeway for their practice, where there is an environment that bolsters their confidence to act on their convictions). They are also extraordinarily talented—at helping to create that bolstering environment, at envisioning against-the-grain practice, and at accommodating their communities without compromising their principles.

There are several tensions that either are addressed explicitly or simply appear implicitly throughout this volume because they are inherent when bringing together the perspectives of critical pedagogy and whole language. These concern curricular topics and directions, exercises, and system questioning.

There is a tension between students having a significant voice in their own learning and teachers playing out a critical perspective. The latter can seem like an imposition (a "front-loading" as Jerome Harste calls it [1994, personal communication]), interfering with the former. After all, if the curriculum is supposed to be centered on students' interests and if students are supposed to be able to "negotiate" the curriculum, how can the teacher insert her own interests? But negotiating entails both students and teacher; the teacher is not just an intellectual servant in the classroom, trailing behind students to pick up the ideas students drop. The teacher's interests also have a place in topic determination. Moreover, the teacher's knowledge and perspectives are always embedded in the ways teachers direct or even facilitate inquiries. What makes a critical direction for a topic seem like an imposition of the teacher's agenda but a noncritical direction seem like neutral guidance is that the former disrupts prevailing ideologies. But both critical inquiry and noncritical inquiry are "teacher-directed." It is naive to think otherwise, to imagine that the teacher is a cipher—that the teacher's implicit (often unexamined) perspectives and issues are absent when she helps students pursue a topic. It is also naive to think that students' interests are theirs alone and are, thus, "innocent." Students develop their interests through complex interwoven webs of influence and socially shaped "tendencies." Even young children sometimes question aspects of those webs (though I would guess questioning of the social shaping of their idiosyncratic predilections is more rare). But running throughout the social shaping as well as the webs of influence are media-produced messages. Thus, putting students' interests at the center of curriculum is, at some level, putting the media's interests—and therefore corporate interests—at the center. In fact, no matter whose interests (in the sense of curiosities) drive the curriculum, some interest group's interests (in the sense of benefits) will be enhanced.

At the same time, it remains important—for reasons of democracy and for reasons of student engagement—to broaden opportunities for students to have a significant voice in determining the ideas on the table, the topics to be studied, the projects they will undertake, the tasks that should make up those projects. "Negotiating the curriculum" means making room for students *and* teacher to make such decisions. Many of the contributors to this volume have walked that tightrope between the students' interests and the teacher's agenda and show us new ways of resolving this tension.

A related issue implicates preplanned language exercises. A whole language perspective includes an understanding that reading is both a social practice and a meaning-making process—a language process. That is, reading is not getting words but making sense (with various systems serving the sense making). That understanding of reading (and writing) as language points to the need for immersing written-language learners in situations of real language use, i.e., situations where language is being used for communicative purposes, not where the language event is primarily about teaching or evaluating students' language proficiency. In the latter case, it is exercises that prevail, language evoked for the purpose of taking part in language instruction just for the sake of instruction or for taking part in language evaluation just for the sake of evaluation. Whole language teachers' understandings of language lead them to avoid exercises and instead to teach language in or closely related to contexts of actual use.

That particular theoretical understanding of reading and language is not central to a critical perspective. And so there is another tension, with a different face depending on one's "origins." Educators with whole language roots easily avoid language exercises but may find themselves struggling to maintain a focus on systemic critique in the curriculum. Educators with critical pedagogy roots more "naturally" find ways to foreground social justice and critique but may struggle with how to avoid assignments whose purpose is primarily instruction in or evaluation of written language. Some of the contributors to this volume refer to their own efforts to go outside their "roots" in relation to either sustained critique or sustained *use* of (rather than exercises in) written language.

If sustaining critique goes against the grain, locating a problematized curricular topic within a *system* (of domination, of privilege) is even more outside the norm. Critical whole language education would have teachers questioning the ways systems (e.g., of race privilege, gender dominance, corporate interests) are implicated in specific actions, texts, or situations. Many of the contributors to this volume discuss their efforts to tie their curricular study to such systems.

The contributors to this volume are heroes to me. They stick their necks out, and they stick to their principles while working in generally uncharted territory, all in the service of a more democratic and just society. They enlarge my understanding of educational practice and my view of educational possibilities. I hope they do the same for other readers.

Note

1. The term "whole language" has taken such a drubbing in the media (a deliberately unfair drubbing, it should be added), that it might make better marketing sense to avoid its use in this volume. But avoiding it for such reasons would undermine the work of all who have contributed to this volume.

Reference

Shannon, P. (1990). *The struggle to continue: Progressive reading instruction in the United States.* Portsmouth, NH: Heinemann.

CHAPTER ONE

On Critical Whole Language Practice: Why, What, and a Bit of How

CAROLE EDELSKY

Arizona State University

I'm a worrier—especially about who and what is close to me. Anyone who knows me knows that. So it's no wonder that I would worry about whole language, a movement and a perspective that has been "close to me"—part of my work, my thinking, my identity—for almost two decades. But just because I'm a known worrier doesn't mean that my worries should be discounted (although even I will admit that worries concerning my own family could be minimized). When it comes to whole language, unfortunately, my worries have been all too justified. I have worried about (and still worry about) imposters and appropriation; i.e., people and programs claiming, without basis, to be "whole language" (Altwerger, Edelsky, & Flores, 1987). I have worried about (and still worry about) extermination; i.e., forces aiming to legislate or smear whole language out of existence (Edelsky, 1989). And I have worried about (and still worry about) perpetuation; i.e., whole language practice unwittingly contributing to systems of injustice (Edelsky, 1994). All three of these problems spoil whole language's chances for achieving its

Parts of this chapter are revisions of sections of an article entitled "Education for Democracy," which appeared in *Language Arts* 71.4 (1994), 252–257. The second half of this chapter is a revised version of "On Justice, Equity, and Petards," the keynote address for the Whole Day of Whole Language, NCTE, Orlando, Florida, 1994.

goals, which, as I understand them, have always included an increase in democracy and shared power.

Using the label "whole language" for what does not emanate from a whole language perspective is obviously misleading. But it is also a danger. It says: When comparing whole language with other educational practice, compare *non*-whole-language-going-by-the-name-of-whole-language practice with other practice that is also non-whole-language-going-by-the-name-of-something-else. When there is no noticeable difference among these various non–whole language practices, proclaim that whole language (represented by an imposter) has no particular advantage. The result of appropriating the label "whole language" without the substance is a loss of support for and interest in understanding whole language more deeply, and a concurrent lessening of chances for whole language to be a force for increasing democracy and shared power.

Clearly, wiping whole language out of existence would have the same ultimate effect. What is not so clear, however, is the mix of people, forces, and conditions working to eliminate whole language. For example, Far Right extremist groups paint whole language as a cause of educational deterioration, but so do some liberal, secular investigative reporters (e.g., Tashman, 1996). Recently, the interests of religious extremists and corporate profiteers have opportunistically coincided, first in attacks on public education (especially on whole language, with its evidence of professionalism, innovation, and responsiveness) and then, ultimately, in efforts to take over public education. A public school system weakened in resources and public esteem is a better target for privatization. As is to be expected considering my first worry—the labeling of non–whole language practices as "whole language"—much of what is subjected to smear campaigns is not whole language at all (e.g., substituting literature for basal readers in teaching separate skills; instituting journal writing with assigned topics and then grading the journals; failing, in the name of student-centeredness, to offer students instruction or coaching). Regardless of (in)accuracy, these efforts may well produce their desired effect. Certainly, the accelerating push for state and national legislation makes whole language an "outlaw" practice. If, however, whole language goes, so does the potential for it to be a positive force for social justice.

The paradox is my third worry: If, instead of going, whole language stays—at least if it stays as currently practiced—it also loses its potential for being a positive force for social justice. While whole language foregrounds concerns for democracy and equity in relation to the structure and organization of the classroom (e.g., in structures for classroom interaction, teacher-student relationships, curricular authority, the workings of evaluation, and so on), it does little in the way of theoretically foregrounding democracy and equity outside the classroom. Nor is there widespread awareness among whole language educators of how undemocratic hierarchies and inequitable systems pervade what happens inside the classroom (e.g., relations among peers in writing workshops, interpretations during literature study, and lines of questioning in inquiry projects). Without such concerns and awareness, whole language may implicitly condone structural inequities, may reinforce dominant blame-the-victim messages that deny structural inequities, and thus may simply offer a more humane, "kinder and gentler" way of perpetuating the status quo.

It would be a terrible irony if whole language were to stand in its own way (although, if one listens to certain critics [e.g., Field & Jardine, 1994], that is an inevitable outcome). In this chapter, I will argue for the need for re-theorizing whole language so that it can stand more firmly on the side of democracy, I will offer a few preliminary ideas for that re-theorizing project, and I will present some suggestions for re-theorized whole language practice.

What's the Problem Here?

If whole language is to promote democracy, justice, and equity, whole language educators must recognize the undemocratic nature of the existing political system in the United States. Despite secret ballots, rhetoric, and governmental structures, the United States is a long way from being a democracy. In a democracy, people participate meaningfully in decisions that affect their lives (Shannon, 1993); they genuinely negotiate important societal goals (Johnston, 1992). The participation is a participation among equals, negotiation among equals, not participation in which a few are more equal than the rest. Moreover, it is significant participation; not merely a vote on options determined by others behind the scenes, but a say in what the options are in the first place.

That does not describe the situation in the United States. In the past decade, while the majority of people in the United States have become increasingly poorer, a small minority have become increasingly richer (Shannon, 1993). The growing disparity in wealth has been the consequence of deliberate governmental and institutional policies (e.g., tax policies, budget appropriations, Federal Reserve policies). The vast majority of people have no opportunity to participate significantly in those policies; instead, large corporations, through their lobbyists, are the ones whose influence counts. It was governmental policies, not public action, that allowed savings and loans' profits to go into private pockets while losses were and still are billed to the public (Greider, 1992)[1]—a case of privatizing profits but socializing losses. It is tax and budget policies that cut Aid to Families with Dependent Children while continuing to provide ample welfare to corporations (e.g., subsidies to a corporation from the U.S. Department of Agriculture for selling its products overseas, tax breaks to mutual life insurance companies, allocations of *un*requested funds in 1995 to "defense" corporations—the same corporations that contributed more than $900,000 to political campaigns in 1994) (Franklin, 1995).

Wealthy corporations have overruled the wishes of the majority of citizens for years. As Greider details, the majority of people in the United States strongly favor safer cars, but for more than twenty years corporate resistance has prevented enactment of laws for improving auto safety. Similarly, the majority of people in the United States value cleaning up the environment, but one environmental protection effort after another has failed because corporations have been able to exert undue pressure in creating definitions for terms like "ample margins of safety." Moreover, the intent behind workplace safety laws or clean environment regulations that do exist has been repeatedly under-mined by big companies that find it less costly to engage in lengthy litigation to negotiate down the fines rather than to clean up their acts.

The public clamor for reform of health care has been sub-verted by a corporate takeover that offers neither the choice and quality of fee-for-service care nor the universality and security of national health care (Amsel, 1996). In little more than a year, an oligopoly of insurance companies removed decision-making power from physicians, provided incentives for *not* treating, and now makes billions by *not* supplying medical care.

A system in which wealth buys the right to overrule majority wishes is not a democracy. A system which privileges corpora-tions not only to write laws (through their lobbyists, who pro-vide exact wordings to the committees charged with writing regulations to implement laws [Sidener & Mayes, 1996]) but to decide which ones to obey is not a democracy. Neither is a system organized so that only moneyed interests have ready avenues for shaping public opinion and governmental activity.

The public airwaves are available almost exclusively to big corporate giants. That arrangement permits corporations to act as "spin masters," not only in individual news items and pro-grams but in entire domains of activity. Thus, there are television programs and entire channels devoted to a business perspective and business issues but none devoted to labor's perspective and workers' issues (Nader, 1996). Tobacco companies control dis-semination of information on nicotine and influence federal appropriations for research on tobacco (Weiner, 1996). And a recent (1996) telecommunications bill not only owes its exact wording to telecommunication lobbyists, but it also owes its pas-sage to campaign contributions from telecommunication giants (Ivins, 1996). In Arizona, lobbyists who promote the interests of their employers do the research for legislators on pending legisla-tion and serve right along with legislators on special legislative committees (Sidener & Mayes, 1996).

Lobbying power is related to campaign financing. As Charles Lewis wrote in *The Buying of the Presidency,* "We don't just elect politicians; we also elect their patrons and their patrons' priorities. It's a package deal" (1996). The irony is that the term "special interests" is often used to refer to women, minorities, and welfare recipients—those who can hardly afford to act as patrons in political campaigns or to fund a strong lobbying voice.

In a democracy, everybody is supposed to have an equal say: one person, one vote. But in the United States, the democratic political process has been betrayed by "organized money" (Greider, 1992). What is "good for business" then—such as media mergers that have replaced hundreds of separately owned newspapers, radio and television stations, film companies, and book publishers with just twenty multimedia conglomerates—is noted by critics as "bad for democracy."

It isn't just corporate power and decreased democracy that are closely related. So are wealth and poverty. As recent stock market shifts in the mid-1990s show, when employment goes up, the prices of stocks go down. When the workforce can be cut, or shifted to the lower-wage regions of the world, profits rise. Race and gender are similarly related to resources and democracy. When resources determine influence, while systemic race and gender gaps in jobs and income persist, minorities are deprived of access to equal participation.

I am not saying that all rich individuals conspire to over-power all individuals who have less. Rather, it is a *system* that is at work here, a system that exists for favoring the wealthy, for privileging corporations, for giving greater power to men, for privileging whiteness. The individual exceptions (the African American high school principal with a white secretary, the female boss of the male worker) are simply the variations tolerated by a system of privilege, a system of conferring unearned benefits (McIntosh, 1988). If a clerk refuses to cash my check, or if a police officer pulls me over in traffic, I have the unearned benefit of being able to take for granted it is not due to the color of my skin. I have race-based privileges (often augmented by my social class; frequently, diminished by my gender). These systems of privilege or systems of domination—corporatism, classism, racism, sexism— are what impede democracy because democracy is supposed to work without system-derived privilege or prejudice.

To understand systems of domination, it is necessary to note the relationship between politics and economics. Politics is about who gets what, where, and how—who gets money, jobs, diplomas, good health care, high-quality literature in classrooms, turns at talk, respect, and high social value (resources are not only material and public—they are also social and personal). Democracy is one way to decide who gets what. It is one political approach to economy, to the allocation of societal resources. Undue influence, from a grossly uneven allocation of resources, subverts democracy because those who have already "gotten" set things up so that they'll keep on getting.

The "manufactured crisis" (Berliner & Biddle, 1995) of public education offers a textbook case for such a cycle. In a society with unequally distributed property, funding schools through local property taxes ensures unequal funding for schools. Tax breaks for corporations further ensure that even in one locality the cost of public schools will be distributed inequitably. Since 1957, the corporate share of local property taxes has declined from 45 percent of the total to 16 percent (Berliner & Biddle, 1995). Homeowners and small businesses have had to pick up the slack. Not satisfied with this handout in the United States, corporate interests in both the United States and Canada (Barlow & Robertson, 1994) embarked on a disinformation campaign to teach the public that their schools had failed (Shannon, 1996). Data refuting the supposed failure of public schools have been suppressed (Berliner & Biddle, 1995) or given scant coverage. The goal has been to create an image of schooling-in-shambles, of public institutions no longer deserving public support. As Barlow and Robertson (1994) write, corporations were then modestly waiting in the wings, ready to humbly offer themselves as the solution to a crisis they manufactured.

The corporate intent is to earn profits from privatized education as well as to cut costs and therefore their own property taxes by promoting vouchers, two-tiered certification, "standards" and therefore reduced curricula, block grants, and "strategic planning" (funding only the most "productive units") (Shannon, 1996). In terms of shaping public opinion, the intent is to lay the blame for actual or possible problems in the economy onto a public institution (Barlow & Robertson, 1994). This is one more example of the phenomenon of having the power to create the conditions—in this case, stigmatized and underfunded public schools for the poorest clients, privatized schools for the benefit of corporations—that bring about even more power (lower costs, new sources of power).

The last thing that might help bring about education for democracy, then, is something that would further entrench corporate domination or any other system of domination. Business-inspired materials, business-made television shows like Channel 1, corporate-endowed chairs at universities, and business modes of operation do more than sell brand names; they also sell "a way of looking at oneself and society" (Barlow & Robertson, 1994, p. 144).

At first glance, some of the recent business-inspired "innovations" in education as well as in business (e.g., decentralized decision making, total quality management, and consensus building) may seem like improvements. But we should look again. New corporate models are often business adaptations of the ideas of 1960s antibusiness activists, adaptations that retain some surface features including labels and rhetoric while turning the substance and intent inside out. Thus "empowering management" means helping managers be "self-actualized," not helping them to seize power. "Radical decentralization" becomes a way to justify firing full-time employees and bringing in contractors who hire part-timers who do not receive benefits (Kauffman, 1993). In education, business' call for "radical decentralization" linked with the Christian Coalition's demand for "local control" makes any particular school "a sitting duck to a well-organized special-interest group (the better to control you by, my dear)" (Barlow & Robertson, 1994, p. 136).

The first step in putting an end to systems of domination that inhibit democracy is to learn to *see* them, to see how *systemic* (not idiosyncratic) privilege linked to a system driven by profit prevents people from participating equally and meaningfully; i.e., from having a democracy.

Becoming Part of the Solution

Learning to see these systems of domination requires a critical pedagogy. A critical pedagogy examines what is taken for granted (e.g., having principals for schools or selling medicine for profit) and what is accepted as business-as-usual (e.g., letting a test score keep people out of a job, or women letting men think the idea was theirs). Further, a critical pedagogy works at figuring out where the taken-for-granted, business-as-usual came from, what it's connected to, and whose interests it serves.

Clearly, it is not easy to "get critical" in the United States in general and in schools in particular. In a culture where "don't worry, be happy" could become a bumper sticker, it is difficult to whip up widespread enthusiasm for exposing trouble or, worse, for making the effort to understand the sources of trouble. Add to that educators' desires to please and be liked along with the significant pressures to avoid controversy and to appease the Far Right, and critique becomes even more difficult. Nevertheless, critique—and its partners, hope (something that comes from learning about prior struggles against systems of domination, struggles that *did* have some effect) and action (linking students and ourselves to others who are doing something, no matter how small, to end systems of domination)—are centerpieces of a whole language committed to education for justice and equity.

Re-theorizing

The need for critique, hope, and action prompts another: the need to continually re-theorize whole language. Currently, most progressive theories and practices which contribute to or emanate from whole language theory—reader-response theory, socio-psycholinguistic models of reading, transactional theory in reading, curriculum as inquiry, writing-process practices, and so on—can as easily support *avoiding* looking at white privilege, for example, as they support looking *at* it. It is not that those progressive theories and practices are incorrect; rather, they don't go far enough. They don't actively and primarily—as a first priority—tie language to power, tie text interpretation to societal structures, or tie reading and writing to perpetuating or resisting.

While whole language educators' theories-in-practice *do* consider power relationships in text interpretations, for instance, or in curriculum planning, and while we *do* have an *im*plicit opposition to certain hierarchies woven into our frameworks, we do not make the central topic—the pivot for all the rest—the role of language in perpetuating or constituting systems of domination. Whole language educators' theories-in-practice, therefore, could just as well be a softer way of maintaining systems of dominance. To help unseat them, it is necessary to re-theorize whole language.

The idea of re-theorizing might become clearer with an example from feminist theory. For two decades, feminist theory has argued for the personal as being political, for the theoretical truth of individual women's stories, for disavowing some patriarchal notion of "Woman" that all women are and, instead, for valuing the plurality of women. However, as Carmen Luke (1992) has argued, that theory, along with other postmodern, poststructural theories, paints women into a theoretical corner. If, ultimately, women are so plural, so individually different, then we have no grounds to claim anything about "women's" issues. The "we" has become theoretically unfounded and therefore depoliticized. Carmen Luke insisted that feminist theory is correct in attending to individual women's voices, correct to refuse to accept some essential patriarchy-defined Woman. But still, she urged re-theorizing, thinking through some key epistemological issues, in order to maintain the theoretical value of individual women's experience while foregrounding the global economic and cultural oppression women share. Otherwise the theory itself subverts the project of women's emancipation by theoretically denying that there is any validity to a grouping called "women."

I think there is a parallel here for whole language. Its goal may be societal—increased democracy; more equally weighted participation through decreasing the power of systems of domination; improved education for all, resulting in greater democracy, which results in more equity, which promotes more democracy, and so on. But its focus has been on individuals. Theoretically, whole language presumes that though language expression and language processing are socially situated and constrained by social conventions, they are primarily acts of individuals. As a theory-in-practice, whole language fails to take as its central focus the way language learning and language use are tied not just to people's individual experiences but to people's societal positions, to their structured privilege, to their greater or lesser power, and to the interests of the groups they represent. Whole language educators cannot hope to change what is societal by continuing to theoretically background exactly that: what is societal.

Re-theorizing whole language does not mean discrediting the idea of reading as a socio-psycholinguistic process. Nor does it mean denying that all language conventions are social practices that change from culture to culture. It does not mean rejecting the notion that people will create different interpretations of texts due to their individually different prior experiences, which are used to create those interpretations of text. It does not mean eliminating inquiry from language pedagogy. Nor does it mean simply substituting the societally focused work of critical language scholars for the process-oriented work of "traditional" whole language scholars.

Re-theorizing whole language to make it live up to its liberatory potential *does* mean highlighting the relationship of language and power. Norman Fairclough's work (1989; 1992a; 1992b) provides fine direction here but it is not sufficient. Illuminating as his work is, it does not attend to all that happens when people learn or use language. It keeps the language-power issue central, but it does not deal with all that is involved, for instance, in learning the difference between "*the* girl has a dog" and "*a* girl has a dog."

Similarly, a whole language re-theorizing project should foreground the political, sociological, historical character of language and reading practices. At different times and in different places, reading has meant a variety of different practices: pronouncing words from a sacred text, signing one's name on a contract, and using bus schedules (Graff, 1987; Luke, 1995). But there is also substantial evidence for the universality of psychological processes in both oral language and reading. When babies say "goed" for "went," a psychological process of unconscious hypothesis formation explains the phenomenon better than does appealing to the social nature of language learning. Similarly, a process of predicting better explains the existence of high-quality miscues. Re-theorizing means, however, that these psychological phenomena have to be accounted for within the fundamentally social and ideological character of language practice.

Whole language theory has relied heavily upon an analogy between first-language learning and written-language learning. That analogy is still productive (e.g., leading to justifications of "immersion pedagogies" [Gee, 1994]). But it may be even more interesting now to begin to think about comparisons between written-language learning and second-language learning. This comparison may be helpful not only because, generally, people have learned an oral language before learning a written one, though not necessarily the oral "version" of the written language in question (i.e., regardless of whether or not a Japanese speaker already speaks English when she learns to read English, she has already learned an oral language—Japanese, in this case). It may be helpful because it can better illuminate the relationship between immersion and instruction.

A re-theorizing project for whole language would need to consider changing its guiding image—a young child learning language at home. A more provocative image might be a child learning to use language in a multilingual day-care center. Or perhaps it would be better to put the child nearer the edge and the community in the center. Gee (1990) and McDermott (1993) both argue for a shift of attention from the child acquiring a language to a language (or a discourse community) acquiring a child. Such a shift would be more congruent with whole language educators' concerns for the classroom community (R. Peterson, 1992), for the inseparability of the classroom community from any activity, including language learning, that occurs there.

Re-theorizing whole language would entail talking differently about pedagogy. Instead of talking about whole language as a perspective-in-practice, maybe we would talk about it as a set of commitments-in-practice (for example, to democracy or to ending systems of privilege or domination). A theoretical/practical question, then, would be what views of reading support such commitments? Instead of talking about accepting and celebrating students' interpretations and compositions of text, we would talk about analyzing the positions texts offer (whether authored by students or others) and the already-available readings cultures offer.

We would need to reconsider the "centers." That is, teacher-centered and student-centered form an oversimplified dichotomy (an issue discussed later in this chapter and also by several of the contributors to this volume); neither process-centered nor inquiry-centered connect sufficiently to goals of ending systemic classism, racism, sexism, and other systems of domination.

Where the Action Is

Whole language has never been "merely" a theory. In fact, what distinguishes whole language from what is currently traditional practice is how its self-conscious, theoretically framed practice feeds into the "practice" of theorizing and vice versa. It is reasonable at this point, then, to turn to the classroom. If critiquing systems of domination—in order to increase democracy and promote justice and equity—were a priority in whole language classrooms, what would those classrooms be like? And what are some of the tensions involved in making whole language critical? The remaining chapters in this volume offer sustained answers from particular classrooms. Here, I will simply skim the surface of curricular goings-on to provide an overview, to suggest some general aimed-for characteristics, and to discuss a few of the problems in making whole language "critical."

Critical Whole Language Curricula

First of all, in a critical, pro-justice, pro-democracy whole language curriculum, the critique and pro-justice, pro-democracy stance is not a subject or a time of the day. It is infused throughout. It appears on bulletin boards (e.g., Bob Peterson, a critical whole language teacher in Milwaukee, has a gallery of freedom fighters on the wall for students to add to). It appears in the classroom library (which would have been selected to include a great number of books dealing with justice and injustice, social issues, and usually muted or absent voices). That critical, pro-equity stance is reflected in math problems, in some of the topics of study, in comments the teacher tosses out for possible grabbing on to when the topic is a noncritical one, in the teacher's comments in discussions, in the questions the teacher poses (whether students pick up on them or not), and in the big projects the class undertakes.

For the most part, that stance "shows up" (though it is not visible) in the teacher's thoughts. *Critical* whole language teachers are always thinking: How can I encourage students to deeply question what's going on around them? How can I get them to see that their interpretations are not only related to their individual "take," but, more important, to already-made interpretations which are available to students depending on their social/cultural identity? How can I get students to see that just as they are interpreting texts, texts are also positioning them to see things in certain ways? How can I bring in the voices and the stories that are usually missing from textbooks, newspapers, and other media?

A teacher with such thoughts, then, is likely—in the midst of talking about something or other with students—to have sudden brainstorms and act on them, like Judy Buchanan did several years ago when her fourth graders in Philadelphia brought in clippings about the fall of the Berlin Wall, at which one half million were present, and another clipping about a march on poverty in Washington, D.C., at which there were an estimated five hundred thousand demonstrating. It occurred to Judy to ask the children if they thought one half million was bigger than five hundred thousand. And then they speculated about why one math phrase would be used to describe one situation and a lesser sounding "math synonym" would be used for another.

Scottsdale, Arizona, teacher Mary Langan had one of these brainstorms when she started using materials from her district about Thanksgiving. It suddenly occurred to her that the Native American perspective was missing. And so she asked children the unplanned question that prompted some additional study: Whose story do you think this is? Do you think Native Americans would tell it like this?

Or, in a literature study, when talking about a book like *The Great Gilly Hopkins*, my colleague Maryann Eeds (1994, personal communication) says that if students talk about how Gilly didn't want anything to do with dirty, creepy Agnes, the teacher can say something like, "Troubled as Gilly is, she does seem to *have* more than Agnes. I wonder if that has anything to do with how she sees Agnes." And then the teacher should remain silent to allow that comment to get picked up, being ready to help it become a sustained discussion of social-class tensions if it does.

A critical curriculum is not all spur-of-the-moment, however. Much of it is planned in advance. For example, antiracist Canadian educator Enid Lee (1994) asks: Why study statistics with examples from sports or weather? Why not use unemployment figures for math? Why not work on percentages using figures for race and income levels or gender and job promotion?

In literature study, critical teachers can plan to ask students what they think a book is *really* about or to talk, themselves, about the *theme*. As Maryann Eeds says (1994, personal communication), talk about theme will develop when teachers get beyond a *learned* inclination to stay at the level of character and plot. Teachers can tell students that authors usually write because they feel they have something to *say*. Theme talk, of course, permits probing into themes. When injustice is mentioned in connection with *Roll of Thunder, Hear My Cry*, the teacher can say, "Let's go back and look at this tonight; let's study where and *how* Mildred Taylor shows us injustice. Who got something out of that injustice? Let's look more closely at this."

Bess Altwerger (1994, personal communication) advises teachers to plan to be the ones to bring up sexism, racism, or classism in literature studies, being careful to initiate those themes by starting with the students' own experiences. In a discussion of *Bridge to Terebithia*, a teacher might ask: "How did you girls feel about the way the boys reacted to Leslie's speed as a runner? How did you boys feel? Has anything like that happened to you? How did you feel? Where does that come from?"

The point is not for the students to come up with the teacher's "right" answer. Rather, it is to raise the question, to start to *notice* what I have been calling "systems of domination." Maryann Eeds argues that literature makes it easier to notice them. Additionally, literature is written to make readers *care*. Bess Altwerger claims teachers can do a lot to get students to then *investigate* the injustice, beginning with their own lives. And, Bob Peterson (1994b) adds that teachers can help students begin to *act* to interrupt the injustice.

In mini-lessons, teachers can talk about writers' beliefs and perspectives, how they are revealed both deliberately and unwittingly in authors' writings, how those beliefs benefit some people and hurt others. At the same time, teachers can resist making individual authors personally responsible for those beliefs, letting the systems of domination and resulting ideologies off the hook. For instance, teachers and students can look at newspaper copy, television scripts, and ads and try to find the "hidden" messages bought from writers by corporate media and advertisers. And then, in small group or whole-class conferences about the students' own writings, teachers can bring up the issues of writers' perspectives and who benefits from them.

A whole language teacher working from a critical perspective sometimes gets topics of study by starting with objects children bring to class (like pottery shards on the playground). Sometimes, teachers start with topics they know are long overdue for study, topics that are often left out but that have rich potential for critique, for revealing systems of domination—topics like hunger or homelessness or working people's history or immigration. Rather than organizing the curriculum around holiday themes and seasons, whole language teachers usually organize curriculum around what students seem tuned in to. But too often in "traditional" whole language classrooms, teachers stay on the surface of children's interests and either skim over or avoid exploring what is *really* on students' minds (Jerome Harste, 1991, personal communication). Often, that is not the latest movie or TV-promoted product; it is divorce, gangs, parents' jobs, unfair play on the playground, unfair distribution of turns in the classroom.

But regardless of the topics studied—whether they are far from or close to children's deepest concerns, whether they are "heavy" or "light," whether they start out as manifestly concerned with justice and equity or not—and regardless of the structures for studying those topics (structures like workshops for writing or reading, clubs for reading or science, circles for authoring or inquiry), the critical whole language curriculum poses certain questions over and over: Why is it like *this?* Who benefits from it being like this? Is that fair? What else do we need to know to get to the bottom of this? What's left out? Which voices are*n't* heard? What does*n't* this material tell us?

Aside from shorter-term topics, of course, in whole language classrooms there are long-term projects. In *critical* whole language classrooms, those projects are often prompted by local concerns. For example, several years ago, Clint Penka, in

Phoenix, sponsored multiyear projects in which fourth through sixth graders renovated the outsides of houses in their barrio. The students wrote proposals to local businesses to get materials and instruction on scraping, sanding, and painting. They also tutored children at the school associated with the homeless shelter. The intent was to have children work on and *study* housing, in particular, housing inequities—who owns and who rents, where landlords live, where homeless people used to live and what happened to those homes.

Another example. In Gilbert, Arizona, a small group of Kathy Mason's multiage primary students noticed for the first time the basals that had been in boxes all year long (Mason, 1994). They took them out, found in one of them a version of Cynthia Rylant's *The Relatives Came,* and began on their own to compare the basal version with the trade book. They were incredulous, saying things like, "This one isn't poetic. It's like a dead battery. It leaves me with a different feeling," and "this one is like one big flashcard." For several days, they studied the entire basal set—textbooks, workbooks, teacher's manual— becoming more outraged each day at things like a script in the teacher's manual. One child asked, "Why do they tell you what to say? Didn't you go to college?" They wrote to Scott to complain, but then to be polite, changed the salutation to Mr. Foresman:

Dear Scott [crossed out] Mr. Foresman,

I feel embarassed by your books. Why does Water Wiggle? How to Talk to Dears, The Big Blank Piece of Paper, Oh etc. Etc. Etc. Hippo, You be the Bread and I'll be the Cheese, BathtubEgel. A lot of people have complaints here are some The book you give the teachers are like one Big flash card. I donot like your comp. [company] becase your throwing away poetic language. I know what literature is and this is not literature. The books here are just Books not literature. Kids reading your books think there reading literature But there not. those Books are a crime. Please close your comp. [company] or get a real writer.

Sined
Luke D. Zeller

These six-, seven-, and eight-year-olds started a research group on the following questions, posed on their own initiative: How much do basals cost? Why are they as they are? Do grownups know how bad they are? Why do authors permit their stories to be changed? They read Ken Goodman's (1988) "Look What They've Done to Judy Blume" and Goodman, Maras, and Birdseye's (1994) "Look! Look! Who Stole the Pictures from the Picture Book?" They asked Ken Goodman to come from Tucson to study the problem of "basalization" with them. (He did.) They learned firsthand about a system—profit above all—that is behind basal publishing.

General Characteristics of Critical, Whole Language Curricula

From all the aforementioned examples of critical whole language projects and curricular "goings-on," I would list the following as general characteristics (adapted from B. Peterson, 1994a).[2]

1. No (or Few) Exercises

Such a curriculum is not full of exercises (exercises in reading, in science, in history, etc.) (Edelsky, Chapter 5, 1996). If students are asked why they are doing what they are doing, they would say something substantive or something connected to the out-of-school world (e.g., to find out why there's so much violence, or to really get into this book, or to let my grandma know I love her). They would be less likely to say something procedural or institutionally connected (e.g., I'm doing this to get a lesson on pioneers, or I'm doing this to get a good grade in reading).

In order to be a non-exercise, students have to see it as *their* thing; they have to come to own it in the sense of buying in. That is, from *their* perspective, they would see what they are doing as something with real import in their own lives or in the lives of people out of school.

Often, what they are doing would be part of a long-term project. If the project is big enough or long-term enough, then it can accommodate "lessons" or "strategy sessions" without having these turn into exercises.

What makes something an exercise is not the task itself but its purpose. When the talking or reading or writing is done strictly for the sake of instruction in talking or reading or writing or evaluation of talking or reading or writing, it is an exercise. The "same" thing (a lesson on headline writing, for instance) done for the sake of the newspaper which the class puts out—if the child believes the lesson is truly for the newspaper and not merely instruction for instruction's sake—is not an exercise.

2. Grounded in Students' Lives

Grounding curricula in students' lives means that students' questions, interpretations, and experiences are the *starting* point for much—though certainly not all—of the curriculum; students' discoveries and questions are a big factor in what is pursued for study. This also means students play a big role in planning how to study what gets studied. Grounding the curriculum in students' lives does not mean that the teacher plans open-ended assignments without considering the students and students "fill in the blanks" by responding with anecdotes, writing, and data from their own lives. Instead, it may mean that students and teacher together figure out what to do in the first place. It may also mean the teacher watches students closely to see what issues *underlie* what children seem to be interested in. For example, Philadelphia teacher Rhoda Kanevsky (1991, personal communication) notes that the compelling issue for children may not *necessarily* be dinosaurs (though for some children it is); it is often hugeness or ancientness. Neither is it necessarily cartoon figures themselves; it may be what they represent—e.g., transformation or escape.

Like Freire's (1970) generative themes, topics in critical whole language classrooms often come from students' lives. How the theme or the topic is named, however, is crucial. It makes a big difference whether the topic in adult literacy or culture circles is called "jobs" or whether it is named "not being able to find work." And it makes a big difference in elementary school if the topic remains a superficial Ninja Turtles or, as Paula Salvio described (1994), if it moves to the underlying Ninja codes of honor her students were really attracted to. The teacher, of course, is the one who works with students on framing the topic that students bring in. But it is the students who frequently initiate the topics or bring in the raw material for inquiry. That is one of the main ways student choice figures in the curriculum. It is not students choosing from a smorgasbord prepared by the teacher. It is students-as-partners co-creating the menu.

Most likely, what will be planned will involve *firsthand* learning, not just hands-on activity, a powerful distinction made by Valerie Bang-Jensen (1995). When children count out popsicle sticks to subtract, they are learning hands-on. When children actually make change at the bake sale, they are learning about subtracting firsthand. Critical whole language curricula feature much firsthand inquiry, which frequently begins with what students have also experienced firsthand.

3. Offers a Safe Place

Making the classroom a safe place means the teacher has set up structures and norms of interaction that get everybody (students and teacher) to take care of each other, to listen respectfully to each other, to help each other learn—all that is implied in the notion of building a classroom community out of an assortment of people connected only by administrative accident.

These first three features, as I've discussed them, probably do not seem strange to whole language educators. After all, non-exercises, grounding curriculum in students' lives, and creating communities constitute "vintage" whole language. These features are also fundamental for critical curriculum. But there's more—and this is where the shift begins.

A curriculum that provides safety is also a curriculum in which students are encouraged to voice genuine (not merely acceptable) deeply felt interpretations, some of which may promote *in*justice and *in*equity—like children saying that boys shouldn't play with dolls or girls with trucks because God doesn't like that. In a critical classroom, the teacher has to protect *all* interpretations, has to work mightily not to dislike the child of a Ku Klux Klan member, must never punish students for their positions (which usually reflect what the parents think). At the same time, the teacher has to make sure that *any position can be interrogated even as it is protected.*

A critical whole language curriculum has to offer safe space for the teacher too. Teachers should be able to present their opinions—but always as one more *opinion.* Bob Peterson says that when teachers "pretend to have no opinions on controversial topics, they send a message that it's OK to be opinionless and apathetic about important issues" (1994b, p. 40).

A critical pro-justice curriculum has to provide the kind of safety that lets teachers and students figure out how to have the tough, honest conversations about race, gender, and class that put all the pain and problems on the table but yet strengthen, rather than weaken, intergroup ties. Such is the work that Esther Fine and her colleagues are doing at York University and in a Toronto elementary school (Fine, Lacey, & Baer, 1995). The label "conflict resolution" (Fine, 1994) hardly captures the complexity and significance of that project.

4. Takes a Critical Stance

Being critical means more than focusing on social studies types of topics in a questioning way or emphasizing discrimination or stereotypes. It means studying (not knowing the answer in advance, but *studying*) exactly how decisions are made, or how a climate is created or how interactions take place, or how something happens in ways that either perpetuate or disrupt hierarchies based on race, class, or gender.

Let me say a little more about "studying." A critical curriculum does not presume a few, clear answers to everything (e.g., "It's all because of patriarchy"—or racism, or heterosexual imperialism, or capitalism). Those "answers" may be at the base of a critical perspective, just as there are "answers" at the base of a traditional perspective (e.g., "It's all because of particular individuals" or particular forces that come together coincidentally at a particular moment). But the "clear answers at the base"—that is, the ideological premises—are not what is studied. What is studied are the issues that grow out of the premises, the many other questions and answers that lie between initiating questions and ultimate answers. For example, between the initiating question "Why do people watch so much TV?" and the "ultimate" critical answer "to promote a system of capitalist profits" are a host of unknowns to be investigated (Who watches? How is TV watching promoted? What choices exist for watching? How are choices made available? How is TV watching represented? and so on). Similarly, many other questions and answers dangle between the initiating question "Why are there so few women in certain career positions?" and the "ultimate" traditional answer "because of some wrong-headed prejudices on the part of particular people." In each case, critical or traditional, *it is the questions in between that are being studied.*

No one studies anything without having some set of premises. Those premises are assumed (that is what a premise is), not studied. "Studying," therefore, does not mean an empty, premise-less head searching for pure, perspective-less truth. It means asking a set of questions which start from certain premises and then letting those questions lead to other questions and answers.

One of the major premises in a critical perspective is that people live their lives within systems. Thus, being critical means *studying systems*—how they work and to what end—focusing on systems of influence, systems of culture, systems of gender relations. A *non*critical approach *studies* (does not have the answer in advance, but studies) *who did what*. Both perspectives consider individuals, but being critical means questioning against the frame of *system*, seeing individuals as always within systems, as perpetuating or resisting systems. Being *non*critical (in both traditional *and* whole language classrooms) means seeing individuals as outside of systems, maybe influenced by them, but in some important sense separate from systems and therefore separate from culture and history.

In order to have critique infuse the classroom, in order to float just the right critique-inviting balloon in a literature study, in order to initiate certain topics, pose critically provocative problems involving numbers, set the stage for critical projects, keep those big questions in mind, and so on, the teacher has to have or be developing a critical perspective herself.

It's the same old story regarding whole language. In order for the teacher to sponsor literature studies that focus on meaning making rather than skills, the teacher has to have or be developing a whole language perspective. The same can be said for a critical perspective. The question is "Assuming they want one, how do teachers *come to have* a critical perspective?" Again, it's the same as the answer to the question "How do teachers develop a whole language perspective?" They read things written from a critical perspective; they join with others who have a critical perspective; they try watching events closely, asking, "Why is it like *this*?" (i.e., they become event watchers in addition to being kid watchers).

5. Pro-justice

A curriculum aiming for justice and equity must, obviously, be pro-justice and pro-equity. There is a deliberate, active search for materials that try to promote justice, for projects that could reveal the less dominant sides of issues, for resources that feature voices that are not usually heard.

6. Activist

These last two features of a critical curriculum—deliberately bringing in nondominant perspectives and acting on behalf of those who are oppressed by systems of domination—are the most threatening of all for many people. When students start to see inequities, critical teachers want them to care about those inequities, to *feel* the unfairness, to *want* to do something about it. Critical whole language teachers do not want students to become apathetic, cynical, hopeless—to conclude that there is nothing they can do; that's just the way it is.

A critical curriculum *informs* students about activists of all ages (e.g., Hoose [1993] describes children's work in tackling social problems). After all, activists and equity movements are also part of a cultural heritage, even though that information is rarely foregrounded in school curricula. It is important to seek out resources that show what ordinary people have done, usually by banding together with others, to change things on behalf of the less powerful. Those resources include people who students can interview, songs written about resistance, literature about activists, and movies and videotapes about rarely taught events.

A critical curriculum also encourages students to *take action*—like writing to Scott-Foresman, or even marching in political demonstrations (e.g., Peterson, 1994). Some of the chapters in this volume provide other examples.

What Are the Tensions Here? or, Is Critical Whole Language Educational Practice an Oxymoron?

There are two main camps—one more conservative, the other more progressive—criticizing the enterprise I am advocating in this chapter. Both camps object to what looks like the same thing: imposition. However, "imposition" means something quite different, depending on which camp is doing the objecting. The more traditional mainstream camp's claim is that critical, projustice practice makes education political. It imposes a perspective which amounts to brainwashing. The "traditional" whole language complaint is that critical, projustice practice makes education traditional—that is, it imposes the teacher's will, making education teacher-centered.

Imposition as "Brainwashing"

Conservative critics say critical curriculum makes education political and propagandistic. But all education—all curriculum—is political. Any curriculum supports *something*, some view of the world. When an illustration in a text paints Indians as stealthily creeping up on white settlers and the accompanying text says "the Indians attacked," that supports the white view of the Indians as savages, the wars as unprovoked, the whites as having a right to what they now have, the Indians as deserving what happened to them. That representation is political. And when nothing is said in school about Cuba or Haiti or Rwanda or the Timor in Indonesia or El Salvador or the neo-Nazis in Europe, that *non*mention supports powerful interests. That lack of presentation is political.

The reason a critical curriculum seems more political than the dominant noncritical curriculum is that who and what it supports is nondominant and, therefore, unfamiliar. Educators and also the lay public are accustomed to curricula that support dominant interests (whether that curriculum is a mainstream textbook-driven, skills-based curriculum or a whole language curriculum that focuses on studying bears and dinosaurs and ahistorical motivations of characters). Such familiarity and taken-for-grantedness of the support makes it invisible. A critical curriculum, however, is different—and therefore visible.

But it is not propagandistic. A critical curriculum does not supply answers. It supplies questions. Now it is true that part of the answer is built into the question, but that is true for any question (including research questions). The reason questions associated with a critical curriculum seem to harbor answers while mainstream curricular questions do not is that critical questions are not the usual questions. The latter, however, also have part of the answer built into them. For example, embedded in a common question like "What is the author's point?" are such premises/ answers as "authors *intend* to provide conclusions," "points originate with authors," and (often implied) "balance is a virtue." Such premises are political (and ideological) in that they support a particular view of the world.

A critical curriculum does not tell people *what* to think. But it does pose some new things to think *about*. Those who want to prevent schools from offering a critical curriculum are the ones imposing barriers; they are telling teachers and students what *not* to think about.

Imposition as "Teacher-Centeredness"

And then there is the criticism from progressive educators: A critical curriculum is not child-centered; it does not come from children. I think that complaint is based in part on an oversimplified view of "children's interests" and an underanalyzed notion of both "child-centered" and "teacher-centered." The criticism fails to acknowledge how much of students' interests are often planted or at least intensified by advertisement and parent and peer preferences (which in turn are media-influenced).

The complaint that critical practice is teacher-centered fails to note that some teacher direction is a necessary part of teaching— e.g., in scheduling, questioning, supplying the room, and so on.

The issue, therefore, is not teacher direction per se. It is how much and what kind. I think most who oppose teacher-centeredness would nevertheless accept a teacher bringing up a topic or bringing in resources or making a suggestion for a project. But they would probably not like to see the "whole language" label tied to lessons planned in detail in advance by the teacher or to packaged activities that can be passed out at workshops or to activities in which students' participation is limited to filling in from their own lives the blanks which the teacher has created.

Even recognized whole language "models" influence students' interests. Laminack and Lawing (1994) describe Lawing's work in organizing and selecting from what children contribute, thus *shaping* what to study and how to study it. In writers' workshops, teachers emphasize certain questions that students then learn to ask (e.g., "Where did you get your idea?" "What are you going to do next?"). Those are good, important questions in which an entire theory of writing is embedded. Whole language teachers believe it is important that students begin to internalize and therefore genuinely ask those questions. But those questions do not originate with students. It is teachers who teach students to ask those questions.

Good teachers of any persuasion highlight what is problematic in order to push students to think more. Posing critical questions to highlight issues of justice and equity and noticing and studying the roots of what is taken for granted is no different than what teachers in "child-centered" classrooms do—except that it attempts to make the taken-for-granted visible, a practice that is not typical in child-centered classrooms.

The complaint about critical, pro-justice curricula not being child-centered is also due, in part, to a somewhat mechanistic view of the impact of culture and history on curiosity and desire. It does not acknowledge how much of what students bring in, suggest, ask about, choose—the usual sources of child-centered curricula—is tied to the current historical and cultural moment.

While conservative critics deny that there are *perspectives* embedded in every curriculum (none are neutral), whole language proponents deny that there are *social* (i.e., *cultural and historical*) *influences* embedded in *every aspect* of even the most child-centered curriculum (nothing comes only from the child). Whole language educators tend to see people as unique individuals, with culture as an extra, as something that merely contributes to human uniqueness. Too many whole language educators fail to take the critical view that people are *thoroughly* cultured and that choices are *thoroughly* historical (for instance, five hundred years ago, the options would have been different and so would the meaning of a constant option, like parenthood) or that people's responses are *at all times* gendered. Critical anthropologists (e.g., Clifford & Marcus, 1986) argue that ethnographers "write" culture. But a system of culture has first "written" each of us.

There is a history of considerable, though too often implicit, disagreement over the goals of education. The currently victorious default choice (default because it "wins" without any extended public discussion) is that education serves the marketplace. Education is for job training and for maintaining the nation's competitive position in the global economy.

But there are other possible answers. One of them is that education in a proclaimed democracy properly serves the public; i.e., the interests of citizens in a democracy. That position advocates educating people so that they help to bring that democracy into existence by unseating systems of undue influence. A pedagogy that is both whole language and critical contributes to that project.

Notes

1. Greider (1992) provides names, dates, meetings, and quoted sources and numbers documenting the decidedly undemocratic situation in the United States in which "significant participation" is only for the few.

2. Bob Peterson has written extensively and powerfully about his own work as a critical, pro-justice, pro-equity, whole language teacher at La Escuela Fratney in Milwaukee. I have borrowed his list of characteristics, added some of my own, and subjected all of them to my own interpretation.

References

Altwerger, B., Edelsky, C., & Flores, B. (1987). Whole language: What's new? *Reading Teacher, 41*(2), 144–155.

Amsel, L. (1996). Bad medicine. *Tikkun, 11*(1), 25–28.

Bang-Jensen, V. (1995). Hands-on and first-hand experiences in the context of reading and language arts. *Language Arts, 72*(5), 352–359.

Barlow, M., & Robertson, H. (1994). *Class warfare.* Toronto: Key Porter.

Berliner, D., & Biddle, B. (1995). *Manufactured crisis: Myths, fraud and the attack on America's public schools.* Reading, MA: Addison-Wesley.

Clifford, J., & Marcus, G. (1986). *Writing culture: The poetics and politics of ethnography.* Berkeley: University of California Press.

Edelsky, C. (1989). Politics, politics, politics. Keynote address, annual meeting of the Virginia Reading Council, Norfolk, VA.

Edelsky, C. (1994). Education for democracy. *Language Arts, 71*(4), 252–257.

Edelsky, C. (1996). *With literacy and justice for all: Rethinking the social in language and education.* 2nd ed. Bristol, PA: Taylor & Francis.

Fairclough, N. (1989). *Language and power.* London: Longman.

Fairclough, N. (1992a). *Discourse and social change.* Cambridge, UK: Polity.

Fairclough, N. (Ed.). (1992b). *Critical language awareness.* London: Longman.

Field, D., & Jardine, D. (1994) "Bad examples" as interpretive opportunities: On the need for whole language to own its shadow. *Language Arts, 71*(4), 258–263.

Fine, E. (1994). Peacemaking as a tool for change. *Primary Voices, 2*(4), 2–5.

Fine, E., Lacey, A., & Baer, J. (1995). *Children as peacemakers.* Portsmouth, NH: Heinemann.

Franklin, D. (1995). Ten not so little piggies. *The Nation, 261*(18), 670–671.

Freire, P. (1970). *Pedagogy of the oppressed.* New York: Seabury.

Gee, J. (1990). *Social linguistics and literacies: Ideology in discourses.* London: Falmer.

Gee, J. (1994). First language acquisition as a guide for theories of learning and pedagogy. *Linguistics and Education, 6*(4), 331–354.

Goodman, K. (1988). Look what they've done to Judy Blume: The basalization of children's literature. *The New Advocate, 1*(1), 29–41.

Goodman, K., Maras, L., & Birdseye, D. (1994). Look! Look! Who stole the pictures from the picture book? The basalization of picture books. *The New Advocate, 7*(1), 1–24.

Graff, H. (1987). *The legacies of literacy: Continuities and contradictions in western culture and society.* Bloomington: Indiana University Press.

Greider, W. (1992). *Who will tell the people? The betrayal of American democracy.* New York: Simon & Schuster.

Hoose, P. (1993). *It's our world too: Stories of young people who are making a difference.* Boston: Joy Street.

Ivins, M. (1996, January 16). Make way for Gold Rush of '96 for stake in Electronicville. *Arizona Republic,* B5.

Johnston, P. (1992). Assessment as social practice. Paper presented at the National Reading Conference, San Antonio, TX.

Kauffman, L. (1993, May 24). Democracy in the suites. *The Nation, 259,* 712–713.

Laminack, L., & Lawing, S. (1994). Building generative curriculum. *Primary Voices, 2*(3), 8–18.

Lee, E. (1994). Taking multicultural, anti-racist education seriously. In Bigelow, B., et al. (Eds.), *Rethinking our classrooms: Teaching for equity and justice* (pp. 19–22). Milwaukee: Rethinking Schools.

Lewis, Charles, with the Center for Public Inquiry. (1996). *Buying of the Presidency.* New York: Avon.

Luke, A. (1995). When basic skills and information processing just aren't enough: Rethinking reading in new times. *Teachers College Record, 97*(1), 95–115.

Luke, C. (1992). The politicized "I" and depoliticized "we": The politics of theory in postmodern feminisms. *Social Semiotics, 2,* 1–20.

Mason, K. (1994). Response to basals. In P. Shannon & K. Goodman (Eds.), *Basal readers: A second look* (pp. 179–184). Katonah, NY: Richard C. Owen.

McDermott, R. (1993). An anthropologist reads from his work. Paper presented at the annual meeting of the American Educational Research Association, Atlanta, GA.

McIntosh, P. (1988). *White privilege and male privilege: A personal account of coming to see correspondences through work in women's studies.* Working Paper No. 189. Wellesley, MA: Wellesley College, Center for Research on Women.

Nader, R. (1996). Imagine that! *The Nation, 262*(1), 10.

Patterson, K. (1978). *The Bridge to Terebithio.* New York: Crowell.

Patterson, K. (1978). *The Great Gilly Hopkins.* New York: Crowell.

Peterson, B. (1994a). Teaching for social justice: One teacher's journey. In Bigelow, B., et al. (Eds.), *Rethinking our classrooms: Teaching for equity and justice* (pp. 30–38). Milwaukee: Rethinking Schools.

Peterson, B. (1994b). The complexities of encouraging social action. In Bigelow, B., et al. (Eds.), *Rethinking our classrooms: Teaching for equity and justice* (pp. 40–41). Milwaukee: Rethinking Schools.

Peterson, R. (1992). *Life in a crowded place: Making a learning community.* Portsmouth, NH: Heinemann.

Rylant, C. (1985). *The Relatives Came.* New York: Bradbury Press.

Salvio, P. (1994). Ninja warriors and Vulcan logic: Using the cultural literacy portfolio as a curriculum script. *Language Arts, 71*(6), 419–424.

Shannon, P. (1993). Developing democratic voices. *The Reading Teacher, 47*(2), 86–94.

Shannon, P. (1996). Mad as hell. *Language Arts, 73*(1), 14–19.

Sidener, J., & Mayes, K. (1996, January 21). Dollars and bills. *Arizona Republic,* A1.

Tashman, B. (1996, April 16). First, let's fail the teachers. *Village Voice* (Education Supplement), 3–6.

Taylor, M. (1976). *Roll of Thunder, Hear My Cry.* New York: Dial.

Weiner, J. (1996). The cigarette papers. *The Nation, 262*(11), 11–18.

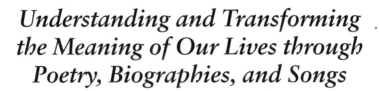

CHAPTER TWO

Understanding and Transforming the Meaning of Our Lives through Poetry, Biographies, and Songs

CECILIA M. ESPINOSA
William T. Machan Elementary School, Phoenix, Arizona

KAREN J. MOORE
William T. Machan Elementary School, Phoenix, Arizona

Background

Our school is a work-in-progress—a project where we teachers have the freedom to put our theory into practice, and the expectation that we will continue to grow in our knowledge about teaching and learning. This professionally enriching state of affairs is largely due to the vision of our principal and the teachers she has hired. Parents who grew up in the neighborhood and attended the school as children often comment that they were afraid to send their children to our school because they remembered what a horrible institution the school was. These same parents now wholeheartedly support our school, the work we do, and the community.

Our school, located in Phoenix, Arizona, is in an inner-city neighborhood whose population has changed tremendously during the past decade. During that period, the Spanish-speaking minority became the majority. Currently, our newest students are people who have just arrived in this country. Our teachers and administrators have worked to help make the school not just an institution but a part of the community, and so our school has many connections with the local university and social and health agencies. These other institutions bring us a wealth of knowledge and expertise; they also use our campus as a laboratory and teaching ground.

The flexibility we enjoy allows us to have multiage classrooms. Therefore, we can come to know the children and their families and build trust over a longer period of time. Knowing the children well helps us develop a curriculum that has depth and relevance to our lives. The work we present below grew out of these opportunities.

The Farmworker Study

Our kindergarten through second-grade multiage classes had been studying about "the desert" for about six weeks. We had studied it from many different points of view. We had read the work of some authors who live in the desert and dedicate their lives to writing about it. We had filled the classroom with desert artifacts brought by teachers and children. The children had done research about animals and plants. We had taken a couple of field trips to different places where we could observe firsthand the desert habitat. Parents had volunteered in the classroom with their expertise about desert plants and their medicinal uses. Each week the children's talk about the desert had became more and more complex and knowledgeable. We thought our "desert study" was coming to an end. We were planning to integrate our knowledge into different projects in order to make an exhibit or presentation about the desert and invite other classes and parents to our "celebration."

Then we came across some work of Tish Hinojosa, a Mexican American singer and activist from San Antonio, Texas. One of her songs, "Bandera del Sol," had already become a symbol for our school that year. Many classrooms sang it and used it as a community ritual. Lately, singing had become a very important part of our school life. It seemed that when teachers and children joined in singing songs that described peace, hope, love, and injustice, then our spirits, our minds, and our actions joined together as one voice. These magical moments, when our hopes were connected to make what seems impossible become possible, confirmed what the Chilean poet Pablo Neruda had reported in his autobiography (*Confieso Que He Vivido*) about the Turkish poet Nazim Hikmet. Once, when Hikmet was being terribly tortured, accused of trying to incite the marines to revolt after reading his books, he began to sing, quietly at first, but later very loud with all his strength. He sang all the songs he knew, all the poems he knew, the songs of the people, songs of the struggle; he sang everything he knew. By singing he overcame his torture. Neruda's response to Hikmet was, "You sang for all of us, we have no doubt in what we need to do. We all know now when we need to start singing" (p. 274).

As we became more familiar with the work of Tish Hinojosa, we understood better about the "need to start singing." We discovered and learned the words to many of her bilingual songs that dealt with injustice and change. Soon Tish Hinojosa's songs inspired our young poets and writers to write their own songs. Samantha and Jessica dedicated hours to writing them. An excerpt from their lyrics for "Peace and Love," one of our favorites, deals with topics of great concern to the children—gangs, drugs, and guns:

> My promise is to care for the world
> no gangs of danger, but say now is peace
> I am going to sing all day long Peace for the World
> Not drugs, not gangs, not even bad guns
> Stand up and say no guns for the world
> guns are not for me and you.

It was during the time when our classes were studying the desert that we heard Hinojosa's song "Something in the Rain." In this song she talks about the struggles of the farmworkers over the use of pesticides in the grape fields in California, about children being poisoned by pesticides and crying at night from the pain, about parents watching helplessly as their children suffer. This song evokes issues of human rights, of respect for the land and its people, and of the insatiable need of some people to make a lot of money regardless of the consequences. Yet, at the same time, the song is full of hope and humanity. We took some time as a class to pay attention to each one of the words and ideas

chosen for this poem/song. We reflected individually and collectively. Our discussions were full of feeling and evoked many
scary thoughts. Through this song we experienced images of children dying or being born with impairments because someone
wanted to make money. We could hear the pain of the parents,
and their desperate need for these practices to stop.

> There must be something in the rain
> Well, what else could cause this pain. . . .
> TISH HINOJOSA, *from "Something in the Rain"*

As the children became interested in what was happening to
the farmworkers in California, they raised many questions and
issues. Some of the children were aware of farmworkers' labor
conditions because they had relatives who were working or had
worked in the grape fields in California. So we decided to change
the direction we had anticipated for our desert study. We
embarked on a journey of inquiry in which there was no "knowledgeable leader" (no "teacher"). We had never intended to take
this path, but the children's questions and interest gave us no
alternative.

We went to the public library, made phone calls, and talked
to people in order to become better informed about farmworkers
and desert agribusiness. We found out about different organizations, such as La Causa, that could help us gather materials and
locate guest speakers. A law student who had taken a semester
off to volunteer with the migrant workers in California came to
talk to our classes. He represented La Causa—the workers'
movement initiated by César Chávez. He was full of passion for
his work as a volunteer and for the possibility of enacting
change. The children sat around him for more than an hour, listening to him and asking him questions. His words were very
serious and convincing as he talked to us about the poverty and
abuse that still exist in spite of all the work of César Chávez. He
asked us not to buy grapes and to wear the buttons he gave us
that said "NO GRAPES." He reminded us to take the time to ask
managers at supermarkets where the grapes came from, and to
voice our opinion if they came from a place where pesticides

were being used. He taught us that as consumers we had the power to make changes.

He told us about César Chávez's ideas, his love for his people, and his dreams and hopes. We learned from him how much César Chávez had read and studied different laws in order to be knowledgeable and to be able to help his people. He stressed that the struggles of farmworkers still continue due to poor working conditions, low salaries, and pesticide use that persist years after César Chávez death. Finally, he showed us some films with interviews and explanations about the effects of pesticides in the fields and the surrounding areas. The films showed many Hispanics united and taking a stand on the farmworkers' situation.

Soon we realized that we needed to learn and study in depth the life and work of César Chávez. He was going to give us strength to change and deepen our understanding. As a class we read his biography, and kept a close watch for any information the news had about his life, work, and ideas. We also went to see a play about his life and work. After the play one of the children said, "He was like Martin Luther King. He wanted people to be treated with respect."

Slowly, César Chávez and his work impacted our hearts and lives. He was a model to us for putting into practice one's ideas and beliefs. One day the school lunch included grapes. Many of the children refused to take them. The cafeteria manager was upset and asked, "How could they choose not to take the fruit?" However, the children were determined not to take them, and didn't mind explaining why. A few parents visited one day with concerns because their children would not let them buy grapes any more. They complained, "Don't you know that grapes make it easy for us to pack lunches and snacks?"

One day the school librarian had a "Breakfast with Books" for children and their parents, and she served grapes. One of the children told her, "Don't you know you are not supposed to buy grapes? They are putting pesticides in the fields, and the children are being born sick. You need to put them away. Haven't you heard about César Chávez?" The librarian had no choice but to remove the grapes. On another, occasion when we were making posters for a bake sale, the children wrote "NO GRAPES" in the middle of the advertisement for the items we were going to sell. The children had taken something they learned at school, applied it to their lives, and took action. They were also challenging us to do the same and to be more vigilant about the way we lead our lives, both personally and professionally.

This experience taught us that it *does* matter how we use our time at school and that it matters what kinds of studies we choose to do with the children. With the right kind of opportunities and experiences, children learn to care deeply about the world, to be eager to take action and to fight for justice.

Now as we reflect on these events, we think that as teachers we probably did not take this study far enough or deep enough. For instance, the children could have created their own play about César Chávez, his life, and his ideas. Our lives at school are fast and full of interruptions. There is really very little time to reflect, and to take the time to see all the possibilities of moments like the ones we described in the paragraphs above. We know that these young children would have been able to express so much of their knowledge about César Chávez through enacting his story in drama.

Biographies

After the study of César Chávez, we struggled to make more connections that were valid for the children. We were looking for our next step. Since we teach multiage classes, most of the children remain with us for three years. We wanted to provide them with related, but not repeated, experiences in the years to come. Therefore, we began the following year with a study of biographies about people who had fought for human rights, animals, the environment, and so on. Students signed up for groups that would each study one of these people. The groups were led by a teacher assistant, a student teacher, and a teacher. Our goal was to fill our classroom environment with the lives of people who had made a difference in the world: e.g., Helen Keller, Rachel Carson, Rosa Parks, Vilma Martínez, Jane Goodall, Martin Luther King Jr., and Benito Juárez. Starting that year to learn about the lives of people who stood up for their beliefs gave us a vision to follow and a center to be grounded in. It also helped us in making decisions about how to lead our own lives. How was it that Helen Keller learned to control her temper? And what inspired her to become an advocate for unsighted people? What made Rosa Parks finally say one day that she wasn't going to give up her seat anymore? How did Benito Juárez manage to become a lawyer when, as an indigenous person, he was not allowed to go to school? How did Vilma Martínez overcome the oppressive societal thinking that women did not have a place in college or that bilingualism was a problem rather than a resource? What inspired these people to take a stand? Who inspired them?

The biographies were intended to make these famous figures become part of our students' lives and also to inspire them. We wanted them to see that fighting for one's own and others' rights is a struggle everywhere; we have to think globally about it, but we must start with the vision of people's rights in our own homes and classrooms.

Not all the biographies we studied were "teacher-initiated"; many were chosen spontaneously or with very little teacher intervention. One day in Cecilia's class, Julisa, a second-grade fluent reader, did not seem engaged in her reading. She would pick a picture book, finish it, and move on to something else. After conferring with Cecilia, she decided to read the book about the life of Benito Juárez. She started reading the book that same morning. By the end of reading time, Julisa was still reading; she read all through the morning and asked to take the book home. As soon as she saw us the next morning, she told us she had stayed up very late, past her bedtime, because she could not stop reading, and she wanted to share the book with the rest of the class. So Julisa shared "everything" that she had learned about Benito Juárez the day before. Even when we wanted to move on to something else, she said, "Wait, I am not done yet, I have more to tell you." The children listened to her intently, asking questions and giving their opinions. Julisa said she wanted to write a book about Benito Juárez. For many days afterward, she kept reading about his life and taking notes. As she wrote about Benito Juárez not being allowed to attend school because of his race, Julisa said, "I understand now. He had to go to a special school for indigenous people; he couldn't attend the same schools other people attended."

What was amazing to us was not only that Julisa learned such "lessons," but also that she was able to elevate what "reading" meant for the whole class. In only "one day and one night," as she said, Julisa discovered the power of reading someone's life *into* her own. Benito Juárez will be a part of Julisa's life for many years to come. We were truly fascinated when we heard Julisa say, "Wow, yesterday I didn't know anything about Benito Juárez, and look at me now. I know so much about him."

These studies of those who fought for their rights and beliefs helped us to remember that the human spirit has amazing capabilities, even in the midst of very difficult circumstances. It is our responsibility as teachers to help maintain this vision of our students being enthusiastic, successful learners so that we can help them see the possibilities, and at the same time so that we can see the possibilities for ourselves.

Standing up for one's beliefs and one's rights is always difficult, but it is especially hard for our students, given the complex issues they confront. Many of their families are immigrants, many are undocumented, and many families have escaped poverty and political persecution in their native land and have come here only to continue their suffering. The language they speak isn't necessarily highly valued in our society. The news and the media continuously present them from a very negative point of view. Most do not have access to medical care, and they are constantly afraid that "la migra," the immigration service, might come and take them away. Many of the places they rent do not meet even the basic standards of safety and health. Their landlords are not always the most helpful, and so they learn to live quietly because often the consequences of speaking up are damaging to their already fragile sense of "security."

For instance, in our school neighborhood there is a very large apartment complex, notorious for its drug traffic and prostitution, where many of our children live. Originally, the apartment had both a front and back entrance. To cut down on the amount of traffic going through, the managers closed off the back exit with a large fence. The front entrance is on a very busy street, so the school district would not allow the bus to stop on that street to pick up the children. The children were forced to walk a long distance around the complex to meet the bus in the back, in front of the locked gate. Many children climbed the steel-pointed gate or squeezed through holes in the chain-link fence. After several children were injured, the managers greased the gate so that it could not be climbed. When parents complained to the managers about this unsafe and unfair condition, they were told that if they complained to anyone else, they would be evicted from their apartment and reported to "immigration." A parents' group that was formed to talk about children's rights and safety in the community began to focus on this issue. The attitude of the parents who talked about it was that nothing could be done. It was only because administrators from the school district, members of the media, and some state legislators became involved that the problem was able to be mediated. The bus driver now has a key to the gate.

Many people at our school have been fortunate enough to work closely with Patricia Carini, former director of Prospect School, and current director of Prospect School Archives. She has influenced our thinking and our teaching in terms of seeing children through their strengths and building on those strengths. She has written (Carini, 1986) that

> Given the attitudes currently dominant in our society, I believe that it is important—indeed, crucial—that those of us deeply concerned with children and childhood learn to be attentive to, and to draw upon, children's strengths (and our own) in order to modify and counteract these adverse influences. This requires vigilance in guarding the rights of all children to an environment conducive to growth and to an education. It also requires the ability to observe and build from children's strengths as thinkers, learners, and persons. Finally, it requires us to create classrooms and other environments that are responsive to the broad and diverse range of children in terms of interests, potentials, and needs. It is, I think, only from a firmly grounded knowledge of children's

strengths that we will be able to offer effective alternatives to current and proposed school practices that undermine children's long-term potential for growth. (pp. 3–4)

Our children bring to the classroom a beautiful language; strong family ties; minds, hearts, and bodies full of hope; an intense desire to learn and to share who they really are. They also bring aspirations, high expectations, dreams, wonder, freshness, and a world full of possibilities. These are just some of their strengths. It is up to us to make sure that we create the space for all their strengths to work for them.

News

The time we set aside for "news" is one of these spaces. We have struggled for years to balance between frivolous news conversations that hop from one topic to another without really affecting our thinking, and the kinds of conversations that really make us think. For example, one year we paid attention to the way the media portray Hispanics and followed the news stories over a period of time. In class, we discussed a series of questions about the point of view of the articles: Who is really telling this story? Are we Hispanics really the way this article describes us? Do we all have parties with loud music and barbecues, so that our neighbors can't have any peace of mind? Why would anyone want to make such a general statement like that about a group of people? Why are we portrayed as trying to take jobs away from citizens of the United States? If *we* were writing the newspaper article or reporting for the TV news, what kind of stories would we write about ourselves? What are our many positive characteristics? We believe that if we do this critical analysis when our children are still young, they will not grow up believing that those stories are truthful, but instead will learn to read the paper and watch the news with a questioning mind.

Carole Edelsky (1994) urges teachers to think about how systems of domination are part of all classroom interaction. In our news time, we are trying to foreground and question systems of domination. We do that questioning at other times too. One day in Cecilia's class, during "Buddy Reading," the students were doing a study of fairy tales from a historical, literary, and critical perspective. We had spent days studying the different roles of the characters. We had plans to study nontraditional fairy tales in which females play a different role and witches are considered "smart and educated women." We had decided that in order to really analyze and pay attention to all of this, we needed to study the more traditional ones first. While reading the fairy tale "Snow White the Fairest One of All," Reneé, the fourth- and fifth-grade teacher, asked the children if they knew what the word "fair" meant. A child said, "It means if your mom is going to give you something you get the same as your brother."

We decided to look up "fair" in our thesaurus. To our dismay, many of the meanings were connected to "whiteness." The range of related words included "blond, attractive, gorgeous, beautiful, bright, pleasant, serene, clear, unclouded, clean, equal, equitable, even, honest," all the way to "just, unbiased, impartial, unprejudiced, and open-minded." Seeing "justice" connected with "whiteness" reminded us of Herbert Kohl's (1991) discussion of having to "unlearn" racist habits of mind. Kohl's student Akim challenged Kohl's idea of reading Conrad's *Heart of Darkness* because of its explicit and offensive racism. Kohl says, "Before knowing him [Akim] I was not attuned to many of the nuances of racist implication because I was not the victim of racism. I did not suffer through every offensive phrase I encountered when reading, nor did I experience rage when racism was cloaked in the authority of tradition or the language of excellence" (p. 32). As when Akim confronted Kohl, the day we looked up "fair" was a turning point for us. It helped us see how the words we use every day are closely tied to those who are in power. The word "fair" will no longer have the traditional meaning for us; there is so much more behind it. In *She Tries Her Tongue, Her Silence Softly Breaks*, Marlene Nourbese Philip (1989) writes, "Language creates a bridge; to speak another language is to enter someone else's consciousness. Speech, voice, language, and word—are all ways of being in the world" (p. 16). Together we are learning to be "awake" in the world, to become conscious of "the ways of being" embedded in the language we learn and use.

Poetry

Poetry has a very important place in our classes. After many months of daily exposure to poetry, the children's assignment was to find their favorite poem from among all the poetry books in the class. While some of the children took the assignment quite seriously, others did not. Some children chose poems without paying much attention to aesthetics or intellectual weight. We had many discussions, therefore, about why one would like a certain poem. On the one hand, we wanted to support the children's choices, yet we also wanted to raise the "level" of their choices. We wanted them to be able to find poems that really moved them, that spoke to them, and that awakened something unknown in them.

There was a group of Spanish-speaking children who were looking at some of Rafael Alberti's poetry. One of the children in this group was looking for the poem, "Se equivocó La Paloma" ("The Dove was Mistaken"), a poem that is the favorite among many children in our class, and one that the children had practically memorized. Robert said, "Look, you can study about the life of Rafael Alberti in this book. We could study about his life." An intern from Arizona State University, Aída, happened to be there, and the children began to talk with her about Rafael Alberti. She had studied in Granada, Spain, and was also fascinated by the work of Alberti, García Lorca, Machado, and other poets of that period. The next time she came, she brought with her many books about Rafael Alberti and his poet friends. Every time Aída came, she worked with the children, helping them to take notes and "translating" the words of these books for adults into words and stories that the children could make their own.

This was another time when the children were engaging in inquiry that was quite unexpected for the "teachers" and when the teachers' knowledge was also very limited. But we learned. Rafael Alberti is another one of those poets who has fought for the rights of others. He became a poet of the oppressed and the persecuted and was himself persecuted and then went into exile for thirty-nine years. He was active during the Spanish Civil War, and became personally devastated when his friend and fellow poet, Federico García Lorca, was killed because of his beliefs and ideas.

One of the most persistent questions the children had was whether Rafael Alberti was still alive. They said, "If he is alive he must be older than ninety years. How could we find out if he is still alive?" One day while Cecilia was working on the Internet, she decided to find out if there was any information about Rafael Alberti. To her surprise, there was an article from a newspaper in Madrid, announcing that Rafael Alberti had been hospitalized on New Year's Eve and was very ill. The next day, during announcements and sharing, Cecilia shared the news about Rafael Alberti with the children. The classroom filled with silence. Another great poet was dying. Although Alberti was miles away, he had become very close to us, and it was hard to imagine that we wouldn't have any more new poems written by him.

That same day, another group of children, having noticed all the talk about Rafael Alberti, began to show an interest in the work of Gabriela Mistral. They went to other classes and gathered books about her poetry and her life. Here was another wonderful poet—and a teacher for twenty years—who had dedicated her life to putting books in the hands of people, writing poems for children, and helping reform schools and create libraries. Her desire was to write poetry for the poor and the most needy. Many children in our class wrote poetry inspired by the work of Gabriela Mistral. The following poem by Viridiana is one of our favorites:

Paz

Paz para
los niños
paz para
los jóvenes
paz para
los maestros
paz para
los animales
paz
para tener
un mundo feliz
y con amor

Por Viridiana, 8 años

Peace

Peace for
the children
peace
for the youth
peace for
the teachers
peace for
the animals
peace
so we can have
a world
with happiness
and love

VIRIDIANA (AGE 8)

Working with poetry in our classrooms and reading essays by Adrienne Rich (1993) and Alastair Reid (1996) have helped us to re-view poetry as: poetry of the people, poetry for the people, and poetry by the people. Adrienne Rich says that she had "long known how poetry can break open locked chambers of possibility, restore numbed zones to feeling, recharge desire" (p. xiv). A poem, she argues, "can't free us from the struggle for existence, but it can uncover desires and appetites buried under the accumulating emergencies of our lives" (p. 13).

Adrienne Rich reminds us that in most countries, poetry has been considered dangerous and indispensable. For example, when the junta took control in Chile, there was heightened political repression. The military regime ransacked and sealed poet Pablo Neruda's house. But people from all walks of life came to write messages to him on the boards of the fence. These messages were full of resistance—brief phrases and names that conveyed a world of meanings. Neruda died twelve days after the junta took over power in Chile, but the poet and his life became a symbol of resistance. Alastair Reid (1996) says of Pablo Neruda's poetry, "He did not write poems for literary circles; he wanted them out in the street, read by everyday inhabitants of the language. He achieved just that, in his own time, as has no other poet I can think of. He accomplished what Whitman only aspired to; he became what Whitman had hoped to be" (p. 61).

We want our students to be awakened by poetry in such a way that their thoughts and feelings are given body and shape by its power. We also want them to know about the lives and work of poets like Pablo Neruda, Rafael Alberti, Alfonsina Stormi, Gabriela Mistral, Rubén Dario, Sandra Cisneros, Nikki Giovanni, Gary Soto, and others. As teachers we know that the struggle starts with us, that children won't take poetry as something indispensable unless we do.

Building Community

As a country we talk about the issues of human rights in faraway places, yet violations of human rights are taking place all around us, in our own country, in our cities, towns, and neighborhoods. Every day, the children tell personal stories that touch on issues of human rights.

Ana was in Karen's class for three years. From the first day she was able to express in some way what she considered to be her rights. She was not a child who easily conformed to the schedule of others. She had her own time frame and agenda. When she invested herself in her work, she was unable to stop just because the teacher said it was time to do something else. She could work for hours on writing or art and produce incredible work. This was difficult for us, but we also saw that Ana supported other children in the classroom; she was a good friend, and she showed us through the thoroughness of her work in class projects that she had a commitment to the class. It took time to get to know Ana and an adjustment on our part to be able to let her have her space and her own time frame.

After second grade Ana's family moved out of our school area. One day, in a phone conversation with Karen, Ana said that she wasn't happy in her new school. Spanish-speaking Ana had been placed in an all-English classroom, one with a narrowly prescribed curriculum. "They don't understand me," she told Karen. "They don't listen to me. They don't let me do my art. They don't know me." The closed curriculum and the language restrictions placed on Ana made her feel stifled; she was sure that the teachers at the new school saw her as not very knowledgeable or creative—a far cry from the thorough, responsible, imaginative child we knew. In *Life in a Crowded Place*, Ralph Peterson (1992) says that students must feel they belong and be confident that they have something of worth to offer others, that everyone need not participate in the same way, that voices differ." Ana needed the time and the opportunity to be herself, to make her own unique contribution to our community.

Building a community often means being an advocate for children and their families. This year Karen had a new child in her class who had just come from Mexico. He lived with his mother, his stepfather, and two brothers. A couple of months after the school year started, the family moved in order to be closer to the stepfather's work. Two weeks passed and one day at lunch we were reminiscing about the child and his entertaining qualities. At that moment the child's mother walked in with her children. She told us that for two weeks she had been trying to enroll her children in the school in the new neighborhood. She said the school would not accept the children because she had no identification and could not produce a utility bill or legal document to verify her address. The office staff and, later, the vice principal told her that too many people try to sneak their children into school, and there isn't room for them all. In desperation, the mother had returned to our school to ask for our help. We asked our principal to intervene. After getting the same story from that school, our principal called the district office and challenged their policy. Eventually, a higher-ranking administrator agreed to help. The children were enrolled the same day. Why did it take a principal calling a district office to get children into school who had been denied an education for two weeks?

Throughout the school year, but especially at the beginning, to build a sense of community and to become aware of our own and others' rights, we play games, talk about our expectations, learn new songs together, read books that touch on issues of human rights, and share personal and family stories. Every day we have a time together that we call "Concerns and Compliments," when children learn to talk about and solve their prob-

lems. In a school with a transient population such as ours, it is a
challenge to provide the children with the feeling of community,
safety, and continuity that they need in order to thrive in an academic setting. Nonetheless, when expectations are set for children to exercise their rights and to respect the rights of others,
amazing things can happen.

Enrique started the year with a lot of difficulties in getting
along with other children. He had many problems on the playground; children complained to him and about him. As the year
progressed in Karen's room, through much talk about individual
rights and the rights of others, Enrique became more responsible
in his actions and more responsive to the rights, needs, and feelings of others. He made progress both socially and academically.
The children often complimented Enrique for the progress he
was making. But two weeks before the end of the year, Enrique
was caught throwing rocks at the house of an incapacitated man
who lived near Enrique's bus stop. The man was frightened by
the violence. The man had dogs which Enrique and some other
boys teased. Another day soon after, Enrique and a friend
thought they had broken a window, so instead of getting on the
bus and coming to school, they ran and hid in the neighborhood.
Other children who had witnessed what had happened reported
it to teachers. The children were very upset. We were worried
about Enrique and his friend because they were not at school,
and nobody—not us, not their families—knew where they were.
The police were called in to look for them. They found them setting fires in the alley of their apartment complex. The police
handcuffed the seven- and eight-year-olds and brought them to
school—dirty and very scared. We felt such a sense of despair;
the progress we had made during the year as a class and with
Enrique as an individual seemed to have disappeared. We had
worked so hard on thinking independently and making good
decisions. This felt like a major setback, and we were angry and
disappointed. But then we saw that the other children in the class
were also disappointed. Moreover, they were not only disappointed in Enrique; they were also concerned about the elderly
man who was being harassed by Enrique and the other boys.
Even more impressive, instead of voicing anger, our students
commented that Enrique needed our help and support more than

ever; rather than punishing Enrique, they said we should help and guide him through this difficult time. We came to realize that even though, as a community, we were not perfect, the struggle was a process and our job was to keep working at it.

Our work with justice changes every year. We keep some basic principles in mind, like working toward bringing the idea of human rights into our classroom and into our everyday lives, as well as keeping a watchful eye in order to see the possibilities the children and life bring to us. We think of this type of work as a craft, a dance, a poem—the form the artist encounters as she works with the rock or the marble, a piece of clay we give shape to as we work with it. We are never sure what will happen, what will come out of it, what next year's children will bring to our class. We discover as we work together. And we create stories like these, which help us understand our lives.

References

Carini, P. (1986). *Building from children's strengths.* North Bennington, VT: Prospect Archive and Center for Education and Research.

Edelsky, C. (1994). Education for democracy. *Language Arts, 71*(4), 252–257.

Kohl, H. (1991). *I won't learn from you: And other thoughts on creative maladjustment.* Minneapolis: Milkweed.

Neruda, P. (1973/1993). *Confieso que he vivido.* Barcelona, Spain: Editorial Seix Barral,S.A.

Peterson, R. (1992). *Life in a crowded place: Making a learning community.* Portsmouth, NH: Heinemann.

Philip, M. N. (1989). *She tries her tongue, her silence softly breaks.* Charlottetown, P.E.I.: Ragweed.

Reid, A. (1996, June 24/July 1). Neruda and Borges. *The New Yorker,* 56–67.

Rich, A. (1993). *What is found there.* New York: Norton.

CHAPTER THREE

Exchanging Ideas and Changing Positions: The Importance of Conversation to Holistic, Critical Endeavors

MARIE ELAINE BOOZER
Ohio State University

LISA BURLEY MARAS
Pennsylvania State University

BILL BRUMMETT
Geneseo (New York) Central School

If there is no struggle, there is no progress. Those who profess to favor freedom yet renounce controversy are people who want crops without ploughing the ground.
FREDERICK DOUGLASS, *1817–1895*

There are few Americans who would not "profess to favor freedom," yet *saying* that one believes in freedom is not equivalent to *exchanging ideas* about what freedom means and how it should be realized. To do this, citizens must first reflect both upon their own lives and the lives of others. In sharing these reflections and using others' reflections to further our own, we are able to critique ourselves and the sociopolitical systems to which we belong. This critique allows us to visualize more just ways of living and to find the means by which to actualize those visions.

As holistic, critical educators, we believe that talking with each other and with our students helps us move from merely professing freedom to making freedom a reality. We believe that conversation is the mechanism that not only drives our inquiry-based curriculums, but allows us to ask ourselves and our students questions about inequality and to seek ways to responsibly address privilege and oppression. Conversation connects us to others engaged in similar struggles, affirms our individual efforts, and pushes us toward greater reflection.

A focal point of our current professional conversations is two student-led inquiries that led us and our students to challenge attitudes, behaviors, and systems that subjugate various groups of people. The first occurred in Bill and Lisa's intermediate multiage classroom. Through their study of group homes and their interactions with residents of a local group home, students became more aware of how their personal attitudes and actions affect others in their community. The second, underway in Lisa and Marie's fourth-grade classroom as we wrote this chapter, centers on students' attempts to overthrow an unjust schoolwide reward program. As the project increasingly permeates their lives, students are making connections between the reward program and similar institutions both in and out of school. This chapter provides a summary of each inquiry, our reflections upon the critical nature of these inquiries, and our current conclusions regarding the importance of exchanging ideas through classroom conversations.

Group Homes: Reflecting on our Attitudes and Actions

Curriculum planning in Lisa and Bill's multiage classroom centered on the "Authoring Cycle" (Harste, Short, & Burke, 1988). Rather then focusing on the transmission of predetermined facts to students, curriculum based on the authoring cycle begins with learners' life experiences and is directed by the questions they have about those experiences. Through collaboration with others and reflection upon their experiences as a result of those collaborations, learners revise their thinking and formulate new questions. Since curriculum is the means whereby class members support each other in exploring those questions, conversation is vital to the development of curriculum. Thus, in Lisa and Bill's classroom, class meetings were frequently held not only for presenting and sharing knowledge, but for engaging in each other's life experiences and for discussing reactions and concerns about those experiences.

Following this framework, numerous conversations in which class members shared experiences related to group-home residents arose as part of daily sharing time. For example, Lydia[1] recounted the summer and spring vacations her family had enjoyed, vacations that included one or two residents from the group homes where her parents worked. Lydia also shared stories of relationships she and her parents had had with particular residents. Kelly gave us frequent reports on her brother, a group-home resident. When he came home for his monthly visits, Kelly's excitement spread through all of us. Afterward, she filled us with the details of their time together. Cheryl talked with us about her multiply handicapped grandmother. Though not a group-home resident, Cheryl's grandmother, like many group-home residents, was not able to fully care for herself. For months we shared Cheryl's grief and lent her our support as she shared her family's predicament. Several students read *Summer of the Swans* by Betsy Byars (1972) and discussed the relationship between Sara and her mentally retarded brother.

As members of the classroom, Bill and Lisa also shared their personal experiences related to group homes. Living adjacent to a local group home, Bill described his life as a neighbor and reminisced about the public hearings and open houses that occurred when the home first opened. Bill told the class about scaring dogs away when they cornered residents, and of conversations he'd had with residents during his daily walks. Lisa also shared some of her early teaching experiences, including those with profoundly disabled students, children whom many people believed could not learn and were frequently ignored by many school personnel. All of these conversations, as well as many others, were not limited to a single day, but were scattered throughout the year, allowing time for a rich history to develop among the class members. Each experience planted the seed for another, nurturing and supporting what had come before and what was to come after.

Pulling It Together

In mid-April, Bill and Lisa looked at state-mandated curriculum documents to determine what areas they had not yet explored with students. A major area that still remained was local history. True to the "Authoring Cycle," they began the study by brainstorming with students lists of things they could study. The list they generated included items one would expect to find in such a study—life among the Iroquois or as early settlers, formation of the town, land forms, industry, crops, architecture, art, and famous people. Unlike lists produced in other classes, however, this one also included local issues prevalent in classroom conversations and in the media—the humane treatment of animals, the opening of a new Wal-Mart store, the proposed backfilling of an abandoned salt mine, and the treatment of group-home residents. As students talked about each topic on the board, they abandoned some and combined others. Finally, students insisted that their study of local history begin with explorations of community issues rather than merely factual information. As a result, students divided into three groups to study Wal-Mart, the salt mine, and group homes. Although all three occurred somewhat simultaneously, the intensity of each took precedence at different times, sometimes involving the entire class. The group-home experience took its turn in the limelight during the last few weeks of the school year.

While gathering information about group homes from books and other publications, students decided that human resources would provide an angle not available in print. Accordingly, they organized visits with staff from local group homes. The visitors discussed the history of the homes where they worked, as well as the way the town's history affects acceptance of their residents. (Many families had moved to the town decades earlier to be near family members who lived at a nearby asylum.) As speakers answered students' original academic questions regarding circumstances that lead to placement, group-home organization, and employment opportunities open to residents, more personal questions began to emerge. Questions such as "How do residents feel about their placements?" and "What occupational goals do residents have?" led students to set up visits at a group home and at a semi-independent apartment setting shared by two former residents.

Interacting with Residents

Before the group-home visit, students had viewed residents' lives as half-empty glasses, being unable to attain the things that they themselves aspired to. As a result, students weren't prepared for the enthusiasm and lack of self-consciousness with which the group-home residents and staff greeted them. Residents of the group home openly and honestly discussed their experiences in setting and working toward social, behavioral, and financial goals. They shared rooms filled with personal possessions and family mementos, rooms amazingly similar to those the students shared with siblings in their homes. Students beamed at the bicycles, stereos, and dolls owned by residents and listened intently as each described how he or she had saved money to buy particular objects. The welcoming, proud nature of residents and the realness of their rooms broke down any tentativeness we had.

Tom, a former group-home resident now living in an apartment, also shared his home with the students. Unlike the group home, Tom's apartment was sparsely furnished. He talked with candor about the difficulty he and his roommate, another former resident, had in paying the monthly bills with the low incomes they received from their jobs, and about the difficulty of maintaining relationships he had with other residents. Still, his enthusiasm and pride in his accomplishment, one he had worked toward for three years, allowed him—and us—to view his situation not as one that would overcome him, but as one that he would relentlessly try to overcome.

Although most of us experienced the group-home residents as loving individuals eager to share their lives, a few students initially did not. Snickering as the residents spoke about their possessions, these students laughed and made snide remarks to one another in voices only those closest to them could hear. Some students were so caught up in the lives before them that the remarks went unnoticed. Although Bill caught their eye, effectively silencing them for the moment, these students were eventually swept away by the force of the residents' welcome as the tour continued.

Personal Examinations

Conversations after the visit with group-home residents became more personal, more focused on the lives of the residents and less focused on organizational aspects. Since students worried about group-home residents having full access to stores and not suffering discrimination for their disabilities, Bill and Lisa introduced several picture books about children with disabilities. Students began to discuss times when they had experienced discrimination in one form or another, empathizing with one another, as well as with the group-home residents. During one of these conversations, Bill described an incident in a local coffee shop in which a group of men, knowing one resident's penchant for picking up loose change, glued a quarter to the floor, then laughed at the resident's efforts to remove it. This served as the catalyst for students rethinking their own treatment of residents.

Perhaps the most powerful example of the personal reflection that began to occur in students was seen in Mark and Nicholas. During a class meeting, these boys confessed to a discriminatory act:

> Looking one at a time at his classmates' faces, Mark shared, "In the doughnut shop a whole group of us picked on Donald. I knew we shouldn't have, that it was mean, but everyone was doing it." Beside him, head hung low, Nicholas added, "We called him names and teased him about the way he walks." The boys continued, lips puckered, barely holding in their emotions as they described the episode, intent on saying what had been festering for weeks.

The initial reaction of class members was to absolve the boys of their behavior, until Kristin, whose mother works with the visually impaired, reminded us that everyone is guilty of discrimination and that it is our responsibility to try to stop it. Everyone shared stories in which they had been the victim of or a participant in discriminatory acts. Many stories related to name-calling and teasing, often with reference to words like "retard" or to being in a "special class for dumb kids." Students described the hurt they had caused or suffered and began to discuss more caring ways of acting toward others. By reflecting on their own experiences as givers and receivers of cruelty, they came to see discrimination in a more personal way and to understand ways in which they supported or challenged further discriminatory attitudes.

Armed with a growing desire to include group-home residents in community events, Bill and Lisa's students decided to invite them to the annual school talent show. Several residents accepted.

Personal Connection without Personal Responsibility

In the group-home study, students began to explore how people are treated unfairly at personal levels. They learned to see residents as individuals with dreams and goals similar to their own and to respect them as valuable in their own right, rather than pity them for what they couldn't do. They also learned to consider the effects that their own actions have on others. In this sense, the study was personally transforming for many students.

Most students, however, felt neither a personal responsibility nor a personal commitment toward really helping the group-home residents become an integrated part of community life. We studied group-home living and talked about societal ideologies that lead to perceptions about residents' lives, but we did not actively study or critique systemic issues related to group homes. Consequently, students could not move beyond the personal. For example, after visiting the group home, we discussed our changing view of what it means to live "a full life," but we might have actually studied societal mechanisms that generate and perpetuate the views we originally held. Questions such as "What ideologies and practices encourage us to think that success should be defined in terms of financial independence, living apart from one's family, and owning particular material goods?"; "How and why has this view changed over history?"; and "Who benefits from or is harmed by this view?" have the potential to help students see how our personal actions are created by and help to create the societal structures in which we live. Likewise, Tom's struggles provided an excellent starting point for studying wage discrepancies and job rankings, both of which are part of an economic system that allows a minority to prosper while a majority barely scrape by. Yet we did not study these and other systemic elements, partly because the year ended, and partly because we did not notice them ourselves, so that we could suggest to the students that we study them. Thus, the group-home study was personally transformative for many participants, but it was not what we now consider a critical study, one that goes beyond the personal and attempts to understand the sociopolitical systems to which we belong.

Through our current conversations, we now also recognize a variety of activities that might have moved us from critical talk to critical study and action. Students might have written editorials with or about group-home residents. They might have studied how residents are treated by people in sales and service positions at local businesses or the extent to which various buildings are accessible to people with physical disabilities. Efforts by religious organizations to reach out to residents or by businesses to provide adequately paying jobs for them might also have been studied. Community events that mix all town residents might have been planned. We might have involved parents in any or all of these possibilities, or even suggested that families find ways to engage in more meaningful relationships with residents. Unfortunately, the school year ended before we identified these and other avenues.

Super Stars: Overthrowing an Unjust Reward System

When Lisa took a fourth-grade position at another school, she carried with her the understandings of language and learning that framed her work in the multiage setting. Because she believes in the power of collaborative communities, she immediately engaged children in conversations, asking them to help make classroom decisions. Since Marie and Lisa share similar interests in critical literacy, Lisa received approval for Marie to conduct research in her new classroom. Just as Bill and Lisa had previously operated as collaborative teaching partners, so did Marie and Lisa operate in the new setting.

During the second week of school, Lisa received a memo about "Super Stars," a schoolwide reward program. When she asked the students to explain the program to her, Lisa discovered that each teacher could choose five students a month to receive awards. Lisa questioned her qualifications for being able to choose students for various awards, leading one student to suggest that every person has different opinions about what the qualifications ought to be. Another student protested that since Lisa is the teacher, her opinions count more than the opinions of students. Lisa challenged the role of omnipotent, omniscient teacher, and asked students how they would feel if she were to pick any one student for the Teacher's Pet Award.

Once students began to recognize the subjectivity with which rewards are often given and the emotional effects of such awards, Lisa asked how they might participate in the program and yet be sensitive to these issues. Eventually the class decided that everyone should receive the Good Friend Award because of their efforts to form a caring community. Lisa submitted the entire class and a parent volunteer posted everyone's photo and name in the display case in the school's main hallway. Within a few days, however, Mrs. Wase, the principal, reprimanded Lisa for nominating the entire class, insisting "It can't be everybody or it means nothing. There isn't space in the display case and it's too much to print in the newsletter."

Acceptance or Change?

A few days later a memo arrived in Lisa's mailbox reminding teachers to choose only five students per class for the Super Star awards. When Lisa shared the memo with the class, several students protested that only choosing five students would be unfair because the class works as a team. Lisa agreed and told the class that they could either accept the changes and figure out a way to participate in a system they believe to be unfair or share their concerns with Mrs. Wase in the hope of helping the system to become more fair. When one student suggested that Lisa could talk with Mrs. Wase, Lisa replied that she had talked with Mrs. Wase and that Mrs. Wase needed to know that the dissatisfaction was coming from the students. Lisa then suggested that they share their opinions through letters. The class agreed with the idea and two-thirds of the students wrote letters at home that evening. During the following week, the class edited their individual letters and devoted some of the daily writing time to writing a group letter that everyone signed. Three students then delivered the letters to Mrs. Wase. The class also decided not to participate in the Super Star program until they received a reply.

After Mrs. Wase received the letters, she repeated her previous rationale to Lisa, voiced her discomfort with Lisa's support of the students, and implied that she might share the letters with the School Advisory Board. Lisa suggested that Mrs. Wase might want to talk with the students, which Mrs. Wase agreed to do the following week. When Mrs. Wase did come, however, she repeated the rationale she had initially given Lisa and attempted to use analogies to convince the children of the merits of the awards. Mrs. Wase told the class she had shared their letters with the School Advisory Board but that the School Advisory Board had decided not to change the program during the current year. The students did not make any contributions to Mrs. Wase's forty-minute talk.

When the date for nominating Super Stars drew near the following month, Lisa asked the class for suggestions. Several students were adamant that the School Advisory Board and Mrs. Wase did not take their opinions seriously. Marie asked if there were others in the school who were dissatisfied with the Super Stars program, and several students responded that they knew other kids who also disliked it. From this conversation, the class created a survey that asked, "Do you think the way Super Stars is set up is fair? Why or why not?" and "Would you like it changed?" Although the results were quite unscientific, the majority of students and family members surveyed agreed that the current system was unfair. Given these results and the approaching winter holidays, the class tabled the issue until January.

Talking to Understand

When school resumed in January, the Super Star issue was again a focal part of conversation. Although a majority of the class still wanted to completely withdraw from the Super Star program, several students who were previously against participating in the program had received awards from the music teacher and were now in favor of the awards. Barbara, a student who had received multiple "stars" during each of her former grades, particularly favored our participation in the program.

The discussion became intense as Barbara contended that receiving the stars made her "feel good" and that not receiving them encouraged her to work harder so she could get one the next month. With increasing forcefulness and loudness, student after student expressed frustration about putting forth great effort and not receiving awards, about the fact that some people receive awards for what they ought to be doing anyway, and about the affective consequences of these and other frustrations. When Barbara insisted that the awards inspire her to learn, Lisa and other class members felt personally insulted by Barbara's statement; they viewed the class as a supportive environment, and her statement implied that they were not supporting her. As the attacks progressed, Lisa noticed that students were arguing not to understand others, but to convert people to their point of view. Knowing that such would only lead to coercion, not understanding, Lisa tabled the conversation. Later, Barbara had the opportunity to state her position to the class without interruption. Some students were swayed by her talk—it *does* feel good to receive an award; parents *are* proud when their child's name is published in the school newsletter; every other class in the school participates; rewards encourage some people to compete; and some people *are* better than others at certain things. Since they could not all agree on what to do, a committee, composed of members from both sides as well as undecided parties, formed to examine the issue more closely.

When the committee was unable to devise any adequate solutions, the issue returned to the classroom forum. Some students wrote about the issue in their bimonthly learning reflections. Others spoke to Lisa and Marie privately or in small groups and, still, consensus was nowhere in sight. When some students wanted to operate on the majority-rule premise, Lisa introduced the term "tyranny of the majority" and illustrated it with examples. Afterward, the class decided that only a unanimous decision not to participate in Super Stars would suffice.

Rethinking Positions

Since the school year was now half over, Lisa and Marie decided to press the issue and assigned position papers for homework. (Position papers were not new to students, as they had previously written statements on how they should treat each other and on how they learn.) After reading the position papers and discovering three out of twenty-six class members were still in favor of participating, Marie and Lisa planned a discussion to help students consider the issues more deeply. Lisa and Marie would not identify the dissenters, though they might choose to reveal themselves.

To begin, Marie quickly surveyed the class to determine how many people had received Super Star awards in previous grades. When the class adjusted the results to estimate the number of total students receiving awards per grade level, the average was approximately 20 percent. Stephanie, one of the holdouts, quietly commented, "I thought everybody got one sometime."

Next, Lisa acted as the chart-paper scribe while Marie brainstormed the pro's and con's of the Super Star program with the students. Unlike many discussions, during which some students fidget or carry on private conversations, students tended to look directly at the speaker, to share stories about their own experiences with the program, or to ask one another questions and make connections among points listed. Occasionally, students contradicted themselves or offered weak rationales for a point, either pro or con. In such cases, class members quickly pointed out the flaws. By the time the hour-long discussion ended, the chart paper was filled with four pro's and seventeen con's.

At the close of the session, Marie and Lisa again asked students to consider their positions in light of the conversation. Marie or Lisa spoke individually with the dissenters, assuring them that if they really believed in their position, then they should stick to it. All three dissenters indicated that given the most recent conversation, they were rethinking their views: perhaps it is not okay for one person to feel good when many others do not; perhaps competition is not as effective or as enjoyable as collaboration; and perhaps it does not matter if some people *are* better than others at certain things if we are all helping each other. When Barbara wrote in her reading log that we should be doing what the other fourth-grade classes were doing, Lisa reminded her that if she really believed that, then she must want us to do all the things that the other fourth grades were doing. As Barbara described things she liked about our classroom, the differences from other classes became startlingly apparent; Barbara also began to rethink her position.

Two days later the class gathered to discuss their positions. Lisa had barely introduced the topic when a turning point occurred:

> "I've been talking with my dad and my friends," Barbara announced, "and I think we shouldn't participate in Super Stars."
>
> Relief immediately swept through the group. "You're kidding!" Harriett gasped while Harry reached over to hug Barbara. Marty and Ray shared a high five, several students applauded, and others cheered.
>
> "It's about time," sighed Ed. "How come you changed your mind?"
>
> "Well," answered Barbara, "I've been listening to how people feel about them and I think that if they're not good for everybody, we shouldn't have them." Again, students clapped and cheered.[2]

The blind vote was unanimous, but the conversation continued about the role talking had played in this process.

Inviting Others to Converse

Students were aware that class members had come to understand each other's positions through talk and wanted to invite others to also talk about the issue. To do so, they needed to inform people of their decision. We brainstormed ways to do this, finally deciding that a letter to parents and everyone at the school would be appropriate. Students formed small groups and wrote drafts. The next day each group combined and revised their drafts into a single class letter. The letter included their decision, how that decision was made, the reasons behind the decision, and a suggestion for how the program might be changed to address the problems students found with it. Every class member hand-wrote two sentences in the final document and signed his or her name. Lisa photocopied the letter and placed copies in teachers' mailboxes just before the end of the school day.

The ramifications were immediate. As soon as the last bus left, Mrs. Wase called Lisa in to her office. Teachers who normally left fifteen minutes after the students stood outside the principal's office for almost an hour waiting for Lisa to exit. Lisa heard their angry voices outside the office and kept Mrs. Wase talking. Inside the office, Mrs. Wase told Lisa that she should have told the students to live with the system as it was until the end of the year, that children must earn the right to speak out against something by living with it. Mrs. Wase implied that students were not capable of the thinking evidenced in the letter and that an adult must have authored the letter they copied. Lisa explained that her job is to support children in exploring things, like Super Stars, that are important to them. Lisa stated that she was honest with Mrs. Wase and the other members of the interview committee that hired her, that she was and remains committed to critical literacy. She then offered to resign. Mrs. Wase declined the offer but said she would "yell" at the class because she thought their actions were wrong. Lisa referred to the reforms that Jesus Christ and Martin Luther King Jr. had instigated, to which Mrs. Wase replied, "Yeah, and look what happened to them."

Just after the bell rang the following morning, Mrs. Wase hesitantly entered the classroom but immediately told the class she was displeased. She asked if everyone in the class had agreed with the letter, and to her surprise, everyone either nodded or said, "Yes." Mrs. Wase told the students that the Super Star awards motivate students to work harder and celebrate individual achievement. She told the class that each class is part of the school family, that "when we're part of a whole picture, we go along with it."

Throughout Mrs. Wase's lecture, the students were attentive, but silent. When she asked, "Does anyone have anything you want to tell me?" the students maintained their silence. She asked the students to think more about Super Stars and told them, "Even if you don't like something, you should go along with it and not try to change it." She invited them to send a representative to the next School Advisory Board meeting in April and left.

As soon as Mrs. Wase was out the door, the conversation began. Students were insulted that she had ignored the content of the letter and that she had not respected the enormous amount of time and thinking that was behind its creation. In addition, they expressed fear of her and related their silence to that fear. When Lisa admitted that she had been reprimanded and that other teachers were also mad at her, a spirit of solidarity arose. Cries of "That's not fair," "Why should they care," and "We have the right to share our opinion" filled the room. Ray, a student who initially didn't trust Lisa's desire to share authority, asked if he should stay after school to make sure Lisa was okay. Someone asked if Lisa was going to quit, and all voiced relief when she said she would support them in whatever they chose to do next.

A Second Attempt

Once students expressed their initial emotional reactions, Lisa and Marie reminded them that they came to their decision through months of arduous conversation, talk that Mrs. Wase had not been a part of. The class decided that they would invite her to come talk *with* (not at) them and would determine strategies for overcoming their fear.

The day that Mrs. Wase reprimanded the class was also the first day of a week-long school-evaluation process implemented by a team of teachers, administrators, business executives, and parents from other districts statewide. A member of this team was in the class during her lecture. After the students' discussion of the episode, the team member told Lisa and Marie, "I can't help thinking of the American Revolution and the Declaration of Independence. This is what ought to be happening in classrooms." Later that afternoon he spoke with Mrs. Wase about the incident, apparently admonishing her for shutting down any conversation that could have occurred. Mrs. Wase later told Lisa about the conversation and that she wanted to talk to the students again.

Because of various factors, it was two more weeks before Mrs. Wase returned. Throughout those two weeks, however, conversation repeatedly returned to the Super Star issue and how we might approach our conversation with Mrs. Wase. A few students volunteered to start the conversation and to make sure people were sharing points from our list, either by directly asking them to share, or by referring to someone's name when they talked about a point. As soon as Mrs. Wase sat down, Ed began to speak and Mrs. Wase began to take notes. Others jumped in with little hesitation so that during the next forty-five minutes, students articulated numerous examples, opinions, and rationales for their position. Mrs. Wase asked questions, made comments, and attempted to clarify points she'd previously made. Lunchtime stopped the conversation, so Mrs. Wase agreed to return afterward.

Rights and Responsibilities

Whereas the tone of the morning conversation had been one in which all parties seemed to be seeking understanding, in the afternoon Mrs. Wase reverted to her original stance. Using her notes from the morning session, she twisted students' words to fit her objections to the class's actions. This time, however, neither the students nor Lisa remained silent. In summarizing students' comments, Lisa stated, "We want people to understand our position. It's like *The Great Debate,* a book we read about women's suffrage. We're a minority that feels differently from the majority, but it's our right to have and share our opinion." Mrs. Wase became flustered and fell back on her position as only one member of the School Advisory Board and therefore unable to make decisions on her own. Due to a scheduled assembly, the conversation again ended.

At the writing of this chapter, the Super Star saga has not yet ended. Students are preparing to talk with the School Advisory Board. They realize that the award system may not be changed for the following year or possibly for any year. Nonetheless, our conversations continue. Students periodically draw parallels to grades, the Honor Roll, and fitness awards. We discuss the fallacies in advertising and other propaganda that perpetuate the "work hard and get ahead" ethic, including the Army's "Be All You Can Be" slogan and personal and family experiences about barriers that keep many people from rising up the economic ladder. Above all else, we recognize that it is our right to have a stance that goes against the majority, that it is our responsibility to try to explain that stance to others, and that we need support from others as we work through understandings and try to effect change.[3]

Pushing It Farther

Unlike the group-home study, the Super Star study demonstrates children taking action to rectify an unjust system. The critical potential of the study, however, remains limited by three major factors. Because of Lisa's tentative (at best) relationships with other faculty members, students were unable to organize other students and extend their crusade into all areas of the school and district. Parents were only indirectly involved in our conversations because of union and school policies that inhibited interaction. Thus, who we were able to directly affect was limited.

In addition to being limited by interpersonal factors, curriculum mandates also limited critical potential. Lisa and Bill began the group-home study as part of a study of local history. In the multiage setting, there was a great deal of professional flexibility which they could employ. In the fourth-grade setting, however, both topics and when and how the topics would be taught were prescribed. On several occasions human rights issues arose during class conversations, but we could not leave the mandated curriculum to let these issues take center stage. Indeed, we only explored the history of women's suffrage with any depth because the required science units showed some topical overlap. Even then, Lisa and Marie only cursorily extended the issue of suffrage to other groups or to inequality still experienced today. As a result, questions such as "Whose interests are served?" and "How is this part of our entire system?" were discussed in relation to a variety of issues—gender roles, body image, sweatshops, and others—but were only acted upon in relation to the Super Star issue. Time to examine sources outside our own experiences and opinions was almost nonexistent.

Like the group-home study, the Super Star study did not systematically explore the social myths that created it. For example, we acknowledged that Super Stars and school programs like it do not benefit the majority of individuals, but we did not delve into the hierarchies that they perpetuate. We recognized that we learn better in collaborative settings, but we did not examine the systems that discourage or sabotage collaborative efforts. Studying questions such as "Which ideologies and practices encourage us to think that systems in which there are winners and losers can be just and fair?"; "How did these views develop?"; and "How do they differ from ideologies and practices in other societies?" would have helped us to understand the broader sociopolitical context of our actions. Our conversations and our actions were critical, but our investigations were not.

Additional Factors Inhibiting Critical Potential

In addition to those previously mentioned, there are other factors that inhibited the critical potential of both studies. Conversation, a crucial component to the genesis of each inquiry and the transformation of individuals, constantly changed direction. As such, dialogue might heighten around certain things for a while, then shift to something else. Passion alone is insufficient for exploring all the issues that could arise; it must be accompanied by commitment to do so. Once the commitment is evident, however, there must also be avenues to help learners explore an issue.

Both inquiries utilized the wealth of experiences and knowledge of class members, along with the perspectives of speakers invited to the class. In addition, a few resources directly related to discrimination were available. We discovered, however, that texts written *for* children about social issues are difficult to find. Novels such as *The Great Debate* (Tedrow, 1992) and *Summer of the Swans* (Byars, 1972) are excellent discussion starters, and books such as *The Kids' Guide to Social Action* (Lewis, 1991) provide helpful suggestions. Some magazines, such as *Time for Kids,* do occasionally address issues of social justice, although references for students to pursue are absent and the topic is typically dealt with in a superficial manner.

In some ways, the lack of critical analyses written for children became a stumbling block for us. We were accustomed to filling the room with printed materials related to whatever inquiry topic we were studying. Since inquiry topics are generally related to science or social studies topics, such resources are not difficult to find. When students investigate social issues, however, a different strategy is necessary. In retrospect, we realize that we needed to read critical analyses to children and to help them synthesize the information such analyses contain. Books and magazines from our home libraries—*The Manufactured Crisis* (Berliner & Biddle, 1997), *America: What Went Wrong?* (Bartlett & Steele, 1992), *The Progressive*, and *Mother Jones*—include references to documents we might have obtained copies of for students to scrutinize as well as organizations that could have been contacted for further information. Investigating issues from original sources might have taken more time and effort, yet the students would have been analyzing primary and secondary documents rather than someone else's analysis watered down for children. We allowed the lack of materials written specifically for children to inhibit our critical exploration, though we now realize such a lack does not prohibit critical study.

Perhaps the most significant stumbling block we have found to helping students recognize and challenge injustice is our own energy level. Like any teacher, we often find it difficult to juggle the demands of administrators, parents, colleagues, and students; yet when curriculum is developed as a joint venture by all class members (as it is within an "Authoring Cycle" framework), the demands become more manageable. Teachers and students support one another in their efforts to understand and act upon interests and passions. In so doing, a solidarity develops, a shared commitment to each other and to the topic of study. We know that this solidarity is strengthened as we discuss social issues from a critical perspective; we suspect that critical investigation strengthens it further.

A commitment that exists solely among students and their teachers is insufficient to maintain the energy necessary for challenging oppressive ethics or for attempting changes within a school or town. Connections to other people with similar goals is vital. During the group home study, Bill and Lisa were in constant conversation with each other as well as with their students. Because they both valued what was happening, they were able to talk about what else could be done, not whether it should be happening. Likewise, Marie and Lisa provided strength for one another throughout the Super Star study. "When it was just me," Lisa once stated, "I questioned my sanity. It seemed like everyone around me—at least all of the adults at my school—were against me and what I stood for." Through our frequent conversations with each other, with colleagues in other settings, and with ourselves as we read professional texts, we were constantly reminded of commitments to rectifying inequality. When the controversy was at its peak and our energy waned, these reminders helped us to continue.

Conversation as the Key

In *Life in a Crowded Place,* Ralph Peterson (1992) states, "Conversation requires a willingness to give of oneself and to receive of others" (p. 51). Sharing a minority stance with someone in authority, as the students did in the Super Star study, or baring one's soul, as Mark and Nicholas did in the group-home study, does not occur in an environment where support is lacking or where people are afraid to trust each other. Such revelations and their subsequent transformations can only occur where there is a shared sense of community, a common respect for all individuals and their ideas, and an intense desire to understand those ideas. This chapter attempted to demonstrate this claim in our holistic, critical classrooms.

As holistic educators, we recognize the role of conversation in curriculum development. Rather than assuming that we know what children need to know or what they are interested in, we are kid watchers, observing the choices children make and the strategies they use. We make curricular decisions on the basis of what we see and hear, but we also invite our students to talk with us about these decisions so that they are not mere recipients of a curriculum we devise, but rather are the co-creators of the curriculum. Without conversation and the community which supports it, the shift to shared authority cannot occur.

As critical educators, we also recognize the role of conversation for understanding, critiquing, and transforming the systems which we help to create and in which we live. As with the Super Star study, critical talk may lead to critical action without critical investigation. (Likewise, we suspect that critical conversation can also result in critical investigation without critical action.) Nonetheless, neither critical study nor action can occur without conversation, for it is the means by which we identify injustice, explore the roots and consequences of that injustice, and determine how we might attempt to alter ourselves and our society to rectify that injustice. If conversation cannot occur, then transformation cannot occur.

Conversation, then, must be a key component of any critical endeavor. Without the exchange of ideas, we are limited by our own position, unable to imagine possibilities. Without possibilities, there is no change, and freedom remains an abstract concept rather than a closer reality.

Notes

1. Pseudonyms are given for all students and colleagues to protect their anonymity. The names of school programs and committees are also fictitious.

2. Although we are aware that this can be interpreted as velvet-gloved coercion, it was not. The intent was to come up with a solution and a plan of action. We were prepared for, and expected, the solution to include dissenting views. Had Barbara not changed her mind, our solution would have been different. Her statement surprised all of us, and although her agreement was not necessary, it did make the process of coming up with a solution easier.

3. Two years later, we can report that students requested but never received an invitation to speak at a School Advisory Board meeting. Super Stars, however, was discontinued, something we learned from a memo placed in Lisa's box during the last week of school, almost three months after the students' letter. One student commented, "It's like they're afraid to talk to us." The Super Star system was replaced by each grade level giving their own end-of-quarter awards. Allan later told Marie, "It's not that different from Stars. But we did something important." Laura added, "it was the most important thing we did, to change something in a big way. Maybe some day we'll change something else."

References

Bartlett, D. L., & Steele, J. B. (1992). *America: What went wrong?* Kansas City, MO: Andrews McMeel.

Berliner, D. C., & Biddle, B. J. (1997). *The manufactured crisis: Myths, fraud, and the attack on America's public schools.* White Plains, NY: Longman.

Byars, B. (1972). *Summer of the swans.* New York: Viking.

Harste, J. C., and Short, K. G., with Burke, C. (1988). *Creating classrooms for authors: The reading-writing connection.* Portsmouth, NH: Heinemann.

Lewis, B. A. (1991). *The kids' guide to social action: How to solve the social problems you choose—and turn creative thinking into positive action.* Minneapolis: Free Spirit.

Martinez, E. (Ed.). (1991). *500 years of Chicano history in pictures.* Albuquerque, NM: Southwest Organizing Project.

Peterson, R. (1992). *Life in a crowded place: Making a learning community.* Portsmouth, NH: Heinemann.

Tedrow, T. L. 1992. *The great debate.* Nashville: Nelson.

Templeton, J. W. (1996). *Our roots run deep: The black experience in California, 1500–1900.* San Francisco: Electron Access.

CHAPTER FOUR

¡Sí Se Puede! Teaching for Transformation

REBECA GARCÍA-GONZÁLEZ
University of San Francisco

PILAR MEJÍA
*Principal on Special Assignment, San Francisco (California) Unified
School District*

WINNIE J. PORTER
César Chávez Elementary School, San Francisco, California

There was a time when very few teachers at César Chávez
Elementary School practiced whole language or critical pedagogy. Twelve years ago our school was considered one of the
worst public schools in the San Francisco Unified School District.
Today, the commitment and vision of teachers like Winnie Porter
is bearing fruit in the form of the progressive working environment which attracted Pilar Mejía, our principal, and Rebeca
García-González, a younger teacher. In this chapter, the story of
the school's past and recent transformation is told from the point
of view of three Latina educators who believe in the practice of
critical pedagogy and whole language.

Winnie Porter

From Hawthorne to César Chávez:
The Name Change

I was born in Peru and came to the United States when I was six
years old. I was thrust into an English-only classroom, and went
from public schools to parochial schools in San Francisco. I went
to college, got a job as a waitress, and then took up teaching. I

taught for one year at a Catholic school and for about five years as a substitute teacher.

I came to Hawthorne School at a time in my life when I did not have a vision or a direction. I accepted the job teaching Spanish bilingual kindergarten mainly for financial reasons and because I wasn't sure what else to do at the time. I just knew that the direction I had been headed in was not the way I wanted my life to go.

When I arrived at Hawthorne, I was shocked by the physical condition of the school. Every room in the school had boarded-up windows and tiles falling from the ceiling. On warm days, the smell of urine permeated the whole building. The school had about six hundred students, in grades K–5; most of them were from poor Latino and African American families. The staff was friendly to me, but everyone seemed cautious. The principal was hated and feared; the teachers kept their heads down and their classroom doors closed. It was not a happy place. You could see sadness not only in the faces of the staff members, but also in the faces of the children. I think the thing that struck me the most was the filth throughout the building, from the corners of the floors to the doorless toilet stalls and plugged-up urinals in the students' bathrooms.

After working at Hawthorne School for a few years, I began to identify my goals. I was becoming an activist and a loudmouth, as I realized that everything I did in my classroom was a political statement. I had read about racism, but as a white-skinned Latina, I'd blended in. Here, I had racism staring me in the face. The Black and Latino kids in this school, and their families, had been abandoned and forgotten by the school district. I saw the oppression in the faces of my students; I felt their hopelessness. I understood that they did not see the education that we were offering them as something to be valued. I realized that teaching them to read and write was not enough: If I didn't help them challenge the status quo, I wouldn't be teaching them what they needed.

By the end of the 1980s, our school had gone through dramatic changes. A core group of teachers started organizing, working together, and holding daily meetings. The physical plant was renovated, with a new boiler, roof, windows, playground, and bathrooms. We even had an incredibly beautiful mural painted on the front of the school.

The most important changes, though, had to do with the philosophy of the school. Slowly many of the original staff members left and were replaced by more progressive people. Determined to give our students a decent school, we ousted three principals, became vocal in the district, and developed good relationships with two consecutive superintendents. We argued and debated and laughed together, becoming a team and developing a program for our school. As we gained control of the structure of the school, our curriculum began to change, reflecting the lives and the problems of our students. It was a totally exhausting, thrilling, passionate time—not a job but a calling.

I had become involved with the California Teachers Association/National Education Association (CTA/NEA) early on, and the union had been crucial in helping us with our struggle to take over the school. Through my involvement with the union, I began to have many opportunities to develop myself as an educator, attending conferences and training sessions and becoming a trainer myself. I met and talked with people like César Chávez, Mary Hatwell Futrell, Jonathan Kozol, Stephen Krashen, and so many others who inspired and motivated me. I traveled throughout the United States, visiting hundreds of classrooms, talking with hundreds of educators, and reading voraciously.

During these years I also began to have very intimate relationships with the families of my students. Very often I would have four or five siblings from the same family, not to mention the cousins. In a sense I became a part of their families. I visited their homes, went to birthday parties, *quinceañeras*, weddings, and funerals. I helped families with immigration papers, health care for the children, landlord problems, domestic violence, and more. I began to have a very different understanding of what it was to be a teacher. Certainly, my university experience had not prepared me for this.

And yet, as involved as I and the other teachers were, I realized that although we had always told the parents and the community that we wanted them in the school, it was still largely rhetoric. The school was not a place where parents could feel comfortable or welcome. Parents needed a distinct purpose to come to school. When we had general parent meetings, very few parents attended. But when a particular teacher held a parent meeting with a particular purpose, massive numbers of parents attended. I realized that we had to change our approach with parents and that we had to be very clear about the role that parents played in the school setting. We needed to get them involved with their kids, and with their kids' education—not just to have them in the building doing chores or selling food at events.

By the late 1980s, our school was well on its way to becoming the kind of school I had envisioned. We had changed our governance structure to become a teacher-driven school. We were continuing to evolve our curriculum to reflect the lives and the needs of students, now including Chinese and deaf children. We had a new principal, Pilar Mejía, who had been chosen by our school community. Parents were organizing and taking a more active role in the school. Our gay and lesbian teachers were slowly coming out to the whole school community. It felt good to be a part of this school, but yet for me and others there was still the feeling that something was missing.

It was during César Chávez's funeral in 1990 that Betty Pazmiño and I realized what the missing piece was. We were approached by Angie Fa, one of our school board members. She told us that she and the school board wanted to rename one of the San Francisco schools after César, and would we like it to be our school? Without hesitation Betty and I said yes, and we took it back to our school community immediately.

Of course, this was the missing piece. As long as our school was named Hawthorne, it could be any kind of school. Most of the students did not know who or what Hawthorne was. Many of them could not even pronounce the name. Few of the staff members could name the books he had written or tell anything of his life. Nathaniel Hawthorne had nothing to do with our school, the neighborhood, or the community. César Chávez, on the other hand, had so much in common with our school, neighborhood, and community. Many of our students of various ethnic groups could tell stories of their relatives working, marching, and fighting alongside César. Naming our school after him would send a clear message to everyone regarding what our school was all about.

During the two weeks after the funeral, our school went through an incredible power struggle. On the one side were those like me who desperately wanted the name change. On the other side were those who had strong ties to the old name and were furious at the idea of changing it. Never before had there been such a strong division between any two factions.

Betty and I presented the name change to our staff in the form of a petition to the school board. Many of our colleagues eagerly joined in by helping to circulate the petition among the parents and the neighborhood community. We held meetings for the staff, the parents, and the community. Arguments both for and against the name change were very heated and passionate. Several individuals tried to argue that since the Mission neighborhood was becoming increasingly Asian, it would be inappropriate to name the school after a Latino. Those of us advocating for the name change argued that César had worked with and for people of all ethnic groups.

I remember sitting in an impromptu teachers' discussion that was heated and very divided. One of the teachers whom I felt very close to tried to explain why changing the name was not important. She was arguing that the school could be named anything: "It could be called Smith School or White School." Her attachment to the name "Hawthorne" was in the history that was attached to it. She could not let go of tradition. No matter how much we argued back and forth, she could not understand why we felt so passionately that the school had to be named after someone significant in the lives of our community. I remember this teacher friend of mine leaving in tears. I felt torn, wanting to run to her and comfort her. I wanted to tell her that everything was going to be all right. We had so much history together; we had struggled and fought together to transform our school. Yet I was frozen. I knew at that moment that our lives had now taken different paths. I knew that this was the moment when our struggles were no longer the same. I couldn't go to her because there wasn't anything that I could say to her to make her feel better. The name change had severed our relationship.

It was through these experiences that I began to see my students through different eyes. I wanted them to attend a school that was named after someone they could see themselves in, someone who looked and talked like them. I wanted them to know that there were people out there fighting for them and their families. I wanted them to see themselves as part of history, that they too created it. After all, wasn't this what education was for? Didn't children deserve to attend a school named after someone relevant in their lives? Someone who could inspire them and help them see how education could make their lives better?

Changing the name of our school brought about results that we had not anticipated. The year after the name change, several teachers left our school. A group of parents pulled their children out. The new name attracted numerous educators who wanted to be a part of our school community. We were approached by several community organizations to become involved in various projects. Two local artists requested to paint a mural on the back of our school honoring César and the farmworkers.

The greatest change that has come about as a result of our new name, I believe, is in the attitude and commitment of the staff. Those of us who struggled through the name change have been transformed by the process. We cannot work in a school named after such a great leader as César Chávez and be complacent and accepting of the unjust conditions in our world. If we do not take the side of the oppressed, we are not being neutral; we are supporting the oppressors. We no longer see teaching as limited to the four walls of our classrooms through a narrow curriculum designed by somebody else; we now see teaching as ensuring, through curricula designed by us and for our students, that our students learn from and about the world. We must look at children holistically, as physical, spiritual, and emotional beings. Teaching and learning must be conceptualized through a holistic lens. Students have to be seen within the context of their families, their communities, their histories, and their struggles. We as teachers cannot work in isolation. We must work in partnerships with families and communities. Together we can help students interrogate their own realities, analyze them, see them from different perspectives, and ultimately work toward changing them.

Pilar Mejía

The Protest

As I drove home from school that Wednesday evening, I felt so proud to be principal of César Chávez Elementary School. I felt proud of Nate and Sam, two of our fourth-grade students, who were mature enough to go back to school to report what happened to them at the local grocery store. I felt especially proud that we had a school where the adults were so ready to listen and respond to their complaints.

Nate is new to our school. His mom transferred him in when she heard about our African Centered program. He is a very dark, handsome child with gold rimmed glasses and an easy smile. Sam has been there since kindergarten. He is from Ethiopia. His older sisters speaks their native language, but Sam has already lost it. This is the first year he has had a truly wonderful teacher. He's had a hard life—not only at our school, where he ended up with those tired old teachers who dislike children, but also in his home life, where he is being raised by his grandmother. But tomorrow they'll have an experience like no other.

"Guess what happened to two of our students!" I exclaimed to Fernando when I got home. "They went to the store on the corner of 22nd and Folsom, and the guy in the store started yelling at them, accusing them of wanting to steal something. They got pissed and showed him their money, but he just kept harassing them. He even threw a bag of potato chips at them and hit one on the head and then told them to get out! So, tomorrow, some of the classes are going to picket in front of the store."

Fernando didn't share my excitement; instead, he defended the store owner: "I know that guy. We used to go there for sand-wiches when we had the *Los Siete* Free Clinic across the street from the store. He always treated us fine. Besides, you know how kids are—maybe they *were* trying to steal something."

I couldn't believe the man I loved was talking this way, but I continued: "If they were trying to steal something, they wouldn't have come back to the school to tell us what happened. They told one of our volunteer parents, Mr. Garvey, and one of the para-professionals, Brother Mantu. Mr. Garvey and Brother Mantu couldn't believe it, so they decided to go to the store. When the owner saw two grown African American men approach, he got all upset, refused to speak to them, and threatened to call the police. So, they went back to the school and talked to Rachel, Nate and Sam's teacher. Right away, Rachel said 'Let's boycott that store.' So, in the spirit of César Chávez, we agreed to organ-ize a boycott and a picket."

The next day went as planned. The students made signs and discussed the previous day's incident. Rachel and Brother Eli (our other African Centered teacher) helped the students organize. Other teachers heard the news and decided to join the picket.

They took a bullhorn with them and chanted slogans demanding justice as they marched peacefully along the sidewalk. From the school I recognized the chant "*Sí se puede*," a favorite of the United Farm Workers which, loosely translated, means "it *can* be done." Within a short time the police arrived. The store owner had called them. Brother Eli explained what was going on and the two students filed a police report. What an experience for our students!

That evening, when I arrived home, Fernando asked me how my day had gone. I told him about the protest. He didn't say much. I told him that my supervisor called me. Apparently, someone had complained to the superintendent's office. She said that she was very concerned and that she thought it was against school board policy to stage a protest. She also wanted to know if the students all had permission slips from their parents. I showed him the memo that she had faxed to me.

"Well, that makes sense," commented Fernando. "You really can't take kids out to protest if their parents don't know."

"School was already out yesterday, so we couldn't send home permission notes. But, OK, I can admit that was a mistake, and I told the teachers to make sure they get permission for tomorrow, but that's not the point. This is such an important thing for the students to do—to know that they have this kind of power. You know what the store owner said to me when I talked to him on the telephone today? He kept complaining about the Mexicans and the Blacks—that they're always stealing."

Fernando insisted, "He's just some ignorant guy. I see what you're trying to do, but I don't think this is the right way to do it. That old guy has been on that corner for twenty-five years. He works day in and day out. Why not protest in front of Bank of America or some large corporation that pollutes the environment and exploits workers?"

"Yeah, it's fine to do that too, but this is so concrete, so real. It happened to two of our students; they're part of organizing the protest; other students are supporting someone they actually know. You should have heard some of the discussion—even in Winnie's K-1-2 class. And you know what? When they were out there picketing, a bunch of people were happy to see that they were protesting and a couple of Latinas went up to Martha and told her that the guy had been really terrible to them and to their kids, too."

Our conversation ended there. It was late, so I went off to bed—in a bad mood. The next day was Friday. The students went out to protest again—this time with permission slips. The store owner called several times while the picket was going on. He begged me to make the protest stop. I told him I'd come to talk to him after school.

As soon as school was over, Mr. Garvey and Brother Mantu, Nate and his mom, and Sam and I walked to the store. The minute we walked in the old man started complaining. He said that the protesters had been banging on his window and broke the alarm system. Brother Mantu said angrily, "Nobody touched your window and you know it." But the old man ignored him and threatened to call his lawyer.

Mr. Garvey calmly faced the owner and said, "You need to apologize to these two boys." The old man got defensive. He claimed he had never done anything wrong and seemed outraged that he would be asked to apologize.

"OK," I said, "If you're not going to apologize, we're leaving, and the protest and boycott will continue." I turned to walk out of the store. Brother Mantu had a few more angry words with the owner; Mr. Garvey coaxed Brother Mantu to leave. We all walked back to the school, agreeing that the old man didn't want to hear a thing we had to say. I don't think any of us were very surprised at his reaction. I turned to Nate and Sam. "Did you hear him say that he was going to call his lawyer? You've got to become lawyers. You have to go around to people in the neighborhood and get information on how he treats his customers. We have to know if he has a pattern of treating some people better than others. If he takes us to court, we have to be ready."

"Yeah! Some other kids told me that he yelled at them, too!" said Sam excitedly.

"Are you ready to continue the demonstration?" I asked. They both beamed and nodded their heads.

"We're all ready," said Mr. Garvey.

We walked back through the schoolyard, with the huge two-story mural of César Chávez looking down on us. The children in the mural, the farmworkers, Dolores Huerta, the eagle, Dr. Martin Luther King Jr.—all seemed to be smiling at us, giving us strength, leading the way.

That evening, during dinner, I told Fernando what had happened that day, but he didn't say much. "Fernando," I said, "Why aren't you excited about this? This is the most significant thing that has happened in the three years that I've been a principal."

"Well, I don't see why I have to get so excited about it. We look at things differently sometimes. Isn't that all right?"

"Fernando," I began earnestly, "this is about my life. This is why I'm a principal—the only reason I'm a principal. You know I hate being a principal. But I do it because there are so many terrible principals out there—principals who probably wouldn't have even wanted the name of Hawthorne School to be changed to César Chávez. I helped make that happen. That's why I'm there."

"This isn't such a big deal," he said in a calm voice that drove me crazy. "Besides, maybe you're making a mistake. What if you get fired? What good are you then?"

"That would even be better! This is a matter of principle for me. I have to provide this kind of example; otherwise, what kind of leader would I be? I'm certainly not a good administrator. You know that. The only thing I know how to do well is teach. Don't you have any respect for me as a teacher? This is my profession, my life. I know how children learn things. You have to trust when I explain that children learn from real-life experiences that have meaning in their lives."

"What do you want from me?"

"I need your support," I whispered and walked off to bed.

Saturday I went to school to work on my response to the memo my supervisor had sent. I explained why we organized the boycott and picket. I wrote: "We believe that students need to learn that they make history, that they are the future, that it is up to them to challenge and destroy injustice, that they are the subjects, not the objects, of the historical process."

The next few days were such a contradiction for me. On the one hand, Fernando and I were not able to talk about this. On the other, I'd never felt so fulfilled at work.

When the students went out to protest on Monday, they had also prepared a flyer about the boycott. They handed out the flyer to people who walked by and posted some on nearby poles. Nate, Sam, and a few other students went to several classrooms to explain what was going on and to gather more support for their cause. They asked students to boycott the corner store.

Tuesday, there was another demonstration. Again, the owner called the school, but this time he said that he was ready to apologize and that he wanted me to tell the two boys that he was sorry. But I insisted that he come to the school. I spread the word that the store owner had finally decided to apologize! The students could hardly believe it.

I almost felt disappointed. The students hadn't become lawyers yet. I had imagined our students taking this to court, learning statistics and social studies, reading and writing, revising and editing for real purposes. This victory seemed too easy. Still, this was the week we had to give standardized tests, and these had come to dominate everyone's thoughts. I had to draft an agenda for our next professional-development day, finish evaluations, attend ten meetings during the week, and prepare for the yearly earthquake drill, and the following Saturday was the free food-bag giveaway.

Finally, on Thursday, we held the assembly. The usually boisterous crowd of students was strangely quiet. All the African Centered and Multicultural classes, three of the Chinese bilingual, five of the Spanish bilingual, and the 3-4-5 Deaf Education class watched as the old man walked carefully up to the microphone and said he was sorry . . . that he didn't want any trouble. Nate and Sam accepted his apology. Then Brother Eli got on the microphone and assured him that there would be no more trouble if he learned to respect all people including the children who walked into his store. They shook hands and the old man walked out. Brother Eli continued to talk to the students about the power of organized action. "Do you see what you can do? When you get angry, and you feel like hitting or throwing a rock, or getting a knife or maybe a gun, you aren't using your real power. You know what your real power is? It's what you have up here and in here." He pointed to his head and to his heart.

"Why do you come to school?" he called out to the students.
"To learn!" they responded in unison.
"Why do you learn?"
"So we can teach!" they yelled out.
"What is knowledge?"
"Power!" The word shot out into the air like a cannon.
"All power to who?"
"All power to the people!"
"Ashé!"

Rebeca García-González

The Teach-In

Early one Saturday morning, I got a call from my Chicana friend, Martina. She was breathless. "Did you know there's going to be a Latino march on Washington? And guess what—I've been named Western Regional Coordinator!"

I had already heard about the march from Martha Estrella, a Chicana bilingual teacher who had announced it at our faculty meeting. She and other teachers were planning a "teach-in" at a neighborhood park, in solidarity with the march on Washington and with the purpose of making our elementary students aware of their rights as children and as immigrants. Some community members had already been contacted. They had pledged their help with contacts, donors, and some of the services the students would need on that day.

Martha explained to me that the idea had come from Nancy and Greg, two Latino bilingual teachers from our district. They wanted all the classes in solidarity with the Latino march to attend the event. "The purpose would be to bring awareness to the students of their identity, to show our capacity to care for each other. *Raza por Raza.*"

"We have more time to plan than last year," said Martha. "*¿Qué pasa, dónde está La Raza?*" was to be the teach-in's slogan. Her voice was full of emotion. A community artist and activist, Martha had nonetheless never taken on a project of this scope for the school. Her inspiration had come after reading a draft of the story that Pilar wrote about the student protest our school had organized the previous year.

During the next five minutes, an ad-hoc committee was formed. It would meet with the three other elementary schools in the area that had substantial Latino populations. Several teachers immediately offered services and ideas: a list of curriculum ideas centered around "El Día de la Raza"; drafting a letter to the parents with the background for the teach-in; organizing a parent-support committee; calling the press; and faxing other schools.

Two days later the list of curriculum ideas had been distributed to other schools. At César Chávez, the week spent in preparing for the teach-in reminded me of the hectic last days of the school year: One teacher announced an impromptu banner contest, with a panel of judges traveling from room to room to view the entries; the parent letter explaining the teach-in was rewritten three times; Martha ran around looking for a sound system at a low price; and a mistranslated flyer asking parents to join us at Dolores Park erroneously implied to Spanish speakers that the event would be a protest.

I announced the teach-in and the banner contest to the students during our community circle. Imagining the version they would give to their parents that night, I carefully explained its purpose: "It is a time to get in touch with our rights as immigrants in this country. We are not going there to protest—we are going there in solidarity with those Latinos who are visiting the president."

After learning of our plans, my friend Martina, a filmmaker and former elementary teacher, enthusiastically volunteered herself as a speaker for my Spanish-immersion class. "I could come to César Chávez and speak about Chicanismo. I can also show the video we made about the recent Latino marches for immigrant rights," she said. It was then that I realized that if I didn't offer my multiage class a well-planned critical curriculum in preparation, I couldn't expect them to understand the significance of a daylong teach-in or the meaning of solidarity with the Latino march on Washington.

In retrospect, I realize that my choice of general topic (Chicanos) came from a desire to have students study, over an extended period of time, a population to which the government and the majority society had assigned a lower status. For California students, this meant communities of either Chinese or Mexican origin. For the children in my Spanish-immersion class, an example close to their experience meant studying Chicanos. My student teacher Vicky and I decided on "perspectives" as the theme which would guide our explorations of an event in Chicano history, the Mexican-American War.

We had begun the semester with the concept of "freedom," focusing on the origin of the Latin American independence holidays, the *fiestas patrias,* which are celebrated during the month of September. Toward the end of this unit, some students wrote plays on the life of Simón Bolívar during writer's workshop;

another group led by a student of Dutch heritage decided to write on Dutch liberation from the Nazis; and those who didn't join a play decided to write poems.

The Mexican-American War ending with the Treaty of Guadalupe Hidalgo merited a different treatment. While I had to rely on borrowed materials of Mexican and U.S. origin in order to answer the questions that the *fiestas patrias* unit inspired (Did the independence wars bring freedom to Latin America? Did they bring freedom for everybody?), I found plenty of materials available in English and Spanish on the Mexican-American War. The problem, however, was that an overwhelming number of them were written from a perspective excluding the inhabitants of Mexican origin living in the region. We decided to contrast our social studies textbook chapter on the Treaty of Guadalupe Hidalgo with the book *500 Years of Chicano History in Pictures*, written from a Chicano viewpoint. The video based on this book was also included as part of the curriculum.

Seeking a way to introduce the concept of "perspectives," I decided to turn on the TV after recess. The daytime soaps were on, and I asked the students to look for Latino or Chicano persons. I used problem posing to call attention to the issue of representation in our media. "There aren't many Chicanos or Latinos on TV," the students told me. "Why do you think this is so?" I asked. The lively discussion that followed concluded with a student recommending that Latinos and Chicanos buy their own TV stations in order to tell their side of the story. This turned out to be an excellent introduction to the concept; it also became our small-group time task—comparing our textbook with the trade book *500 Years of Chicano History*.

Every morning of the following week, each small social studies group read the history of the Guadalupe Hidalgo Treaty, and met afterward for a discussion of the differences and similarities in both stories. We brainstormed possible motives for these discrepancies. Some children mentioned that the Chicano version sounded "like angry or something," and that their book didn't look so "expensive." Guillermo noticed that the maps used to show the territory were very different. Our social studies textbook showed an enlarged section of the area, making it harder to determine its size in relation to a U.S. map. We also made a list of the terms used in the textbook to describe the Mexican (businessmen, Mexican citizens) and U.S. citizens (settlers, pioneers, entrepreneurs, Californians) and discussed the images these terms brought to their minds. It was hard to facilitate the discussion at this point because both sets of terms sounded positive, so I asked them to notice what was missing: "How would you like to be described, Micaela—as a San Franciscan citizen, or as an independent, resourceful, charismatic San Franciscan citizen?"

Later, I brought out *Our Roots Run Deep* by John Templeton because I wanted them to see an example of a California history textbook written from the perspective of an African American historian. I didn't ask them to read its middle-school-level text, only to observe the book and compare it with the other two. Gradually, the idea that textbooks reflect the perspective of their creators emerged in the form of questions, which I recorded: "How come we don't have a choice of textbooks?" "Why are the other books published in black and white?" After what seemed like a long time, the inevitable question came up: "How come we don't study books written by Chicanos?"

On Monday we saw the first half of the video *500 Years of Chicano History*. Dividing the Chicano history video in half enabled us to keep the sessions short and left additional time for discussion. The students were able to connect the historical background of Mexico shown in the video with their study of *las fiestas patrias*. On Tuesday we saw a segment of a video about Felix Longoria, the Mexican American soldier from Texas, whose remains were refused chapel service by the white owner of a funeral home in his native town. The second half of the video *500 Years of Chicano History* was shown on Wednesday. Sergio Arroyo, a young Chicano Aztec dancer and community activist, watched it with the class and spoke to the students about his own search for identity.

Gabriela Fuentes, our next-door Spanish bilingual teacher, offered to host Martina's visit in her classroom. We joined our classes and set up the monitor in the tiny space between the electrical outlet and the window. It was evident that this was the highlight of the week. Older students wanted to sit in front to meet "The Filmmaker," since I had not told them anything about my friend. What a surprise it was for them to see a short dark woman the same age as their teacher walk in with her husband, a Nicaraguan man with a sweet smile. After introducing herself, she asked for a marker and proceeded to trace the origins of the word *Chicano* on a piece of paper already stuck on the wall.

Next, she asked the students if they had ever heard of how Chicanos from East L.A. spoke. Nobody responded until she gave a short demonstration. Several arms shot up instantly. "That's how my dad speaks at home!" said one of the younger girls in front, a look of recognition illuminating her face. Martina talked about her neighborhood near Lincoln High and about the recent protests staged by Latino immigrants. "Latino and Chicano people are connected all over California," she said. "We farm the land. We take care of the children and clean the houses. We hold many other types of jobs. Because of this we have a lot of power."

After describing how she and other women from her Latino barrio in Redwood City were selling tamales to pay for their trip to Washington, some students from Gabriela's class asked Martina to take two of the banners they had made for the contest to the march. Ester and Elena, two fourth graders from my class, gave her two poems they had written during writer's workshop.

La marcha	The march
La marcha que	The march,
siempre tiene un sentimiento.	There's always a feeling to it.
Todas las noches	Every night
marcha la gente,	People march
cuando tocan las campanas.	When the bells call.
Y la gente	And the people
se levanta a marchar	rise and join the march
para pelear por un comité	to fight for a committee
que vigile la policía.	to watch the police.

ESTER HERNÁNDEZ, AGE 9

- 92 -

La raza	Raza

La raza es como un armor
  sin nombre
una paz con corazón,
una rosa de sentimiento,
un águila en un nopal,
tres culturas de diferentes
  generaciones.
La raza es como educación
  con esperanza,
una calle limpia y amorosa.
Un baile folklórico,
el jarabe tapatío.
La guerra de la república Mexicana,
Una rosa de un charro.
	Raza is like a love
	  with no name
	Like peace with a heart
	A rose of feeling
	An eagle on a nopal
	Three cultures of different
	  generations
	Raza is like education
	  with hope.
	A clean and loving street
	A folk dance,
	El jarabe tapatío.
	The Mexican republic's war,
	A charro's rose.

ELENA NAVARRO, AGE 10

The morning of the teach-in, Vicky and I packed five water bottles, extra school lunches, and a video camera in our backpacks and took the class downstairs to the yard. The organizing committee had planned to have the schools walk to Dolores Park. We were the first ones to line up at the schoolyard. One by one all the classes came out carrying paper banners: "Día de la Raza"; "Immigrant rights"; "César Chávez lives." Some classes had taped signs to bamboo sticks bought for the school's garden, and others waved handmade flags with the farmworkers' logo. On the way to the park, children from the older grades sang spontaneously, oblivious to the curious stares of adult onlookers: "*¡Sí se puede, sí se puede! Oye, ¿qué pasa, Dónde está la raza?*" Many parents joined us for the day, bringing the students' younger brothers and sisters.

We were the first school to arrive. I unfurled the huge black satin banner which identified our school and asked a student to hold it. "Can we eat our lunches now?" asked one of my third graders. Slowly, individual classes from the other schools began to fill the spaces under the lace-like palm shadows. I walked around with a video camera, weaving slowly through the small bodies sitting on the grass, while asking the older children to stand next to their colorful banners and flags.

The master of ceremonies was a young Latino man who immediately addressed his young audience in Spanish and English. The program featured Aztec dancers, a special performance by the Chicano group Culture Clash, two Latino community activists speaking about immigrant rights, one singer, poetry from several middle school students, and performances by two elementary classes.

Back at the school, I borrowed the TV monitor from Gabriela and invited her class to watch the video with us, realizing that it was important to reflect together as a group before going home. After the video the two classes discussed the day. Several boys said that they felt the happiest when chanting on the way to the park, and others felt Culture Clash had delivered a hilarious performance. After Gabriela's class left, I asked my class to do a quick write in response to two questions: How would you organize next year's *Día de la Raza*? What do you feel you have learned after this week?

The comments made by parents and students showed me the importance of critical work carried out through involvement with the community. No other "political" cause had ever received so much schoolwide support. In addition, the written reflections of some students in my class indicated that they were able to connect the March on Washington and the teach-in with their own future as Latinos in the United States. As Alina put it, "We have to learn to march so that no one takes advantage of Latinos."

Conclusion

What does critical pedagogy look like in an elementary school? Over and over, we ask ourselves that question. We know that whatever it is, it depends on the conditions in which it exists. This is a small part of our ongoing struggle and reinventing of the word and the world.

As Paulo Freire taught us: Education is not neutral; it either maintains the status quo, or it is a tool for liberation. We hope our stories encourage others, but we also want critical educators to know that it is not easy.[1] It is much easier to teach in a traditional way. Critical pedagogy does not come from a textbook; no one can tell someone else exactly how to do it. This type of teaching is more than professional activity, even more than personal commitment. It encompasses our entire lives.

Note

1. "Not easy" is an understatement when it comes to educating for a *participatory, public* democracy (Shannon, 1998). Three years after this chapter was written, Bill Rojas, the San Francisco Unified School District superintendent, reassigned the principal despite parent and teacher protests. Although private assurances were given to the community that it would have a voice in selecting the next administrator, the new principal was not among the candidates interviewed by the search committee. By June of 1999, fifteen out of thirty-three teachers had left César Chávez—a disheartening development. But the story isn't over yet. Pilar and the teachers committed to struggling for justice are continuing that work in professional organizations, graduate schools, and as new administrators. And many parents and new teachers in the community, taught by the activism at César Chávez Elementary School, have become increasingly skilled at organizing for their rights. Moreover, two of the school's three parent advocates are now taking courses to become credentialed teachers. Working for justice *through* schools includes working for justice *within* school systems.

References

Martinez, E. (Ed.). (1991). *500 years of Chicano history in pictures.* Albuquerque, NM: Southwest Organizing Project.

Shannon, P. (1998). *Reading Poverty.* Portsmouth, NH: Heinemann.

Templeton, J. W. (1996). *Our roots run deep: The black experience in California, 1500–1900.* San Francisco: Electron Access.

CHAPTER FIVE

Critical Literacy
in a Fourth-Grade Classroom

MARIA SWEENEY

Hawes School, Ridgewood, New Jersey

June 13, 1994. A fourth-grade class in an upper-middle-class, predominantly white New Jersey suburb takes its bows to enthusiastic applause from parents and fellow students. A familiar scene? Not quite. These children created "No Easy Road to Freedom: A Play about South Africa" from scratch. They researched, wrote, staged, directed, acted in, and produced this play and provided background materials for their audience. It was the students' idea to create the play. In the process, they learned far more than most educated adults know about South Africa and the injustices of apartheid, and they experienced the power of working collectively to take a stand on an issue they grew to care about deeply. They also learned what it's like to grow something from the seed stage to a plant in full bloom. Every student, regardless of academic ability, played a critical role. The children experienced their power to make a positive difference in the world.

In reflecting on the experience, one of the students, Maia, wrote:

> I think that everyone in the audience learned something new today. I believe that our play was a form of protest. I am very proud that our class worked together and we made an impor-

A related treatment of this research appeared as "No Easy Road to Freedom: Critical Literacy in a Fourth-Grade Classroom" in *Reading and Writing Quarterly*, 13.3 (1997), 279–292.

tant statement. I think we should put on the play a bunch more times to really get the message into many people's minds. I wish we could show our message to all racists. Most people would never think that a group of fourth graders could ever understand what's going on and send out a strong message like we did, but we did!

Maia's feelings of empowerment and commitment to social justice, feelings I believe were shared by all students in my classroom, evolved during an entire school year of a critical-literacy curriculum which prompted students to confront social inequities and assume responsibility to forge a more just society. I asked students to consider alternative views of events past and present. I asked them to look for missing or silenced voices in the materials we read, and to consistently ask of what they read, heard, or witnessed: Is this fair? Is this right? Does this hurt anyone? Is this the whole story? Who benefits and who suffers? Why is it like this? How could it be different, more just? Through these questions I sought "to give students the tools to critique every idea that legitimates social inequality, every idea that teaches them they are incapable of imagining and building a fundamentally equal and just society" (Christensen, 1994, p. 8).

I strive to create a classroom atmosphere and curriculum that prepares my students to build and participate in a critical democracy. I help my students gain the necessary skills and knowledge to critique their world, unveil injustices and needless suffering, and work for social change. I nurture a strong sense of compassion and equity, and I urge children to get angry and do something.

I don't pretend that my teaching is neutral or objective; education never is. Behind everything taught is a point of view or particular perspective. Value-free education is a myth and, in fact, an impossibility. As Ira Shor states in *Empowering Education:*

> Critical education is not more political than the curriculum which emphasizes taking in and fitting in. Not encouraging students to question knowledge, society, and experience tacitly endorses and supports the status quo. . . . As Freire said, education that tries to be neutral supports the dominant ideology in society. (1992, p.12)

Year after year across the United States, most young children still learn the traditional story of "Columbus the hero who discovered the New World" taught by teachers who consider themselves objective and fair. But this approach to the story actually legitimizes the invasion and theft of another people's (Tainos) land, and it ignores the perspective of those who were "discovered." This is just one, by now obvious, example of the biased way that history and other subjects are taught everywhere.

The radical historian Howard Zinn opens his courses with the following disclaimer:

> This is not an objective course. . . . I am not a neutral teacher. I have a point of view about war, about racial and sexual equality, about economic justice—and this point of view will affect my choice of subject, and the way I discuss it. (1993, p. 29)

Zinn openly reveals his biases. He teaches history that values peace, justice, equality, and freedom and this approach necessarily urges students to look critically at this nation's past.

Those who fault critical educators for imposing our values on children ignore the fact that education which doesn't ask children to pose critical questions, search for alternative perspectives, and uncover untold stories helps reproduce an unjust society. Certain people benefit while most others suffer from current social arrangements. Education which claims to be neutral trains children to take the world for granted and to never imagine a more just society. Therefore, I openly approach all aspects of my teaching with my bias for social justice.

In this article I will attempt to illustrate the possibilities of critical literacy in a whole language elementary classroom by discussing a project my students and I undertook to follow the events leading up to the South African elections in April, 1994. Before describing the project, I will briefly characterize my curriculum.

I use a whole language approach to teaching literacy and infuse issues of justice and equity throughout the curriculum. My students develop their skills and strategies as readers and writers through authentic literacy events. They read whole texts which they have chosen, and they write for their own purposes for a genuine audience in a reading and writing workshop (Atwell, 1987;

Calkins, 1994). During the year we do a few inquiry units (theme cycles) in which topics of study are collectively chosen, guiding research questions are generated by all, and we engage in an open-ended, meaningful inquiry project such as the one described in this article (Altwerger & Flores, 1994; Short, Harste, & Burke, 1996). I begin each year with a general idea of my social studies time line, which includes topics sufficiently open-ended to become theme cycles. For example, my tentative time line this year is Building Our Classroom Community; Understanding the "Isms"; Oral History; Labor History and Current Issues; Critical Media Literacy and Women's Suffrage. I chose these units because they all relate to New Jersey (the official fourth-grade theme), are potent topics for sparking questions of interest to the children, and relate to justice and equality. The length of time devoted to each unit depends on the students' interest. I also allow space for a topic to be chosen by the students.

Human Suffering and Injustice: So Many Questions

Several weeks before the South African elections, my students viewed the filmstrip *Apartheid Is Wrong* (1986). In this filmstrip the children saw signs like "Europeans Only" on a public bench; "Servant's Entrance" above a railway waiting room; and "Peaceful Demonstration: Don't Shoot" at a squatters' demonstration. They saw contrasting pictures of a black shantytown and a white woman being served a cool drink by a black servant. They also saw pictures of mass demonstrations, funerals, and a chart which presented them with the relative populations of white and black South Africans and the percentage of land owned by each group. (Whites made up 13 percent of the South African population, but reserved 85 percent of the land for their own use.)

The children, shocked and angered by what they had seen, responded with questions like "Why do most white South Africans treat people of color so badly? Don't they realize we're all the same inside?" "Why did black men and women have to work so far from their families?" "How could black people be forced to live on horrible lands when this was their country to begin with?" "Who made the laws, and why were the whites in charge of everything if there were so few of them?" and "Why would the government kill people protesting peacefully?"

As we discussed these questions, several children drew on information learned earlier that year to compare the civil rights movement with the anti-apartheid movement and to make a connection between racism in the Unites States and in South Africa. One child recalled examples of peaceful civil rights protests crushed by state force in this country. Although the brutal racism of South Africa was still confusing for them, previous class discussions gave them a mental framework for thinking about issues of oppression, racism, and resistance. A single discussion, however, was insufficient to satisfy their questions, so we agreed to follow closely the South African elections.

This group of children was particularly sensitive to human suffering and injustice. Time and time again that year, they seized upon a social-justice issue I had introduced and expressed such sincere concern that we stayed with the topic longer than I had planned. They were curious and caring, always anxious to understand injustice and respond. This topic would, in fact, stir up their strongest passions and inspire them to take on a project to which we devoted the last two months of our school year. But none of us knew this at the time of the filmstrip.

Learning about South Africa

Soon after we viewed the filmstrip, Bob Krist, a student's father who is a professional photographer, came to speak with our class. He had just returned from a month-long tour of South Africa sponsored by the African National Congress. Mr. Krist showed slides depicting stark contrasts in living conditions between whites and blacks. Sharing several compelling anecdotes of incidents he had witnessed, he told of racist behavior and talk as the norm among most of the whites he had met. Again, the children were appalled and deeply concerned. "Did you tell those people who said that stuff they were racist?" Jeremy asked. Another challenged, "Did you do anything?" Mr. Krist explained that what he witnessed was so profoundly woven into the behavior and thinking of most white South Africans that there was little he could have said or done to change anything. Knowing Mr. Krist personally made his accounts of racial oppression in South Africa even more real for the children and heightened their curiosity about the upcoming elections.

To follow the elections, I clipped articles from the daily papers, printed the hourly news from America Online, and plastered our current events wall with photos. Some students videotaped nightly news reports showing mass demonstrations, views of life in shantytowns and homelands, and the fiery enthusiasm among blacks who were anticipating their first opportunity to vote. Each morning I summarized the news and read quotes from black South Africans reacting to the impending elections.

I was passionate and joyful about events in South Africa and openly shared my feelings with the class. I wanted the children to understand that we were living through an extremely momentous event. At one point one of the students said, "I think this is one of those things that we're going to tell our own kids about someday if we're doing our own oral histories." (Earlier in the year, we had studied oral history and the children had gathered stories of older family members, most of which included memories of important historical events.)

Students began spontaneously writing raps, songs, poems, and opinion pieces on South Africa, both during writing workshop and at home. The following rap written by three boys was eventually included in our class play.

CHORUS: Mandela's free! Yeah! Yeah! Mandela's free! Yeah! Yeah!
         We just brought Mandela free! Yeah! Yeah!
         He used to be a prison resident,
         And soon he'll be our nation's president.

CHORUS: They used to live in fighty towns
         And soon they'll live in mighty towns!

CHORUS: They fought for their freedom,
         They fought for their rights.
         They fought for equality with all their might.

As the children shared their writings, I realized that the strength of their work and the intense energy behind it merited, even demanded, an audience beyond the classroom. Most social-justice units we do culminate with a "real-world" project, something that takes the students' learning and work beyond the classroom. For example, when we studied the "isms," the students made posters condemning racism, sexism, ageism, and classism and celebrating social equality. These posters were hung around the school and later in store windows downtown. After studying Columbus from the perspective of those who inhabited the islands he "discovered," the children wrote picture books telling this alternative view of the story and gave these to our school library. This study of South Africa called for a project that would allow the children to extend their strong thoughts and feelings past our classroom walls. I encouraged the children to begin thinking about an effective project for this issue.

I showed the film *A World Apart* (Menges, 1988), a poignant story, about a white anti-apartheid journalist persecuted by the South African government for her organizing efforts, told from the point of view of her twelve-year-old daughter. The film made a powerful impression on the children and gave them a clearer understanding of the history of apartheid and the resistance movement. Again they were both saddened and outraged by the brutality of the South African government. Several cried at the site of nonviolent protestors being crushed by the South African police, an anti-apartheid leader who was tortured and killed in prison, and the film's star being arbitrarily arrested and torn from her three young children. I reminded the children several times that this was a true story and that much of what they saw was still true today. I wanted to guard against their thinking that the impending elections meant that all problems would be solved in South Africa.

The film helped my students to understand that the upcoming elections were the result of years of struggle and not simply the white ruling elite suddenly coming to their senses. Social protest was a theme we had discussed several times earlier when we studied the labor movement, the civil rights movement, and the suffragist movement. I place a strong emphasis on history as a social process, a process involving real people making moral choices and forging their future. This also includes looking at situations in which people "chose" not to take a stand, where passivity determined historical outcomes.

Critical Literacy across the Curriculum

Just before the elections, a parent with a son in another class at our school complained to me that the elections hadn't even been mentioned in his class. She suggested that my class prepare something to share with other classes. I brought this back to the students, who decided that we should improve the writings they had already done, write more, and create a series of mini-performances based on those writings.

My students assumed that they were already expert enough to create these performances, but I knew that they weren't. I told them that to do this responsibly, we had to do further research and continue our discussions. I decided to devote a substantial part of the curriculum for the following few weeks to this project. In math we studied statistics reflecting differences in wealth, living conditions, and access to power between white and black South Africans. I drew information from a curriculum written by Bill Bigelow (1985) and an excellent booklet prepared by COSATU (1992). Earlier in the year we had done an extensive unit on statistics through which the children learned to gather, represent, and interpret simple and familiar statistical data (e.g., typical family size in our class, school, town). They then studied what I called "statistics for social justice"—U.S. social statistics showing differentials in salaries between women and men and among various racial groups, and contrasting infant mortality rates among various social groups. These experiences had prepared the children to understand the South African statistics.

They restated the South African statistics in their own language, generated new information, wrote problems, and posed questions on the basis of the basic information sheet I had prepared. They then made beautiful posters presenting some of these statistics in words and drawings or graphs, which we later used in a multimedia exhibit supporting the play.

In reading we formed literature groups and read two novels about South Africa: *The Middle of Somewhere* (Gordon, 1992), the story of a family that resists government relocation intended to make way for a whites-only town, and *Journey to Jo'burg* (Naidoo, 1985), the story of a brother and sister's search for their mother, who works far away in the home of a white family. Both books brought my students closer to the thoughts and feelings of typical black South African children and their daily experience with apartheid.

To help my students approach the daily experience of most black South Africans on a more intimate level, I asked each of them to write an interior monologue, a writing device which "prompts students to empathize with other human beings" (Bigelow & Christensen, 1994). It supports students in developing the social imagination necessary to genuinely connect with distant and different others. It puts students inside the experience of another and challenges them to describe a situation from that person's point of view.

Given the vast differences between my students' perceptions of social reality as viewed from a relatively affluent, mostly white suburb and those, for example, of a black South African child of a domestic servant living in a township, writing interior monologues was invaluable in helping my students identify with the people we presumed to teach others about. Because I place a high value on asking children to write only for genuine purposes, I explained that this "exercise" would help them better imagine the thoughts and feelings of the characters they would later portray in our skits.

After reading each book, we brainstormed critical moments in the stories and all major characters. Each child then chose to describe a given situation in a first-person narrative from a particular character's perspective. A few children wrote about various characters' resolve to resist, and I highlighted these for the rest of class in order to ensure that they would not see black South Africans as passive and pathetic. I was impressed by the children's ability to enter into the experiences of others and to capture the pain, confusion, and humiliation felt by so many black South African children.

My students also wrote poems, questions, and personal responses to those novels in their writer's notebooks. My aim was to saturate their thoughts and creative imaginations with the black South African experience. I felt that before we could be qualified to teach others about apartheid and the upcoming elections, we had to work rigorously to understand it ourselves.

We set up a series of charts to keep track of the many questions generated as well as the research gathered to answer them, adding questions and answers each day. Some of the questions recorded were "What is the length of the presidency in South Africa and who will take over after Mandela (assuming he would win)?" "What would Ruth First be doing now if she hadn't been killed by the government and what is her husband, Joe Slovo, doing [the couple featured in the film *A World Apart*]?" "Why didn't Reagan and Bush want sanctions against South Africa?" During this research process we continued following the news and having daily discussions of events leading up to the elections.

At about this time, I showed *Cry Freedom* (Attenborough, 1987), a film about black activist Steve Biko and Donald Woods, the white journalist who brought Biko's message to the world. Both this film and *A World Apart*, shown at the beginning of our study, are long, complex films which were difficult for fourth graders and required extensive mediation on my part. I frequently paused each video to answer questions, clarify situations, and discuss content. The children clearly would not have been able to comprehend either film on their own, but in the context of our research and with my support, they learned a great deal from these films, which contained images of life under apartheid that could not have been conveyed through text alone.

The children were particularly disturbed by the scenes of police brutality, arbitrary arrests, and total absence of justice. Grappling with why "the state" (military and police) might not always protect the people was difficult for the children but important. In an effort to connect racism in South Africa with racism and injustice in the United States, I talked with my students about examples of police brutality in the United States, including the Rodney King incident. I also revealed that I personally had never even considered that the police or military could work against justice and freedom until college, that I had never learned the "underside of history" as a child. I often compared my own sanitized and patriotic education with the way we were learning so that the children would not take for granted a critical view of history and current events. I wanted to ensure that they were somewhat prepared for the years of uncritical teaching they were sure to experience in the future.

And, of course, I again wanted to connect the South African reality of racism and injustice with that reality here in the United States. I continually brought our discussions back home and drew analogies between the two countries whenever possible.

"No Easy Road to Freedom": A Play

By this time the children were becoming "experts" on South Africa—informed and articulate. I asked the class to consider how we might expand the project to create something that would have more impact than the series of mini-performances we had planned to do. One student, who recalled a play my class had done for the school on the Montgomery bus boycott two years earlier, suggested we write and produce a play about the conditions of apartheid, the history of resistance, and the upcoming South African elections. The class agreed.

I have no formal background in guiding play writing or drama with children. However, I find myself using this medium regularly to bring historical events, literature, and contemporary issues to life. I use drama to help children take on the perspectives of others, understand different historical periods, and devise solutions to their own everyday problems. Since the children are engaged in informal drama throughout the year and across the curriculum—in role-plays, simulations, and open-ended skits—they were already comfortable with the medium.

Once the decision was made, I sent a letter to parents which described what we were doing and why, and requested their help. I wanted them to be aware that most of our remaining school days would be taken over by this project and to understand my rationale for this. Fortunately, my teaching situation affords me the flexibility to take on a project that replaces what had been my original curricular time line, but I could never do this successfully without informing and involving parents. Seven parents responded to my letter by offering fairly substantial assistance. A few worked on scenery with a group of children after school for several days; others helped with props, costumes, and a range of other tasks.

The students wanted to show footage from the films they had seen in order to give the audience images of the living conditions of black South Africans, of mass protests, and of other scenes that our play couldn't possibly depict. They thought we could choose a series of short scenes from each film, which we would show during our play's scene changes. I thought their idea was brilliant, but I considered the technical aspects to be daunting. Ultimately, I had a parent and child manage this. They rented the videos again, viewed them at home, and recorded the sections the class decided to show. Later, a few children went to our high school and worked with our district's "video expert" to create a video with these scenes in the order to use them. The three children who worked on this became our technical crew for the play. All three were responsible and intelligent, but too shy to perform. They were thoroughly involved with the play, but truly did not want to appear on stage. They managed these film clips, the sound system, and the lights for our play.

The children were bursting with great ideas, and I realized we needed a system for gathering and responding to their suggestions. I placed a notebook in our discussion area, where the children wrote their ideas whenever they occurred to them. Each day we read through the ideas as a class and decided which to use and how to use them. This was a way of honoring everyone's ideas and saving my sanity, because otherwise children were constantly grabbing me to share their latest brainchild.

The process we used for writing the play was simple, efficient, and drew significant input from every child. The class brainstormed about six scenes on chart paper and discussed generally what each scene would look like. Then the children signed up to write different scenes. I gave each group a work folder, a place to work, and encouragement. They worked for an hour that first day discussing and writing, then brought their drafts back to the class for feedback. We continued this way for a week. When we weren't writing we were gathering more research as the process of writing generated more questions. We called the Africa Fund in New York, the ANC, and the South African Embassy, and had many questions answered. During this process we also referred back to the interior monologues written earlier in order to assist the children in writing more plausible dialogue and action.

Although we had had many discussions linking racism in the United States and in South Africa, I realized that the children were not weaving these concepts into the play, so I decided to directly suggest that this connection be made in the play. I asked the children to brainstorm all the analogous situations here that we had considered during earlier discussions. The list included the following: Jim Crow laws in the South and actual segregation in most places now; police arresting peaceful picketers during a local labor strike; Reagan's refusal to support divestment; the anti-apartheid movement here; statistics revealing a significant differential in the living conditions of blacks and whites in the United States with regard to infant mortality, wealth, and income and education levels. We divided these issues among the play-writing groups, who then went back to find ways of working the information into the play.

One example of this is a dialogue in our last scene between an American visitor to South Africa and a South African—"The ANC Victory Celebration." The American shares an article which refers to the New Jersey system of public education as apartheid. (This was an article that had actually appeared recently in our local paper.) The American goes on to explain that rich suburban districts have far more resources for their schools than urban areas, and given that students in urban schools are predominantly children of color while those in suburban schools are mostly white, this creates an educational system of apartheid.

At the end of one week of scriptwriting, I typed and revised the script and made sure there were parts for everyone, apart from the technical crew. The groups went over the copies of the revised draft and made revisions which were then discussed with the entire class. This process of going through the entire play and soliciting input from all children was tedious, but the children stayed focused and engaged. The children then chose their parts, and auditions were held for the most sought-after roles. The class voted on who would play those roles. Once everyone had a part they were satisfied with, the children set out to learn their lines. For one week their homework was to study their lines and cues every day and read the entire script several times. I wanted to be sure that every child had a strong working idea of the entire play in order to ensure smooth transitions and so that they could all help each other with their lines and staging. We practiced in the classroom every day for about an hour. All the children were directors, giving feedback and suggesting revisions.

During this process, our class was also learning songs for the play, including the new South African national anthem "N'kosi Sikelel'i Africa" and "Sing Mandela Free." The music teacher helped the class learn two of the children's own raps, including the one mentioned above. I also taught these songs to the other fourth-grade classes during our social studies sessions so that they could sing with us during the play.

The scenery for the play included a huge backdrop of a crowd scene, painted by children and parents after school under the guidance of our art teacher. We also hung all of the children's posters which illustrated the statistics we had studied in math and the numerous posters from the Africa Fund. The costumes were black T-shirts with anti-apartheid slogans, made one afternoon with the help of a parent.

The technical crew, with the help of Bob Krist, made a series of slides of South Africa which we used between scenes, alternating with the film clips. They made slides of newspaper photographs showing the long lines for voting, elderly and sick black South Africans being carried and wheeled to voting places, and celebrations during the elections.

This crew also thought we should attempt to make a high-quality video of the play. They suggested that we ask the district's "video expert," with whom they had worked earlier, to bring in his high school students to videotape the play. Once we arranged for the high school students to do the taping, my students became even more serious and committed to creating a high-quality production. There wasn't a single child who wasn't engaged and enthusiastic. No one grew bored, lazy, or disruptive. Students had a strong sense that they were involved in something big and important and so had a responsibility to do it well. I overheard several conversations among the children, discussing how our play was going to make a difference.

One of my four classified students was particularly committed to the play. Melanie, whose previous year's teacher described her as passive, difficult to motivate, and "not interested in ideas," could think of nothing but the play, according to her mother. Melanie played the part of a black servant in a white home, and she decided to refer back to relevant sections in the novels we had read and the film *A World Apart,* in order to get a better idea of how to play the part. She was so serious about her role that she assigned herself this bit of research to ensure that she acted with authenticity. Melanie also stayed after school numerous afternoons to work on scenery, and she involved her mother in organizing props for most of the play. The day after the play she wrote the following:

> I think that we were second hand freedom fighters because we don't go to protests and rallies, but we did a play and showed seventy people what happened in South Africa. I think if everyone chips in we could make South Africa a great place to be and we could end racism everywhere.

Melanie clearly felt effective as a student and an agent for social change. School made sense to her while participating in this project, and therefore motivation came naturally.

The week before the play, my students went in groups of five to all the classes that would be attending the play (grades 3–5), to review background information and leave fact sheets for teachers to use with their classes. We also circulated the book *At the Crossroads* by Rachel Isadora (1991), a beautifully written and illustrated story about children living in a South African township awaiting the return of their fathers, who work as miners and are away for months at a time. The teachers all read this book to their classes and led discussions about it, and reviewed the fact sheets we had prepared. This preparation for the play was critical for our audience to really absorb all that we covered. We also encouraged the teachers to have their students view the posters that were up on stage a few days before the play. Although none of these teachers had devoted much time to following the elections, they all seemed quite willing to spend class time on the preparation and follow-up to the play.

June 13: Performance Day

The play went incredibly well. The children knew their lines and delivered them powerfully. There were no major problems despite the complicated technical aspects of our production—

video crew, slide show, films projected onto a large screen during scene changes. The audience loved the performance. It was obvious they were not only well informed, but well entertained, too. After the play, one of my students spoke to the audience about what they could do to fight racism; for example, give money to the Africa Fund, keep learning about and paying attention to South Africa, join anti-racist groups, take a stand against racism whenever they witness it personally. We also prepared and distributed a set of sheets with this information to all the classes.

The day after the play, Naoko, a student from one of the other two fourth-grade classes, said to me, "What Matt said in the play was right; we do have apartheid in New Jersey. We have apartheid right here in Ridgewood." She then showed me a diagram she had drawn which fairly accurately depicted the racial segregation in our town with Blacks, Whites, and Asians living in distinct neighborhoods. Obviously, there are huge differences in degree between racism and segregation in South Africa and the United States, and the children were aware of this. However, I also think it was significant that children, such as Naoko, made such connections.

The parent of one of my students wrote me a letter after this project, expressing her understanding of and appreciation for its effect on her daughter:

> Throughout the year, you helped the children understand issues of participatory democracy and allowed them to experience it in the classroom. The questions raised by the South Africa project went beyond race issues into broader understandings about the power of each individual's participation in community decisions, the essence of participatory democracy. Experiencing how democracy works, how people can form intelligent and critical opinions and make responsible decisions were at the core of what my daughter learned this year.

This parent was one among five extremely progressive, vocal, and supportive parents who set an unusually welcome tone for a critical-literacy program that year. They loved it, encouraged it, and managed to bring along the rest of the parents. In *A Pedagogy for Liberation*, Ira Shor (Shor & Freire, 1987) discusses the importance of keeping your finger on the political pulse of your workplace and making tactful decisions about what that climate can tolerate. He cautions that to ignore this is to be irresponsible and risk losing one's job and thus an opportunity to make progressive change. Each year I try to get a measure of the politics of my students' parents. I need to know just to what extent I can safely pursue a social-justice curriculum. This is not to say that I ever "sell out" or neutralize my curriculum. I do not. I always approach my teaching from a social justice, critical-literacy perspective. However, some years I must modify and slightly tone down the program.

My work climate during the school year of the South Africa project was more fertile for radical teaching than at any time in my ten years of teaching, so I therefore pulled out all the stops. Other years have been different, and so I have had to adjust my program in response to more conservative pressures. For example, during a unit on prejudice and stereotypes and the history of intolerance in the United States, I was accused of being too negative and "not showing all the good things about this country." This prompted me to seek out current examples from the newspaper of people fighting discrimination and to highlight historical examples of successful social-justice campaigns and individual activists. I have also been accused of not showing "the other side of the story." To this I did not respond that, in fact, the children are drilled daily with the official and status-quo supporting version of the past and present. Instead, when teaching about exploitative working conditions in Nike and Disney overseas plants, I had the children read documents from those companies' public relations departments. The documents were written in response to criticisms from labor-advocacy groups. In reading these documents, the children gained skills in critically analyzing various points of view, considering the interests and perspectives behind texts, and forming their own opinions. Teaching for social justice requires that you find that delicate balance between taking risks and pushing the limits of your particular work world, and maintaining your job for future years of transformative teaching. To be a teacher for social justice, one must also be brave and willing to not always be popular.

When viewed in the larger context of an ongoing struggle for social justice, the impact of our play was modest. But when I consider the effect it had on my students, the strength of the project is heartening. My students felt empowered as social activists and believed they had a mandate and the ability to make a difference. The project was successful because it nurtured the children's sense of their own power to build a more just world. I believe that such an experience can propel children forward as future activists—hopeful, committed, critical, and with concrete skills to effect social change.

References

Apartheid is wrong: A curriculum for young people. (1986). Trenton, NJ: Educators Against Racism and Apartheid. Filmstrip.

Altwerger, B., & Flores, B. (1994). Theme cycles: Creating communities of learners. *Primary Voices*, 2(1), 2–6.

Attenborough, R. (Dir.). (1987). *Cry freedom.* 157 min. Universal City, CA: MCA/Universal. Videocassette.

Atwell, N. (1987). *In the middle: Writing, reading, and learning with adolescents.* Upper Montclair, NJ: Boynton/Cook.

Bigelow, B. (1985). *Strangers in their own country: A curriculum guide on South Africa.* Trenton, NJ: Africa World.

Bigelow, B., & Christensen, L. (1994). Promoting social imagination through interior monologues. In B. Bigelow, et al. (Eds.), *Rethinking our classrooms: Teaching for equity and justice* (pp. 110–111. Milwaukee: Rethinking Schools.

Calkins, L. M. (1994). *The art of teaching writing.* New ed. Portsmouth, NH: Heinemann.

Christensen, L. (1994). Unlearning the myths that bind us. In B. Bigelow, et al. (Eds.), *Rethinking our classrooms: Teaching for equity and justice* (pp. 8–10). Milwaukee: Rethinking Schools.

COSATU. (1992). *Our political economy: Understanding the problems.* Johannesburg, South Africa.

Gordon, S. (1992). *The middle of somewhere: A story of South Africa.* New York: Bantam.

Goggenheim, C. (Dir.). (1991). *A time for justice: America's civil rights movement.* 38 min. Santa Monica, CA: Direct Cinema. Videocassette.

Isadora, R. (1991). *At the crossroads.* New York: Greenwillow.

Menges, C. (Dir.). (1988). *A world apart.* 114 min. Los Angeles: Media Home Entertainment. Videocassette.

Naidoo, B. (1985). *Journey to Jo'burg: A South African story.* New York: Harper & Row.

Shor, I. (1992). *Empowering education: Critical teaching for social change.* Chicago: University of Chicago Press.

Shor, I., & Freire, P. (1987). *A pedagogy for liberation: Dialogues on transforming education.* South Hadley, MA: Bergin & Garvey.

Short, K. G., and Harste, J. C., with Burke, C. (1996). *Creating classrooms for authors and inquirers.* 2nd ed. Portsmouth, NH: Heinemann.

Zinn, H. (1993). *Failure to quit: Reflections of an optimistic historian.* Monroe, ME: Common Courage.

CHAPTER SIX

Teaching without Charisma: Involving Third Graders as Co-investigators of Their Inner-City Neighborhood

PAUL SKILTON-SYLVESTER

Frederick Douglass Elementary School, Philadelphia, Pennsylvania

I'm no Jaime Escalante. I admit that there may have been a time when I would not have minded being the next Jaime of *Stand and Deliver* (Menendez, 1987/1997), or John Keating of *The Dead Poets Society* (Kleinbaum, 1989), or even Sir of *To Sir, with Love* (Braithwaite, 1959), but the charismatic teacher/performer is not me. To support my claims of dullness, I offer a written evaluation I received as the leader of a staff-development program for teachers. After giving me the highest ratings as a facilitator and action researcher, one teacher admitted reservations about my oral presentation to the faculty: "... Sometimes you could be a little more livelier [*sic*]," she wrote. Then below this on the evaluation form (which I had crafted) it asked "How could he improve in this area?" Ignoring the third-person form, the teacher wrote to me directly: "It's hard, because it's *your personality*" (emphasis added). Having acknowledged one of my ongoing "challenges" as a teacher, in this article I want to recount a year in which I did have some success, and share some lessons I've learned about teaching without charisma.

During this particular year, my students created in our classroom a child-sized, red brick neighborhood made out of cardboard boxes, called "Sweet Cakes Town." (None of the students could explain to me why they seized upon one boy's odd suggestions for this name.) Every Friday afternoon in

Sweet Cakes Town, my third graders each received a paycheck or welfare payment. Afterward, they went to the local branch of the Fidelity Bank to cash their check, and were then free to spend their money, to open their business, or to report for work. Students paid rent for their desks, and paid taxes to support the classroom's municipal workers and welfare recipients. As the salaries of workers went up or the number of people on welfare increased, taxes had to be raised. In Sweet Cakes Town the businesses, government, and union were owned and run by the students. There were, on average, twenty-four students in my class. Twenty-three were African American and one was Latino. Ninety-three percent of the families in our school were on public assistance. As their teacher, my role in this curriculum was to pose problems about how to make the classroom more like the neighborhood, prodding them to go further in their modeling.

The economy of Sweet Cakes Town was not a make-believe economy; Sweet Cakes dollars were legal tender for real goods and real services. Students could rent a chessboard at the Toys Я Us, rent paints at the Art Supply store, borrow a book from the Free Library, plant a seed at the Wonderful World of Plants store, sell one of their own paintings at the Art Gallery, rent an outfit at the Value Plus clothing store, get their hair cornrowed at Shawntay's Beauty Salon, or go to feed the rabbit at the Sweet Cakes Zoo.

But the lesson that I hope to convey in this chapter is not so much about creating a model neighborhood in the classroom—model neighborhoods and model economies have been created with great success in the past.[1] In this article, the point that I want to make is that good teaching need not wait for some elusive inspiration to strike the teacher; the inspiration can, and should, come from the students. My intention is not for other teachers to re-create Sweet Cakes Town—to "assign" Sweet Cakes Town to a class would surely kill the magic. Rather, my intention is to pass on lessons about how to involve students in creating their *own* understandings of the world, tapping their *own* inspiration. To these ends, I do think that the practice of using a few good questions to guide a whole-class inquiry can be a fruitful one. In advocating this approach, I am suggesting that we rethink what we mean by "curriculum"; from a set of activities and answers, to a set of questions.

After telling the story of Sweet Cakes Town, I will discuss how I think a neighborhood study like this could be improved.[2] When I developed the Sweet Cakes Town curriculum with my students, I tried to help them create a classroom neighborhood which had enough of their own experience in it to make it "real," and enough of their imagination in it to make it hopeful. By virtue of the high degree of their *selves* that my students brought to this model neighborhood, I feel assured that Sweet Cakes Town did in fact have a kind of "realness" for them. And by allowing students to imagine themselves in a variety of social roles, I think that it also succeeded in fostering hope. Having said this, I must also admit that there is more that I think could have been accomplished in relation to the second goal—the imagination/hope connection. While the Sweet Cakes Town neighborhood clearly allowed students the chance to imagine themselves in new *social roles*, I feel less satisfied that the curriculum allowed students opportunities to dream of new *social systems*, or that it allowed them the chance to put their dreams into action in the real world. In the latter part of this paper, I will discuss these dilemmas and suggest some ways in which they could be remedied.

Planning for the Spontaneous Curriculum

There is a paradox that teachers face when we think about letting students' interests influence the direction of the curriculum. The paradox is that we need to know where we want to go with the curriculum, but we also need to be prepared to go somewhere else; to choose to follow the interests of the students and go on a real adventure.

How do you prepare to go one place and keep open the possibility of going somewhere else? In brief, the answer that has worked for me is that I, as the teacher, need to know the terrain well enough to make an informed decision about whether that *somewhere else* is going to be at least as educative for my students as the course I imagined—factoring into this decision that *their* choices have the added educational merit of fostering empowerment, critical decision-making skills, and deepened learning through improved motivation.

The guiding metaphor here is that of preparing for a hike. As a teacher, I think of myself as a wilderness leader. I need to know the terrain in the area we're exploring—the well-beaten path, the little side paths that might turn out to be overgrown, and even the land where there is no path. Children aren't afraid to bushwack, and there very well may be a pond over that hill with lessons to be learned about the food chain and the succession of plants, and all sorts of stuff that we'll want them to learn in a few years anyway (but then we will end up having to use scratch-and-sniff stickers to motivate them). As a teacher, I need to know about that pond so that if students are interested in climbing that hill, I will have knowledge about whether that is a fruitful route, or whether I need to insist on staying our course.

When we are not with them, students are, of course, doing their own exploring. Every morning, around the globe, there is a march that occurs as children walk to school, performing countless investigations of the physical and social world: experiments of physics, and biology, and sociology, and anthropology; investigations into the holes in the pavement, the dead animals in the empty lots, the odd ways of different kinds of storekeepers, and so on, day after day. These are the same children who come into our classrooms and sit down at their desks and continue to fiddle with little gadgets until we, as teachers, approach and the gadgets disappear into the recesses of their desks.

When I'm at my worst, I can only see these students as disruptive. I can't find ways to align my program with this march. They just won't learn! When I'm at my best, I join their march; I find ways to make my program go where they are going—back out into the world. I do this with the confidence that once the expedition has begun, I can always find ways of extending their informal inquiry into formal (i.e., "school") knowledge.

An important way that we, as teachers, can "join the march" is by framing curricula around holistic terrains rather than abstract terms or disconnected subjects. The first step that I take in preparing to teach a curriculum—and this happens sometime around mid-July when I'm starting to get nervous about the upcoming year—is that I have to decide what, in the broadest terms, we're going to study. Are we going to study the neighborhood, or the pond in the local park, or the skyscraper that is being constructed downtown? And here my metaphor for curriculum planning merges with real life: In the tradition of the school where I was trained as an intern teacher, the Bank Street School for Children, I really do tend to pick a terrain—a place where issues of science and social studies and math and reading are whole and live and real, in a way that is so suited to the way children learn that not one of them in their right mind would dream of opting out of the first field trip. What child doesn't want to see how they put up a skyscraper?

My assumption is that children learn things as wholes. As a child, my teachers took me to museums to learn about art. Maybe I did learn something about art (although I can't recall what that may have been), but I also learned what the go-go joint looked like that we passed on the bus, and how the coatroom worked once we got there. It's debatable how educative those lessons were. But what if we could pick a place to take the class where all, or most of, those connected lessons *were* educative? That's what I try to do when I pick the focus of our study.

But, of course, it's not that simple. We can't just study what we and our students would want to study; for most teachers there are guidelines for what we must and must not teach, dictated by the mandated curriculum (as enforced by the principal) as well as the material that we know is coming on the standardized tests. In the case of the Sweet Cakes Town curriculum, I used a checklist of objectives to allow us to follow student interests as much as possible while keeping track of what mandated objectives we had come upon so far. In the preceding summer, I made a list of these non-negotiable objectives on my computer, listing the source after each one. Then I added my own objectives to this list. This list of objectives became my list of intellectual "sights" that I wanted to make sure that my students "got to" on our hike, preferably for a number of visits. I kept this list at the front of my plan book, and recorded the date each time we "got to it."[3] Many of these mandated objectives came up naturally, but others I had to raise myself.

These lists also suggested to me the terrain to which I would need to take my students. If the standardized curriculum said that I was to study "The City," and the standardized test focused on ways that technology has changed peoples lives, I probably would not choose to take my students on a trip to the Schuykill River (although there are many lessons about cities that students could learn from a river). Instead, I might choose to study a skyscraper that was being built, knowing that this was well within the realm of a curriculum on "The City," that it would provide an entry point into discussing changes in building technology, and also knowing that it might lead to issues that I was most interested in: lessons about urban planning, community activism, how laws are made that govern real-estate development, the change from a manufacturing economy to a service economy, gentrification, and so on.

In thinking about the developmental appropriateness of these terrains, I use the following rule of thumb[4]:

Younger	Older
Concrete	Abstract
Nearby	Far away
Close to present	Far into past or future

I think of these guidelines more as an aesthetic preference than as hard-and-fast developmental rules. Here's what I mean: If we know that we want students to study ancient Greece sometime between kindergarten and fifth grade, why not wait until the later grades, when students' powers of abstraction are more developed, so that they can better understand where the place is and how far ago in time that period occurred, as well as some of the more abstract philosophical and mathematical ideals of the civilization?

Playing the devil's advocate now, one might ask, "Could a teacher who really cared about ancient Greece make it concrete and "alive" for first graders?" In my opinion, that teacher probably could, if ancient Greece was already "alive" for that individual. I could imagine it being done using literature, drama, and artwork, for example. But to my mind, it makes *more* sense to have first graders study something that is already concrete, nearby, and in the present (a farm or a local factory, for example), and leave ancient Greece for later.

In my summer planning, once I had decided the focus of the study, I began to do research. For our neighborhood study, I revisited the area that we would be studying with an eye toward "generative themes" (Freire, 1982, p. 93). I drove around the area, noticing changes in race and apparent income level; walked through the stores nearby, seeing the prevalence of Asian store owners; checked out the nearest park, noticing beautiful surroundings but an apparent lack of pond life; talked with some police officers at the local station, and learned patterns of crime; and chatted with some older women and learned a few things about the history of the neighborhood.

Then I started to read—not just children's books, but leading scholars of the field.[5] In the case of our neighborhood study, I read current urban sociology, and I reread Wilson's *The Truly Disadvantaged* (1987). I looked for written histories of the area but found only general overviews of Philadelphia history. Then I went to the public library to see what children's books seemed relevant. In addition, I took a friend of mine out to dinner who is an economist and asked her what she thought were the most important concepts for me to teach in a study of an urban neighborhood.

As teachers, we need to have our own "take" on what we're studying. I believe that we have a responsibility to act not only as *co-explorers*, but also as *guides* on the hike. As important as it is that we involve students in the curriculum, it is also important that we fulfill our roles as teachers—as those who have gone ahead, those who have experienced more, to guide students toward those experiences which we believe will be most educative; not just for that moment, but for the times that students cannot know what they might encounter (Dewey, 1938/1963, p. 38).

Unfortunately, the sights on any given trip do not speak for themselves—a dilapidated house can just as easily be seen as an individual problem (laziness) or as a social one (redlining). The "criticalness" of critical pedagogy is not inherent in the terrain that we study, but in the questions we ask and the stance that we take. Sweet Cakes Town could have been a Horatio Alger curriculum, teaching that all one has to do to make it in America is to try, and implying that anyone who has not made it has only themselves to blame. Alternately, it could have been a Karl Marx curriculum, teaching that capitalism is inherently exploitative, and that socialism will bring an end to exploitation. What I had in mind was closer to a William Julius Wilson curriculum, teaching that while individual effort is important, the problems of our inner cities are not due to deficiencies in individual poor people, but to structural changes in a system that was already unfair.[6] While I wanted my students to understand the obstacles to success that they might face, I also wanted them to begin to imagine strategies for overcoming these obstacles.

After I had begun to get an idea of how I wanted to act as a guide (still during the summer), I sat down at the computer and brainstormed lists of possible activities for a number of categories: field trips, opening exercise questions, visitors, movies, art, writing, and each of the academic disciplines. Only then did I start to feel that I knew the terrain and what I wanted to bring to the investigation well enough to lead an expedition.

Using Questions to Guide the Development of the Classroom Economy

When I first initiated the classroom economy in early November, all jobs were "government jobs" and I, their teacher, was the only boss. At the front of our room, a job chart listed government jobs (such as "filing corrected work"), their pay, and the name of the person currently holding the position. (Later, a second chart would be added listing "private sector jobs." What remained as government jobs were those traditional classroom-maintenance chores: collating homework, filing corrected work, watering the plants, etc.) The money that we used was designed by students. Appearing on the different denominations were drawings of Rosa Parks, "Homey the Clown," Don King, and somebody's mother.

In order to apply for a job, students needed to fill out a job application. On the job application, students wrote reasons that they should be hired, examples of their previous work experience, and names of references. I returned these applications with written explanations for their acceptance or rejection. Students became familiar with the boss' criteria for a strong application (to know, for example, that last year's teacher made a better reference than one of their friends). I once observed a boy start an application, then crumple it up to start over, saying "I forgot neatness counts!"

In an instance that showed me how students' desire to get a job could overcome academic weakness, a boy named Ray came to me with a sense of urgency, asking me for help on the job-application form. Ray needed help with the application because his reading and writing were impaired by dyslexia. I told him that I could help him but that he had to wait until silent reading time in the afternoon. Ten minutes later he repeated his request for help on the job application, and I repeated my response. Not long after, I saw Ray out of his seat at the job-listing on the chalk-board. He was struggling to copy words so that he could complete the application without my help. I found his application in my "in" box. It read "I what a job. I what ssr collector." He wanted the job of the collector of books for sustained silent reading time ("S.S.R."). He wanted it bad.

From the School District of Philadelphia curriculum guide (1989, pp. 34–39) I took the idea of having the students fill out a pay sheet at the end of each day. As suggested in the guide, students would be paid for being "good classroom citizens." What I liked about this idea was that it seemed to provide the possibility of bringing economic experience into the classroom. The problem I had was that in the real world, one does not get paid for being a good citizen, but rather for doing one's job; those who are richest are not always the best citizens. With this in mind, I reframed the economic system so that children were paid for "the job of being a good student" rather than being good citizens; I structured the classroom economy to run parallel to an experiential economic study of the outside neighborhood; and I used students' questions and experience about both economies to chart the direction of our study.

During the last ten minutes of each day each child evaluated his or her "job of being a good student" by filling out a pay sheet. On the top half of the pay sheet was a grid for the student to fill in, with one column for each day of the week and a row for each aspect of the "job of being a good student": their schoolwork, behavior, and a "government" job. On the basis of their self-evaluations, students wrote in how much they should be paid. I provided some parameters, such as that schoolwork paid a maximum of twenty-five dollars per day. At the end of each column was a row for them to total each day's pay. On the bottom half of the sheet was a space for them to write their personal goal for the day.

On Friday afternoons, students were paid and had the chance to use their money to buy the use of activities (an easy conversion of the once-a-week period of "student-choice" time). But before students could spend their wages they were required to pay taxes and rent for their desk. Students who were unable to pay rent or taxes went on welfare.

With the classroom economy underway, I asked students questions to help them extend this analogy to the outside neighborhood. In the opening exercise I asked "How is our classroom like a neighborhood?" Students said, among other things, that "both are our place to leave and come home to. . . . Both have different places for different things. . . . Both have libraries. . . . We all have desks like people in the neighborhood have houses." (The analogy between desks and homes presented the possibility of looking at the problem of homelessness, but for the time being I felt that we first needed to establish the economic infrastructure.)

Opening Exercise, November 18

"How can we make the classroom more like the outside neighborhood?"

Once the classroom economy was up and running, the Sweet Cakes Town curriculum unfolded from the question above, which I first asked my students in November, and then every month or so afterward for the four months that we studied their neighborhood. While this question set up the central challenge of the curriculum, there were other questions—usually one per day—that also structured our investigation. In the morning, when students filed into the classroom, an "opening-exercise" sheet awaited them on their desks, which typically included a single open-ended question concerning the neighborhood study.[7]

Their answers to the question of how we could make the classroom more like the outside neighborhood were as follows: "Make stores . . . a snack store . . . a bank. . . . Make buildings from cardboard, cut for windows . . . houses . . . a school . . . art store . . . a museum . . . cleaners."

As I considered their answers, I realized that I had a problem. Student suggestions included stores that I thought would be problematic. For example, they had suggested that we start a snack store. I knew that I did not want an economy that depended on how many snacks I could afford to buy every week, or alternately, one that depended on how many we could squeeze from their parents' good will. For practicality as well as realism, I wanted a relatively self-sufficient classroom economy.

Here, it is worth noting that as I initiated this study, I didn't know exactly where this was all going to lead. This is the unsettling part of involving students in guiding the curriculum: If students are truly going to be involved in guiding the curriculum, then their teacher cannot know (for certain) where it will go. What helped me with the uncertainty about where we were going with our curriculum was to realize that allowing student input did not mean that I had abdicated my role as teacher; I could, and did, take my concerns directly to the students when I had reservations about the direction in which things were going.

In one of my better choices—one that I would learn to make more and more frequently during that year—I took the problem of how to start private stores to my students.[8] In a class discussion I told them my reservations about starting stores, and said that we couldn't do it if we had to keep asking for donations. Their response was that we could make stores out of all the things that we already had and used in the classroom.

Opening Exercise, December 3

"What do we use in the classroom from day to day? What stores could we start to sell these things?"

After brainstorming about the goods and services already used in our classroom, the students came up with ideas for stores that we should have in our economy. For example, because we used (educational) games, the students decided that we needed a Toys Я Us.

Once we knew what stores we needed, students applied for building permits, and builders painted red bricks on boxes large enough to be used as storefronts. Using a razor-blade knife, I cut "windows" out of the boxes so that the merchants could stand behind them and sell their wares through the opening. Students painted signs with store names, which I hung from the ceiling over each establishment. Adding to the realism of the neighborhood, we even had two potted trees donated by a company that rents large indoor plants to corporations.

During the same discussion in which students had suggested creating stores in the classroom, William asked how much a store costs. I turned this question back to the students by asking where we could find out. During the discussion that followed, we decided that we would take a walking trip to the nearby soul-food restaurant named "Ziggie's Barbecue Pit."[9]

Opening Exercise, December 4

"When you grow up, what business would you like to start in the outside neighborhood? What is one question you would like to ask Ziggie to help you learn about starting a business?"

With Ziggie forewarned of the invasion, we set out to learn about starting a business. Ziggie's was a homey establishment, dimly lit with hundreds of snapshots decorating its walls. When we and our parent chaperones arrived, we squeezed in, sitting on the stools at the lunch counter and on the seats from his long-deceased Chevy van. As the press conference began, the regulars listened with curious attention. Ziggie patiently answered the questions about building his business.

Opening Exercise, December 20

"What do we need to know to start a bank in our classroom neighborhood?"

With each business that we added to Sweet Cakes Town, the children had questions to be answered. (For example: "Can any-body get money from those machines at the bank?") The search for answers pulled us out from the classroom and into the neigh-borhood; visiting a number of businesses (including the bank and a factory), inviting visitors to be interviewed, collecting speci-mens from a stream in the local park, and researching topics at the public library.

At about the time that we added stores to our economy, I streamlined our taxation methods with a form that asked stu-dents to subtract their rent and taxes on their pay sheets to find their gross and net pay. From this point, their paycheck included only the net figure. By gradually increasing the complexity of these forms, the students had meaningful applications of math problems at a level which was both challenging and attainable. I once overheard a boy say to himself after correctly filling out his pay sheet, "Yeah, I'm *all* that."

On Friday afternoon we had "wholesale-buying time," in which owners rented merchandise from me. For example, the Art Supply store owners rented the use of our classroom's paints and art paper, and the Value Plus clothing store bought the use of the class costume box. After wholesale buying was completed, we began "retail-buying time." The owners used their purchases to sell or rent goods and services to student customers.

Opening Exercise, April 25

Political poll: "Are you happy with the job that the mayor of sweet cakes town is doing?"

Opening Exercise, April 26

"Name one thing that you can do if you are dissatisfied with the job that an elected official is doing."

As John Locke would have wanted it, the government of Sweet Cakes Town evolved naturally as problems arose between individuals. It seems that Lateef, the owner of the Value Plus store, had been hiring new clerks each week rather than paying the old ones. Just when mob action seemed imminent, I suggested that we start a court. A judge was elected, jurors and lawyers picked, and for the time being, playground justice was held off. On the day of the trial, an African American lawyer came to class to coach both the prosecution and the defense. Witnesses were sworn in on a coloring-book Bible that someone had in their desk. In lieu of a black robe, the judge wore a black velvet evening gown on loan from Value Plus. At one point during the defendant's testimony, Judge Jameson blurted out, "Oh, he is *so* guilty!" giving us a chance to explore the notion of "innocent until proven guilty." In the end, Lateef was convicted and forced to pay all back wages.

Another day, we had problems with loitering students starting trouble during retail-buying time. (I heard one girl explain her inaction: "I don't want to shop. I'm savin' my money for a business.") Students decided that we needed a "no loitering" law and called for an election of a government. When children conducted a poll about which citizens should be allowed to vote, they found the boys saying that girls should not vote, and the girls saying that the boys should not vote. Such outrageous suggestions provided a meaningful context for reading some outrageous chapters of American history: the story of Susan B. Anthony and the Women's Suffrage Movement, and the history of African Americans' struggle for voting rights in the South.

Learning from their history, the class decided on universal suffrage. They designated each group of desks as a different city council district with a sign hanging from the ceiling. They elected a city council representative from each table group and a mayor for the town.

The mayor was popular for nearly a month, until students realized he had hired only close friends to fill virtually all the government jobs, with some friends holding four jobs. We talked about how this happens in real life and discussed what options voters have when their elected officials are not acting on their behalf. Students exercised a number of these options, and the mayor was roundly defeated in his bid for a second term.

Homework, June 2

"Fill out the survey we made by asking your parents their opinion of Mayor Rendell."

By the time students decided that the town needed a mayor, they were already in the habit of going to the source for their information. Philadelphia's Mayor Rendell graciously accepted the children's invitation and came to Sweet Cakes Town to be interviewed about his job. During his visit, students gave him a large bar graph showing the results of the poll they had conducted to survey their parents' attitudes toward the mayor (at that point, the mayor was enjoying an 80 percent approval rating). As a final gesture of thanks, the mayor of Sweet Cakes Town gave Mayor Rendell the (paper-mâché) key to our city.

Opening Exercise, June 11

"Name one need that you see in the neighborhood and would like to address in our service project."

The final project for the citizens of Sweet Cakes Town was a community works project: The students' consensus was to address the problem of small grocers in the neighborhood selling crack cocaine. Here, again, I had reservations: While I wanted to affirm students' desire to address this problem, I feared for the safety of my students if they were to publicly oppose local drug dealers. By now, I was used to taking such problems to my students. After I did so, we brainstormed other ways that we could help to stop the local drug trade, and my students decided to raise money for DARE, an anti-drug organization, by writing a newspaper about Sweet Cakes Town and selling it on the street.

At the end of the year, I asked students to carry the storefronts of Sweet Cakes Town to the trash, but they requested permission to keep them—explaining to me that, if I didn't object, they would like to use them to start concession stands in the neighborhood. I didn't object.

Holistic Instruction, Whole Language, and the Classroom Neighborhood

When children go on a hike, there's no question about what the purpose is—they're exploring; they're curious; they're making sense. It is this purposefulness that I try to make the driving force in my curricula. And if exploring is what we're doing, then putting up fences to divide science from social studies, or art from math, only makes the exploring more difficult. By the same token, purposefulness comes from students doing *actual* exploring, not from *practice exercises* for exploring. From my experience, the best way to preserve students' excitement is to study the real world in all its dynamic mess, i.e., "keeping it real" implies "keeping it whole"—at least that's my ideal.

Teaching, of course, is rarely ideal. In this section I want to describe some of the ways I found to keep things whole and to maintain students' purposefulness. I will then give examples of times when I was not able to maintain this wholeness, explaining the trade-offs I was making in these instances.

One way that the Sweet Cakes Town curriculum was "whole" was that students were involved in the investigation of the neighborhood as a real, live, dynamic entity. This is not to say that we didn't "break it apart" into subsystems, but only that students were involved in this process. Analysis, the process of breaking it down, is the fun part, and if we, as teachers, do all the analysis as we make up our lesson plans, then we rob our students of the fun.

A second way that the curriculum was "whole" was in the way that we modeled the neighborhood. By asking students, "How can we make the classroom more like the neighborhood?" I was asking them to build a unified model, integrating each system as they went.

A third way that the curriculum was "whole" was that students participated in the economy themselves, experiencing the way that different subsystems interacted. For example, the mayor experienced the connections between the political system and the economic system as he balanced the needs of workers for higher wages and the needs of voters for lower taxes.

A fourth way that the curriculum was "whole" was that I created situations—and allowed situations to happen—in which academic skills needed to be used for real purposes. For example, students used their writing skills to write letters to invite the mayor of Philadelphia to visit our classroom; to write nominations for our Neighborhood Citizenship Awards; to create thank-you letters to stores we visited and community members who came to be interviewed about their work; to write their city council person to recommend laws that were needed; and to write contracts between employers and employees. They used their reading skills to read fiction and nonfiction stories that they and their peers had written about the neighborhood, to read books written by "outside authors" pertaining to the neighborhood study during sustained silent reading ("S.S.R."), and to read my chart-paper notes from our many brainstorming/discussion sessions. They used their computational skills to figure out their pay sheets, to perform transactions during wholesale- and retail-buying time, and to estimate and count earnings from the "Sweet Cakes News."

Having listed some of our successes, let me explain some of the ways that I compromised my ideal of keeping the curriculum whole, i.e., connected to my students' purposefulness. First, the opening-exercise sheet that I put on their desks usually included some practice from skills we had learned the day before. These exercises usually took the form of mathematics, phonics, or cartography problems. While I was often able to make the content of these exercises relate to the neighborhood study ("Add the factory we visited to the map below"), I did not kid myself that the students did the exercises for purposes relating to curiosity about the neighborhood. They did them for me, the teacher who marks their report card and meets with their parent at conference time. The addition of drill-and-practice questions to the opening exercise had more to do with keeping the peace than any instructional strategy. Here, my main goal was to get the class off to a smooth start. While this represented a compromise of my ideal of purposeful learning, these practice exercises seemed to lure the less-confident students into the process of learning before they could get started with diversionary tactics. I want to stress that this trade-off represented the limits of my imagination at that moment, but should not be misconstrued to represent the limits of my ideals.

Another compromise I made was to make the first one or two of these practice problems exceptionally easy. Here again my aim was to lower the initiative threshold—to invite in the least-confident students. The danger here, of course, is that students can get used to this sort of "spoonfeeding" and subsequently find it overwhelming to tackle large, multistage problems on their own. In retrospect, I realize that I could have done more to wean students of this practice, gradually raising this initiative threshold and preparing them to take charge of complex problems.

Beyond the "Bootstraps": Critical Pedagogy and the Classroom Neighborhood

Opening Exercise, January 4

"True or false: It takes money to make money (be prepared to say why you chose your answer)."

In the United States, a folk story that is central to our popular ideology is the story of those who have "pulled themselves up by their bootstraps," rising in society through individual effort. There is, of course, truth in the bootstraps myth—effort *does* matter, and children need to learn that lesson. But in the bootstraps myth there is also falsehood—or more exactly, impartial truth; truth that hides other truths. What the bootstraps myth leaves out are both the systemic obstacles to success some groups experience and the systemic advantages held by other groups.[10] In this way, the bootstraps myth is a double-sided coin: one side is the veneration of individual effort, but the other side is the blame that we heap on those who have not "made it."

In what it leaves out, the bootstraps myth is *hegemonical*, a word which literally means "leadership" but is used by social scientists to mean something more. In its meaning coined by Antonio Gramsci, a political figure imprisoned by Mussolini in the 1920s, "hegemony" means domination without the use of brute force (Bennett et al., 1981, p. 187). Gramsci realized that domination is not only maintained by armies, but also through the popular beliefs that produce *consent* to unfair systems (Bennett et al., 1981; Forgacs, 1988). By emphasizing the role of the individual, the bootstraps myth diverts us from facing the systemic nature of inequality in our society, reassuring the rich that they made it because of their effort, and scolding the poor that they failed to make it because of their laziness. Over 900,000 manufacturing jobs left American cities during the period from 1967 to 1977 alone (Peterson, 1985, p. 44), and still, we, as a country, continue to act as if the plight of the urban minority poor is a result of their reluctance to pick up the want ads and get a job.[11]

In thinking about what the future might hold for my third graders, I knew that my students *would* need to try, but I also knew that even those who tried would face long odds; that pulling yourself up by your bootstraps was a different challenge for urban, lower-income African American children than it had been for me, as a suburban, upper-middle-class white child.

There are obstacles that my students would face which had nothing to do with their "will to succeed." First, there are those obstacles black people have always faced in the United States: prejudice, residential ghettoization, poor education, lack of capital, and lack of networks to obtain capital, to name a few. Second, postindustrial changes in the economy have constructed new obstacles to economic success for those isolated in the inner cities: lack of jobs, jobs moving further out of the city where there is poor public transportation, jobs moving out of the country altogether, lack of access to job-information networks, jobs that require higher skills, or, I would add here, that require them to speak differently than they do at home (Katz, 1993; Jencks & Peterson, 1991; Peterson, 1985; Wilson, 1987). In the face of these obstacles to economic success, there are the relatively new self-destructive alternatives, such as crack cocaine or AIDS, which also threaten them.

Here was my problem: How could I avoid the twin pitfalls of (a) stressing the obstacles to economic success, thereby encouraging defeatism, and of (b) stressing the possibilities for economic success, and thereby encouraging the view that those who have not "made it" have not tried? In Sweet Cakes Town my answer was to structure the economy in ways that illustrated the obstacles that they might face, but allow them to find strategies for overcoming these obstacles and to imagine their future as those who have "made it." For example:

- I listed high-paying jobs such as gerbil-cage cleaning, but then explained to the students that this job had moved to a classroom in the suburbs. We talked about how many of the jobs that used to be in the cities are now outside the cities and the strategies that adults use for overcoming this problem.

- I hired fourth-grade students who would work for nothing just so that they could get out of class. These were our immigrant workers. Students responded to this by encouraging them not to work unless they were paid.

- One student received a letter in Sweet Cakes mail with the bad news that a great aunt had died and left the enclosed inheritance check. We discussed the reality that not all people in America begin with the same amount of capital.

- Students also dealt with recessions, layoffs, wage inequities, and alliances of capital. All of these obstacles were taken as a challenge to be overcome, rather than a defeat to be endured.

- After we read the biography of César Chávez, student workers created their own union, named JBS local 308 (standing for John Barnes School, room 308). It took a while for them to coordinate collective action. At first when I lowered their wages, one of them would say, "I'm on strike," to which I would reply, "OK, who wants her job?" At this, many of the students would raise their hands, and the striker would back down. Trying to make this as realistic as possible, I, of course, lowered their wages again—and again. Eventually, they realized that their individual good was dependent on each other, and except for two die-hard scabs, the workers started a strike in unison. A bargain was reached over lunch and later ratified by the rank and file.

There were moments when I felt successful at helping students understand the hegemonical nature of the bootstraps myth and others when I did not. Below, I will give two examples of successes before giving one example of a missed opportunity.

The first example comes from a work period that was interrupted by two students yelling back and forth, "Your mother's homeless! No, *your* mother's homeless!" Once the real dispute was settled, this incident gave us a chance to discuss why some people can't pay the rent and ultimately end up homeless. At first, students could only say that homeless people were lazy (the bootstraps explanation). But when we considered their experience in Sweet Cakes Town, students realized that there might be other intervening factors: layoffs, jobs moving outside of the city or the country, jobs not paying enough, or some people receiving no inheritance. In Gramsci's terms, students were taking a critical stance to the prevailing, hegemonical ideology that people are homeless only because of their own deficiencies, a view that ignores the role of wider social forces.

The second example occurred when I took a sick day and came back to find the room littered with trash and one of the storefronts defaced with graffiti. After student volunteers undid the damage, I used a series of opening exercises to raise issues of anger and responsibility to the community: "What feelings are students showing when they hurt their classroom neighborhood?" "How do some people on the outside hurt their community?" "In the classroom system of jobs, what things make you feel bad, sad, or angry?" "How do some people on the outside help their community?" Through this series of questions, I tried to get students to see that destructive behavior, like doing graffiti, is sometimes the expression of misplaced feelings, such as anger, which could be used to solve the problem. Once again, the point here was not to minimize the responsibility of individuals—just the opposite: I wanted them to use their anger to address the root causes of the problem. The effective uses of anger came up later in the year when we discussed urban riots. "Solve the problem" became our class mantra.

A less-successful example comes from a discussion we had on payday. A student named Rochelle had made so little in Sweet Cakes Town that week that she qualified for welfare. When I came around with welfare checks, the boy sitting behind her objected that she had a fat roll of cash in her desk. "She shouldn't get welfare if she has savings of her own," he objected. I didn't know what to do. I told the class that I didn't know what the rule was in the real welfare system in a case like this. I asked them if they knew, but they did not. Pragmatically, I felt the need to solve the problem soon so that the other children, who had just been paid, could begin retail-buying time. I asked for a vote: "Should people be able to receive welfare if their income falls below the minimum level *even if* they have savings?" Students voted to allow Rochelle to receive her check.

While our vote solved the immediate difficulty of whether Rochelle should receive welfare, we left implicit the important issues that this dilemma had the potential to raise: What is the purpose of welfare? Is it to keep people from starving or to help them achieve self-sufficiency? In a system where capital is the basis of prosperity, where some people start off with vast capital and others start with none, how can we help people accumulate enough capital to become self-sufficient, while still not taking away the initiative for work?

These are the questions that I did not ask. This is the cost when I, as a tour guide, do not know the terrain well enough to know the questions to ask.

Improving the Sweet Cakes Town Curriculum

In Sweet Cakes Town, we spent a good deal of energy enacting how the world *is*, but not enough on how the world *could be*. In this section, I will offer my ideas about how a neighborhood study like Sweet Cakes Town could be reframed to offer students an opportunity to imagine new social systems, and then to implement these ideas in the outside world.

Any talk of imagining new social systems, of course, begs the question of what goals we hope to achieve, and from what values these goals emerge. The values which I am suggesting that students "try on" in this curriculum are the values taught in classrooms nationwide during the African American holiday of Kwanzaa. The "Seven Principles of Kwanzaa," or the *"Nguzo Saba"* (Karenga, 1988), are as follows:

Umoja ("Unity"): to strive for and maintain unity in family, community, nation, and race.

Kujichagulia ("Self-determination"): to define ourselves, name ourselves, create for ourselves, and speak for ourselves instead of being defined, named, and spoken for by others.

Ujima ("Collective Work and Responsibility"): to build and maintain our community together and to make our sisters' and brothers' problems our problems, and to solve them together.

Ujamma ("Cooperative Economics"): to build and maintain our own stores, shops, and other businesses and to profit from them together.

Nia ("Purpose"): to make our collective vocation the building and developing of our community in order to restore our people to their traditional greatness.

Kuumba ("Creativity"): to do always as much as we can, in the way we can, in order to leave our community more beautiful and beneficial than we inherited it.

Imani ("Faith"): to believe with all our hearts in our people, our parents, our teachers, our leaders, and in the righteousness and victory of our struggle.

Whereas the Sweet Cakes Town curriculum unfolded around one key question—How can we make the classroom more like the outside neighborhood?—my revised curriculum would begin with this same question, but then, using the Nguzo Saba, add two more, forming a series of three linked questions to guide the yearlong curriculum:

1. How can we make the classroom more like the neighborhood? (September to November)

2. How can we change the classroom "neighborhood" to put into action the seven principles of Nguzo Saba? (November to March)

3. How can we use what we have learned in the classroom "neighborhood" to put into action the seven principles of Nguzo Saba in the *outside* neighborhood? (March to June)

These questions, posed repeatedly to the class as a whole, would serve as a prompt for collaboratively planning the curriculum.

Imagine, if you will, a fictional third-grade class using the curriculum described above. It is November, and so far during the year, the class has concentrated on the first of the three questions ("How can we make the classroom more like the neighborhood?"). Students have created their own classroom neighborhood. We can now begin to imagine what might transpire as we begin to ask them to apply the principles of Kwanzaa to this neighborhood.

One could imagine what the students might say when asked, as a part of the second question, to apply the principle of Ujamma (cooperative economics) to the classroom neighborhood. Let's say something happened, like the incident in which Rochelle wanted to collect welfare even though she had some savings. Students might look at the assumption that Rochelle should not have any savings, decide that this was not cooperative, and then look for ways that we could create a more cooperative system. Then they might decide to start a fund to help people like Rochelle start businesses so that they could get off the welfare rolls. This fund—which could be a public or private enterprise—might pay Rochelle one dollar for each dollar she puts aside for the purpose of starting a business, and then provide an entrepreneurial mentor. Later on, if we started a stock market, the unused portion of this fund could be invested so that profits benefitted the smallest capitalists.

Later in the year, their teacher might bring their ideas on cooperative economics back to them with the third question: "How can we use what we learned in the classroom neighborhood to show the seven principles of Nguzo Saba in the *outside* neighborhood?" Maybe students would focus on getting grown-ups to start a fund for beginning businesses. On the other hand, students might decide to do a fund-raiser and create a fund themselves, with a board of directors to take applications for the money. Students could then try to come up with businesses that they could start in the outside neighborhood.

The actual scenario might look like these examples I have suggested, but probably not. One would have to be prepared to go somewhere completely different, led by the interests and convictions of the students (remember: teaching as guiding a hike).

As we know, teaching values is sticky business. It is much easier to pretend that we are just teaching skills, as if our curriculum could be free from ideology. After all, if I were the teacher of the class discussed above, how could I justify teaching the values of the Nguzo Saba and not some others? Is it just a matter of me (as teacher) imposing whatever values I deem righteous? In answer to these questions, I think there must be some sort of dialectic between the values of the community and the values of the teacher. I designed the curriculum described above for the African American, urban, lower-income area where my school is located. I am not suggesting this as a universally appropriate set of guiding questions. I probably would not use the Nguzo Saba to raise issues of justice in the all-white, upper-middle-class suburb where I grew up. The cultural reference points are different there, as are the students' relationships to inequality. I would, however, find other ways for raising issues of the individual's responsibility to ideals of justice, in ways appropriate to who they are and the community they come from. I would also need to choose ways that are appropriate to who I am and where, I believe, there is an opening for justice. I think of the variety of possible approaches to issues of justice like the spokes of the wheel, starting from different points on the periphery but converging on a common point in the center.

Conclusion

We, as teachers, have good reasons to not study inequality with our children: It's ugly and unfair, and looking at it may cause our students pain. Ultimately, this is why it took me so long to do

Sweet Cakes Town: I had to figure out how it could be other than a curriculum of bitterness and defeatism; how I could look at systemic obstacles without denying the importance of individual effort. Similarly, if I had been a suburban teacher, I imagine that I would have had to figure out how to study inequality without it being a curriculum of guilt and condescension; how one could look at systemic advantages, again without denying the importance of individual effort.

As teachers, we must face our responsibility to abandon the innocuous curriculum that "does" Martin Luther King Day but looks away from the inequality between suburbs and cities, that does coed gym but doesn't talk about how girls and women are mistreated, that talks about Dr. King's dream of equality but not about hatred of homosexuals, that does litter cleanups but doesn't talk about environmental racism.

Our students face the stark realities of inequality every day. Whether or not we find ways to talk about them, as our students ride from the dilapidated inner city to the immaculate suburbs, they *will* find some way to make sense of it, just as you and I did—and do. For my African American students, this might mean deciding that their neighborhood is a mess because their people are lazy (as some have told me); or it might mean deciding that all white people are just selfish (as others have told me); or it might mean deciding that the system is unfair so there is no use in trying (as still others have told me).

The point is that in our silence, students are left to understand the world using only their wits and the warped fun-house mirror which is popular culture.[12] For me and my friends, growing up in the suburbs of Detroit, we came to the conclusion that there were some good black folks and some "niggers" (although I knew better than to say the word). We, as suburbanites, needed to look just as hard at inequality as my third graders did. The best thing that we could have studied in social studies is how suburban/urban inequality is reproduced. I know of no teacher and no class that have yet enacted that curriculum, or written the story of its enactment.

The issues I am talking about are "hot" ones. They are "hot" for good reason—they call into question the situation we've come to consider to be normal. They question the hegemony—the mindset of domination. Because these issues are real ones, ones subject to the push and pull of conflicting interests, we probably will not find them in our textbooks. Textbooks are better at certain answers than tough questions. That leaves it up to us as educators to put the focus on the contradiction between what everyone says America is, and what we see from the freeway. Asking students what they see, and what they want to find out, is one way that we can initiate this investigation in our classrooms.

Notes

1. For other classroom uses of "microsocieties," see McCarthy & Braffman (1985); and Richmond (1989).

2. Portions of this curriculum have been excerpted from a previous article (Skilton-Sylvester, 1994). In retelling this story, I run the risk of becoming one of those people I have long made fun of—those who make a career out of a brief period of success early in their professional lives. My reason for retelling this story is that in retrospect, I see important ways in which it could be improved and extended, and wish to include these in the final section of the paper. A logical question about the revision of this curriculum is, of course, why I am presenting this only as a suggestion and not reporting on its implementation. My reason for this is that in the time since I created the curriculum with my students, I have gone back to graduate school at the University of Pennsylvania. While I have been doing research related to the interests in this paper, I have not had my own class with whom I could work through the proposed revisions.

3. Using a checklist to keep track of objectives is something I learned from Donnan (1988, p. 3). For another framework for bringing together students interests and mandated curricula, see Wigginton (1989).

4. I distilled this "rule of thumb" primarily from classes and conversations with Madeline Ray of Bank Street College.

5. This lesson was impressed upon me by Madeline Ray of Bank Street College.

6. In our personal correspondence, Wilson has written that he does feel that the Sweet Cakes Town curriculum was "in the spirit of his work." In a speech given in 1990, Wilson provided a concise summary of his landmark work: "I argue in *The Truly Disadvantaged* [Wilson, 1987] that historic discrimination and a migration flow to large metropolitan areas that kept the minority population relatively young cre-

ated a problem of weak labor-force attachment within this population, making it particularly vulnerable to the ongoing industrial and geographic changes in the economy since 1970. The shift from goods-producing to service-producing industries, increasing polarization of the labor market into low-wage and high-wage sectors, innovations in technology, relocation of manufacturing industries out of the central cities, periodic recessions, and wage stagnation exacerbated the chronic problems of weak labor-force attachment among the urban minority poor" (Wilson, 1990, p. 6).

7. I learned the practice of starting the day with a single open-ended question as an intern at the Bank Street School for Children in Manhattan.

8. The habit of being honest with students about the constraints that I was facing was one that I learned from Elliot Wigginton, referred to earlier. Wigginton (1989) provides an excellent framework for bringing together students' interests and the objectives of the mandated curriculum.

9. In many schools the spontaneity to go on field trips is curtailed by the time it takes to issue and receive signed permission slips. The School District of Philadelphia helps teachers avoid this problem by issuing blanket permission slips which give consent for students to go on walking trips in the neighborhood of the school throughout the year.

10. One example of the way these truths are exposed and hidden can be seen in the variations of the story of Clarence Thomas's rise to a seat on the U.S. Supreme Court. One popular version tells of Clarence Thomas as a self-made man. Another version, told by Justice Leon Higginbotham (1992), reminds us that while Clarence Thomas surely benefitted from his own efforts, he also benefitted from the collective struggles of other African Americans and the interventions by the U.S. government that these struggles had won.

11. While recent news of the country's "success" in moving welfare recipients to work may appear to confirm the belief mentioned above—that "the plight of the urban minority poor is a result of their reluctance to pick up the wants ads and get a job"—it is important here to consider the definition of what constitutes "success." Many people *are* getting jobs in the booming economy of today, but as one critic of the new welfare law has asked, isn't it time we stopped measuring the success of welfare reform by how many people abandon welfare, and instead ask whether our new state welfare programs enable people to move into family-supporting jobs (Pearson, 1997)? While those leaving welfare may not all be flocking to soup kitchens, somewhere around 50 percent of these individuals have not gotten jobs and are relying on relatives,

charities, and street smarts to support themselves (Pugh, 1997; Swarns, 1997). Since the minimum wage has been raised in 1997, those who have taken minimum wage jobs are earning $5.15 per hour—only 71 percent of what it was in 1968 (when measured in real dollars). People working 60 hours at one of these jobs are still below the poverty level of $16,050 for a family of four. People are taking jobs today just as people sold apples on the street during the Great Depression, just as thousands of people in third-world countries sell chewing gum on the street. What is happening is that *we are confusing the exploitation of desperation with the support of initiative*. At a time when American corporate profits are soaring, government deficits are being filled, and executive salaries have increased 182 percent since 1980 (Johnston, 1997), shouldn't we expect more for the neediest Americans?

12. This metaphor I borrowed with the permission of my mentor and friend, Frederick Erickson.

References

Bennett, T., Graham, M., Mercer, C., & Woollacott, J. (Eds.). (1981). *Culture, ideology, and social process: A reader*. London: Open University Press.

Braithwaite, E. R. (1959). *To Sir, with love*. Englewood Cliffs, NJ: Prentice-Hall.

Dewey, J. (1938/1963). *Experience and education*. New York: Collier.

Donnan, C. (1988). Following our forebears' footsteps: From expedition to understanding. In V. Rogers, A. D. Roberts, & T. P. Weinland (Eds.), *Teaching social studies: Portraits from the classroom* (pp. 3–11). Washington, DC: National Council for the Social Studies.

Forgacs, D. (Ed.). (1988). *An Antonio Gramsci reader: Selected writings, 1916–1935*. New York: Schocken.

Freire, P. (1982). *Pedagogy of the oppressed*. New York: Continuum.

Jencks, C., & Peterson, P. E. (Eds.). (1991). *The urban underclass*. Washington, DC: Brookings. Institution.

Johnston, D. C. (1997, September 2). Executive pay increases at a much faster rate than corporate revenues and profits. *New York Times*, D4.

Karenga, M. (1988). *The African American holiday of Kwanzaa: A celebration of family, community, and culture*. Los Angeles: University of Sankore Press.

Katz, M. B. (1993). *The"underclass" debate: Views from history.* Princeton, NJ: Princeton University Press.

Kleinbaum, N. H. (1989). *The dead poets society.* New York: Bantam.

McCarthy, L. P., & Braffman, E. J. (1985). Creating Victorian Philadelphia: Children reading and writing their world. *Curriculum Inquiry, 15*(Summer), 121–151.

Menendez, R. (1987/1997). *Stand and deliver.* Woodstock, IL: Dramatic Publications.

Pearson, A. (1997, September 14). Letter to the editor re: "Getting Opal Caples to work." *New York Times Magazine*, 20.

Peterson, P. E. (1985). *The new urban reality.* Washington, DC: Brookings Institution.

Pugh, T. (1997). Welfare reform one year later: Is it working or not? Many have jobs, but others live hand to mouth. *Philadelphia Inquirer*, A1, 8.

Richmond, G. (1989). The future school: Is Lowell pointing us towards a revolution in education? *Phi Delta Kappan, 71*(November), 232–236.

School District of Philadelphia. (1989). *Social studies: Grade three.* Philadelphia: Office of Curriculum.

Skilton-Sylvester, P. (1994). Elementary school curricula and urban transformation. *Harvard Educational Review, 64*(3), 309–331.

Swarns, R. L. (1997, July 6). Cut off from food stamps but not flocking to soup kitchens. *New York Times*, B13, 16.

Wigginton, E. (1989). Foxfire grows up. *Harvard Educational Review, 59*(February), 224–249.

Wilson, W. J. (1987). *The truly disadvantaged: The inner city, the underclass, and public policy.* Chicago: University of Chicago Press.

Wilson, W. J. (1990, February). Studying inner-city dislocations: The challenge of public agenda research. 1990 Presidential Address. *American Sociological Review, 55*(1), 1–14.

CHAPTER SEVEN

A Conversation
about Critical Literacy

JAMES ALBRIGHT
Teachers College Columbia University

SUSAN M. CHURCH
Halifax (Nova Scotia) Regional School Board

SUE SETTLE
O'Connell Drive Elementary School, Porter's Lake, Nova Scotia

VIVIAN VASQUEZ
American University

Introduction

In the spring of 1995, I (Susan Church) was fortunate to have the opportunity to speak at length with three teachers about their efforts to enact critical literacy practices in their classrooms. Later, I used those conversations to shape a chapter in a book in which I explored how we can bring a more critical edge to whole language teaching (Church, 1996). During the spring of 1997, the four of us engaged in further discussions through e-mail, sharing our current thinking about critical practice and about the contexts within which we are working.

For two of us, the context had changed since our earlier conversation. Jim Albright was on leave from his grade 4 teaching position with the Halifax Regional School Board in Nova Scotia and was immersed in doctoral studies at Pennsylvania State University. I had taken a one-year leave from the same school district, where I had been a district-level administrator, to accept a position as a teacher educator at Mount Saint

Vincent University and to begin work on my doctorate. Both Sue Settle and Vivian Vasquez continued their work as teachers of young children: Sue in a grade 3 classroom in Halifax and Vivian in junior kindergarten (three-, four-, and five-year-olds) in Mississauga, Ontario.

The following is an edited transcript of an electronic discussion that unfolded in fits and starts over several months, as we all struggled to fit the time to "talk" into our busy schedules. My role in the process was primarily as facilitator and editor, and I greatly appreciated this opportunity to learn more from these thoughtful teachers.

Theories of Critical Literacy

I began by asking each of the teachers to offer some thoughts on what guides their work.

JIM: I guess what most guides my work, and my work this year as a student, is my experience as a classroom teacher. That is not the only influence. But I think my teaching, my relationships with students, and my practice as a language arts teacher is where my work begins. From the classroom, and back again, I hope, what also guides my work are the studies I have undertaken over the past few years and people I have worked with in schools and in the university. Although I have mentioned practice, study, and people, I would hope that practice grounds what I do. I understand that many of my colleagues might think I'm way too "philosophical" about my teaching. I want to collapse the teaching/learning binarism or the teacher/learner binarism.

My classroom experience, informed by my studies, has led me to see my practice as more socially contextualized. Schools are contested sites within which there are competing discourses about what is worth knowing, which knowers are to be valued, and how we come to know. Because this has real effects on everyone within these sites, how these competing discourses get played out is ideological. Consequently, as a language arts teacher, I have ethical decisions to make both about what kinds of texts to use in my classroom and about how they are to be taken up to construct which kinds of literacy practices, and, ultimately, what kind of literate persons. During the past two years, I have been exploring notions of critical literacy, trying to orient myself within that discourse, as a way of working through these questions.

VIVIAN: In Susan's book [Church, 1996] I talked about leading a critically literate life. Living that life would be, for me, what guides my living and therefore my work. Now I've taken up a bigger challenge here than I have in the past. I'm out of that zone of safety and comfort that as classroom teachers we can so easily slip into because of the demands that we face from day to day.

Jim, you talked about schools being contested sites, which I think is where the demands made on us are rooted. And I suppose what critical literacy has helped Sue Settle and I to do is, first, to recognize this and then to, as you say, orient ourselves within a critical discourse. For Sue and I this started, I believe, in the summer of 1992, when Andy Manning and Jerry Harste organized a course in Australia. So this journey has been a five-year challenge for us. I don't mean to speak for Sue Settle because I know she has great things to offer this conversation, but I need to include her, as I should Manning, Harste, Church . . . the list goes on, because it is my relationship with others like them that has mediated the ideological sense of critical literacy with what this means for me in practice. So, in fact, in a consumer world, what I consume in order to be the person I want to be or think I ought to be, are relationships. I think it is through these relationships that I am able to engage in an ongoing re-theorizing of what it means to be literate. In terms of practice, therefore, I see the classroom as a site for the consuming of these sorts of relationships, as well as sites for generative conversations driven by theorizing and re-theorizing the world.

SUE: I was first introduced to whole language in 1980, when I attended a workshop led by Judith Newman and some of her students. It led me to enroll in a graduate program with the emphasis on reading. My teaching since then has been guided by this holistic philosophy. In 1990 I began another program of study led by Andy Manning, which focused on teacher research and inquiry. My interest in inquiry has grown and has also had an influence on the classroom curriculum. The experience with critical literacy in Australia that Vivian mentioned made me realize that whole language needed to be pushed, that language is not neutral, and that it is important that children be supported in understanding how language positions us. All of these experiences, subsequent courses, and the conversations I have had with colleagues and friends have had an influence on my thinking. It is those experiences which guide what I do in the classroom, but ultimately, it is the children who help me to determine what we do in the classroom.

SUSAN: You've all described changes in your thinking that occurred through the influence of graduate studies and relationships with particular individuals. What are your current thoughts about critical literacy?

JIM: Over the past fifteen years, I have managed to work myself into and out of a whole language, or what I might now call a strictly progressivist, stance toward teaching and learning. I think I have been lucky in the fact that through Andy Manning, with whom I did graduate work at Mount Saint Vincent University, I gained an appreciation of the Anglo Australian conversation about critical literacy. Reading Allan Luke, Norman Fairclough, and those associated with them has been very influential. Lately, I have been reading some of the genrist research out of Deakin University in Australia. Working this year at Penn State, I have been introduced to what I think is the somewhat different conversation about critical literacy in the United States. My sense is that the word has been appropriated and contested by all sorts of groups of researchers. It seems less influential, more marginalized, perhaps more factionalized because of that. Perhaps my view of the Anglo Australian conversation is a result of distance focusing my gaze. But, it is interesting listening to the American debate and taking courses from one of the central and partisan figures of that conversation, Henry Giroux. Along with people like McLaren, Simon, and Shor, he's argued for a sociology of education that is open to what they call "projects of possibility" and for the need to take up resistant moments in teaching/learning as opportunities for teacher/student agency to create more democratic education. Unfortunately, Giroux doesn't spell this out very clearly and doesn't take up the project in practical terms. Simon does this to some extent, but it is only the Anglo Australians and South Africans who do this.

VIVIAN: I would agree with what Jim is saying here. Unfortunately, the academic jargon that inundates current writings on critical literacy has marginalized public education classroom teachers in general. The last three conferences I have attended demonstrate this; it's either teachers (who are nonacademics) being told what to think about in terms of critical theory and bashed over the head with it, or they are unable to engage in the give and take of conversation. I think not being able to come to common ground supports the argument that what critical literacy ought to be about is a way of framing life, not a way of deconstructing specific texts.

Like Jim, I have had a taste of the Australian and the U.S. take on what it means to be critically literate. I think the lack of teacher writing about critical literacy in practice is the biggest problem. What's out there is primarily being constructed by academics whose audience is, in most part, other academics . . . and so the ball just keeps rolling back and forth, over beyond and in a lot of cases past the classroom. Teachers' voices need to get out there in order for us to move toward possibilities in practice. As for the Australian take, my first impressions of the earlier work led me to conclude that critical literacy was in danger of being programmatized before we could even really figure out what we were talking about.

SUE: I was fascinated with the conversation that has begun around critical literacy. There's so much to think about! It also reminds me that it is a very different kind of discourse from what teachers are involved in on a daily basis. As Jim and Vivian have both mentioned, language has been part of the problem around critical literacy. It's been too distanced from what goes on in the classroom and remained quite often an academic debate. I agree that teachers' voices need to be part of that debate.

JIM: Thinking a little more about this issue of language, we seem to be bedeviled by two problems. One is a kind of discourse of clarity and the second is a form of anti-intellectualism that is so evident in the culture and in the culture of schools. These questions connect or are related to the need to have critical literacy speak to teachers in their practice.

The issue of clarity—why can't you speak plainly without using scary words, for example, ideology or pedagogy—trades on notions that language is transparent. Everything, even what seems to run counter to the way things are represented in the "everyday," is supposed to be able to be expressed directly and unselfconsciously. There's also the idea that reflection-on-practice isn't very helpful from a teacher-as-deliverer-of-program point of view. The anti-intellectualism seems to focus on a discomfort with unsettling knowledge or memories, as if learning was not supposed to be challenging or disquieting (dare I say, disruptive)— just simple, easy, and a smooth transfer of information. This anti-intellectual stance positions teachers who theorize their practice negatively as "out of it," "impractical eggheads," or as just plain uppity.

I think it means that teachers committed to promoting critical practice have to be very tactical in our use of language—in a way to plant the idea and then help others articulate the words. Discourses are porous enough things that, in the struggle between them, if we are conscious about what discourses are being employed and how they position their users, the terrain they contest can be reshaped through a conscious, discursive strategy. Like all good teaching, if we want students to write, read, and think critically, then teachers have to do it too. I guess it is our job to give them pictures of how it might be done.

VIVIAN: I still think there ought to be more public school teachers' voices invited into the conversation and respected for their contributions because most of what's out there in print is still written by academics for academics. This stuff can't be passed down; it needs to be understood as it is lived.

Living Critical Literacy

SUSAN: So, how *are* you living it? What is your work in the classroom like now?

SUE: The learning is ongoing for me. The children and I plan many things together. I try to offer curricular invitations which are open-ended, allowing for a variety of possibilities. Sometimes the whole class will investigate a particular agreed-upon topic. We meet together as a whole group to discuss issues relevant for everyone, and we also break up into smaller groups to pursue inquiries or to explore various areas of interest. Conversation is what underlies what we do. It's the ongoing conversations that determine what we investigate, how we pursue it, and with whom. This is a very simplistic look at the workings of our day. Our classroom reflects the plurality of voices within the class culture. There is a constant interplay of power—a negotiation of social status. There are many dynamics at play, and I often become a mediator between students in conflict to help them see the other person's perspective.

Over the last three years, I have been exploring social justice issues in the classroom. Vivian and I engaged in a written conversation about this in 1994–95. Issues about gender, race, sexuality, fairness, and ableness come up in children's conversations at various times. When these issues come up, I try to open the conversation to examine the issues from a variety of perspectives. I try to take the children's lead. If their conversation doesn't raise issues from the text they are examining or reflecting upon (and I use "text" broadly here), then I don't try to push it in that direction. Other times there have been occasions where certain issues needed to be raised and resolved before other learning could continue. It just depends. Sometimes the discussion continues with the whole group. Other times it continues with a smaller group. Many of the issues come from the children's lived experiences. They are ever-present. The questions that I find hovering in my mind presently is, "How do I help to support the children in being proactive?" When issues are raised, conversations can move very quickly. I want to help the children peel back the layers to examine the underlying issues. I want them to look at other possibilities. How far do I nudge? How far do we dig? We always struggle with how far we take a conversation. How much of what we do is theorizing or philosophizing and how much is actively looking for ways we can help to create a better world within our classroom and without?

VIVIAN: It seems that what exists out there [in published writing] regarding critical literacy in practice, are bits and pieces, isolated incidents. The incidents here and there make one search for the ideal critical-literacy moment; in fact, as I mentioned previously, critical literacy needs to be lived in practice, not in isolated incidents. Nevertheless, I think the bits that are out there are crucial to the lifeline of being critical in the classroom, as well as powerful demonstrations of possibilities.

SUSAN: What it seems to me you are saying is that critical literacy is a stance you take as teachers so that the curriculum emerges from the ongoing life of the classroom. Sue, you mentioned that the issues come up all the time. How, specifically, would you then pursue an issue with the children to help them grapple with the critical questions? Can you give us an example?

SUE: Vivian talks about living a critically literate life. I also think we need to be in the process of learning to view the world through a critical lens or already viewing the world this way in order to help our students do the same. With that in mind, when issues arise in the classroom, part of our role as teachers is to help bring those underlying issues to the surface, and it is the conversations we have that help to do that. Vivian describes it as teasing out the issues. As an example, I can recall one day after recess when several children entered the classroom arguing. Although I couldn't hear their conversation at first, words such as "club" and "it's not fair" popped out at me. Tempers were simmering, and I knew that this was an issue which had to be resolved before it escalated. So I invited a discussion around "clubs." During the conversation, questions arose: Why do we have clubs? Who decides who can join the club? Who gets included, excluded? Why do people have to be tested before they can join the club? Who makes the rules? Are the rules for everyone or only certain members? Through this discussion, we discovered that in our schoolyard, "clubs" were run in very different ways, some democratically and others more like a dictatorship. The children became aware that there were various possibilities for these kinds of organizations. They also began to understand some of the reasons on which people base their decisions regarding these possibilities. The discussion seemed to provide them with more choices and information which could help them to deal with the power relationships on the playground. I tried to connect this to other organizations or systems that exist in our society. I think part of what we try to do is to build on previous conversations with "remember when we talked about . . . ?"

SUSAN: Is this example close to what you mean by "living a critical life," Vivian? How does it get played out in your classroom?

VIVIAN: As I mentioned earlier, I think being critically literate is a powerful demonstration of possibilities. This is something that I have been grappling with over the past year and a half. It has been my latest and current inquiry. At the start of this school year, therefore, I began to construct, with the children's input, a learning wall, an audit trail of learning, with critical literacy, issues of social justice and equity, as the frame used in construction. What has resulted thus far is an exciting tool for organizing curriculum through the posting of various artifacts of learning such as quotes from the children, samples of their work, conversations, comments from parents. It has become a way of visually articulating our evolving theory of learning about the world through a critical-literacy framework. The curricular audit trail allows the children and I, along with interested parents and teachers, to theorize and re-theorize literacy that is just and equitable. The connections that become visible as the trail moves in one direction and then turns back on itself have allowed us to situate incidents within the context of the year, not just as isolated incidents. It has also become a terrific visual demonstration of what a generative curriculum looks like as one issue leads to another, is revisited later on, and then turns back onto itself. I think it also makes visible an argument for critical literacy as a way of living. Some of the issues we have inquired into include gender (what girls and boys can and can't do and are told they can and can't do by others), race, difference, environment, power and strength, and others.

SUSAN: From that description, it seems as if critical literacy happens all the time in your classroom, as an integral part of the way you and the children live and work together. Can you give us any specific examples of what has emerged?

VIVIAN: An important aspect of the learning wall is the inclusion of artifacts that represent systemic injustice. Perhaps a brief overview of our wall might clarify what I am trying to say here. Currently, our learning wall spans the length of our classroom. The first artifact, the cover of the book *Quick as a Cricket* [Wood, 1994], was placed up on the wall in September when an illustration of a toad prompted the question: "Is this animal a frog or a toad?" As we inquired into this question, a conversation began about where frogs or toads might live, leading us into a conversation about the rainforest and what we could do to sustain life in the rainforests. As we pursued the rainforest question through further inquiry, an issue of gender arose when we were reading the book *Where the Forest Meets the Sea* [Baker, 1987], in which there is an illustration of a man cooking over an open fire. One of the children raised a question regarding what men/boys and girls/women can do that led to an ongoing inquiry into how boys and girls are positioned, for example, in the media. Both of these issues—the environment and gender—have been sustained over the school year, as incidents added to our wall are either connected with ones already there or used to generate further topics for inquiry.

An example of the kind of social action the children have taken this year includes sending out letters to parents asking them not to, in the words of four-year-old Leigh, "buy wood from wood shops that get their wood from rainforest trees." Christopher, another four-year-old, sent out letters to lumber yards, stating his and his classmates' position on the cutting down of rainforest trees. Another time, in connection to how boys and girls are positioned, some of the children passed around a petition asking for the inclusion of kindergarten children in school events such as cafes and assemblies. This particular engagement, along with others like it, have led to inquiry into systems of dominance or privilege. One of the newest additions to our learning wall, for example, is the contents of a McDonald's Happy Meal. This particular artifact was erected on our wall as a symbol of what the children refer to as corporations "tricking kids" into buying their product by enticing them with toys. In reference to this, four-year-old Melissa said, "They are smart because they know how kids' minds work, but we're smarter 'cause we know how *their* minds work."

SUSAN: So, the wall is a means of teasing out the issues, of making a record of what the children are discovering and of the critical questions that their artifacts provoke. Your young students show that we shouldn't underestimate the thinking power of three- and four-year-olds. I'd like to ask you, Jim, to comment on the same issue of enacting critical literacy in the classroom. Your teaching has taken you from elementary to junior high and back and now to a university setting. I know that you have explored a variety of ways of working more critically with children and young adolescents. What are you exploring currently?

JIM: I have been working on trying to get a better understanding about critical practice. I have been working with colleagues here at the university on issues that concern broadly the warrant for critical-literacy education in schools. How does that affect the relationship between teachers and students? Issues I have been working on include the contexts for implicit and explicit teaching, concerns about the means and ends of disrupting students' existing literacy practices and discourses, and, recognizing that the classroom is a contested site, how will resistance be taken up and power used in productive ways? I have been collecting and analyzing data from my teaching over the past few months. I am looking at how forms of discursive, disciplinary, ideological, hegemonic power circulate in my secondary language arts methods classroom. I want to see how student resistance gets played out, and I want to construct a critical literacy practice that builds on my emerging understanding of it from various sources. I have been actively trying to collect and assess examples of critical practice from sources in Australia, Britain, and the United States in hopes of constructing critical-literacy practices through curricular and professional development when I return to Nova Scotia.

I spent much of the early part of the term having students examine the theoretical assumptions which supported their literacy education in high school and undergraduate college, and their own assumptions about what are appropriate texts for use in schools, for example, the canon, popular texts, media, reading and writing, subjectivities. I have also tried to use some material from Chalkface Press in Australia to have students work with some close textual analysis uncovering ideology—

gender, race, and class relations—within texts. Students find this kind of close work different from either the traditional or progressivist pedagogies they have had. We try to work on what is the warrant to do this type of critical literacy. This is a project that I seem to be spending much time on in my own studies this term. Our students do spend time working on Internet and hypertext media and do a course on media literacy. In fact, it is the media literacy, almost a form of cultural studies, that students grasp most readily.

What I am trying to do is create for myself and for students pictures of what critical literacy might be like in classrooms. Shor is helpful in discussing his problem-posing approach. I think the textual stuff above helps flesh out Shor's Freirian pedagogy.

SUSAN: I'm interested in knowing more about how student resistance is enacted in your secondary-methods classroom. What have you been learning from your inquiries?

JIM: Student resistance seems to come in forms that cannot be easily predicted, but my reading of Shor has pointed out to me that I need to look at resistance as openings and places to go where generative and topical themes may emerge (Shor's terms). Naming the resistance and then breaking it open with students seems to be key. My students, for the most part, are not like high school students. They are the compliant, good, and academically successful students. But, they have taken up issues such as "working the teacher" as a form of both resistance and ritual performance. I also see silence and preservice teachers' reluctance to theorize their practice as forms of resistance. There has been some debate about the role of the teacher, the juggling that Judith Newman [1991] talks about and the "bedazzlement" or "provocative" role that some critical-pedagogy folk talk about, in the teacher's actively disrupting the everyday assumptions of students' subjectivities.

VIVIAN: I guess I've always talked about this in terms of teasing out issues from the ongoing conversation. Sue Settle and I have talked about this often, agreeing that issues or topics or critical incidents don't always make themselves apparent; they need to be teased out, named, and placed on the curricular agenda.

Constraints and Openings

SUSAN: When we talked a couple of years ago, we all shared a strong sense of the constraints and tensions associated with taking a critical stance. It seems to me that those constraints and tensions certainly haven't diminished but, in fact, may be even more intense in today's increasingly conservative climate. How do you sustain yourself in this context?

JIM: I think indifference seems to be the most telling constraint I face. Part of the problem is that those who are interested in critical literacy are not well networked. Further, there does seem to be some history and miscommunication within critical pedagogy, a term that frightens off those that might be introduced into the conversation. The issue of accessible language and the politics of clarity come to mind. Sometimes, you need a new language to say new things. But we need to be aware of the audiences we are speaking/writing to and with. How do we create a new audience for critical literacy that puts pictures of possibility in their heads, as Giroux would say, a "pedagogy of hope"? How do you engage teachers and learners in looking at literacy practices that open up new ones and that do not make them feel defensive about their past practices? Fundamentally, how do you help teachers see what they do as a practice with larger implications than simply something done in schools? How do you go beyond being "a cheerleader" for critical literacy to something more concrete?

SUE: I feel I often proceed cautiously. I am still feeling my way with an inquiry curriculum. I am still feeling my way in terms of the kinds of invitations to offer students which promote rich, thoughtful conversations. There are those children whom I struggle to help become the "center of the curriculum." I struggle with moving toward a more democratic classroom. I have concerns about what happens when the children move on to other classrooms which do not follow the same philosophies. I know that children have been seen as saucy or disrespectful when they question the status quo. Even if they're told up front that some people will object to their questioning, I still remain concerned for them. I struggle in my own mind with issues of power in the school setting.

I seem to be working longer hours, yet still can't accomplish all that I know I would like to. I am frustrated at times with the slow progress it seems I am making. I continue to struggle with the tensions that continually exist for me as a teacher in terms of time in the classroom, external expectations of what should be going on in classrooms, the valuing of products over process, the conflicts and the politics that exist within a school setting, as they exist in society. I am discouraged when I hear parents admiring the "sameness" of classrooms and what happens in them. Is that really what we want? As the conservative climate increases, I do find it more wearing, more isolating, more demanding. It is not an easy path, but it is the road I—we—are traveling. The climate is a challenging one for everyone—with reductions in funding for education, restructuring, changeovers, curriculum changes, site-based planning. I hear discouragement on the part of many. I hear the weariness in the voices. These are challenging times. There's no question. So where's the hope? I keep wanting to be optimistic. To me, it's with the children. It's the children and their responses that keep me on my path.

VIVIAN: I think the constraints we face, in classrooms, from day to day are very real, although socially constructed. I think that it is our relation to those constraints that ultimately restricts us, not necessarily the constraints themselves. I guess what I am saying here is that we have more space than we often think; it's a matter of how we go about claiming that space and how we feel about the action we need to take toward that space.

JIM: The whole point seems to be about creating these spaces where literacies can be examined. I think we need to focus on the fact that this is possible in almost any setting. We need to contest the pessimism that focuses on what we see as the limitations to our practices. It seems to me that trying to do critical practice will help us create the institutional room to do them—in a sense to create a legitimacy for this new practice.

VIVIAN: Perhaps it is the pessimism vis à vis the limitations we see that is our biggest constraint. In many cases I don't think we really know what our constraints are until we engage in some sort of action. In any case, these constraints, in whatever form they may take, vary between contexts.

SUSAN: I agree with that. The context also influences our own stance—it influences whether we feel pessimistic or optimistic about the possibilities open to us. The broader context within which we are working has an influence over how much space we can create for ourselves. For me, an important factor in creating that space is working within a community of colleagues. It is much harder to sustain this kind of work when I feel isolated and when I lack the support, encouragement, questioning of others who are grappling with similar issues.

SUE: I have been struggling in isolation this year, as I've not been connected on a regular basis to those who are thinking about these issues. Working within a community of colleagues certainly does help to lessen that sense of isolation that we often have as teachers. It's those others that help to keep us on the edge, to use a Harste/Manning expression. It's those others that help to push our thinking.

JIM: Along with the chance for conversation, I think there has to be a project. This goes back to what I wrote about good pedagogy. Students should be actively engaged in putting what they learn to work, making it something bigger than a school exercise. I think this goes for "critical teachers" as well. I think the next step, beyond the conversation whose purpose has been, quite importantly, consciousness raising, personal professional development, and the attainment of academic certification, is this sense of project—moving out to other teachers and to communities. In all our work, we have managed to bridge the gap between the academic world and the classroom. We now need to link classrooms and the community.

SUE: Schools are often not set up to allow teachers to interact, much less take on projects. The daily responsibilities we have in terms of classroom as well as school committees or extracurricular activities are time-consuming, however rewarding they might be. On small staffs it means people are often pushed to their limits in time, making meaningful conversations difficult, though certainly not impossible.

JIM: Maybe it means beginning the conversation there. Why are teachers put in such a position? What are other alternatives? What does it mean to be a professional? What are the structural limits to teachers' work? In some circumstances, perhaps, this is the door into critical pedagogy.

SUE: My last thesis caused me to look at my own teaching experiences through gender. I came to the conclusion that we all create our own realities in relation to our social and cultural ways of knowing. Our reality changes as we perceive the world through different lenses. As I examined my teaching experiences through the lens of gender, I could reposition myself differently and understand the tensions which I encountered differently. Certainly, the broader context (politics, economics, conflicts) has influence on the tensions that are created in schools. I realized a week or so ago that part of the difficulty I've been experiencing in terms of my own work, is the value I place on relationships and the feeling of connectedness to others. Perhaps this contributes to the risk factor in claiming the space Vivian talks about.

JIM: I don't know if we have to give up one to do the other. I hope I am making sense here. One of the fundamental things I have learned from feminism is the importance of relationships and connectedness. The success in taking up any project would seem to be predicated on this. I think we want to be seen as "nice" people. And both at a tactical level and, fundamentally, at a personal level, I would want to be liked by others, even those who might find my language and pedagogy off-putting or threatening. Some people seem to be really good at this. What I hope, though, is that this wanting to be liked—the eros of teaching—does not prevent us from doing ethical work.

SUSAN: That's why I believe having a community within which to work—and that community may not primarily come from those in your workplace, unless you are very fortunate—is so important in helping us to sustain the ethical work. I'm not sure that it is so much wanting to be seen as "nice" as it is needing that community with whom to engage in inquiry. It can be very lonely and alienating to be the only teacher in a school asking critical questions or attempting to enact critical practice with students.

SUE: When I read Jim's comment about schools being contested sites and Vivian's comments about our relation to constraints and how we feel about the action we need to take towards creating that space, I thought, "Well put!" This year I have found in my own practice that, although our conversations within the classroom may often raise critical issues which we discuss, I'm not sure that they inspire action in and beyond the classroom, and I suspect it's because of my own discomfort with issues I haven't resolved myself that inhibits my claiming that space and thereby offering those demonstrations for the children. So that's where I am at the moment. How one positions oneself in relation to the constraints is related to how much space one will claim. That again takes us to issues of power and power relationships within school and society.

VIVIAN: I thought I would add to what Sue has said regarding claiming space toward action, a different way of being in our classrooms, while creating curriculum. I suppose what we are really proposing, in so many words, is to look toward alternate possibilities in order to envisage and actualize how we can better live together and nourish one another and lead critically literate lives. How we actualize curriculum is part and parcel of this. I think this conversation is, in itself, a demonstration of how we may get beyond the tensions. Let's hope that others accept what we have done here as an invitation toward creating their own possibilities while reclaiming some much-needed critical curricular space.

JIM: I think the possibility exists to advance critical literacy if we are aware of our audience and aware of our language. Critical literacy can enter the debate when it focuses itself on literacy practices, education, and schooling by appropriating the language of values that has been so well employed by others in the debate. What kind of students do we wish our schools to create and, ultimately, what kind of society do we want to have? The language of critical thinking and related notions could be taken up to broaden the debate about the kinds of reading we ask students to do. There is the language of relevance to student interests and concerns to employ. Further, the rush to include technology, employment, etc. in schools could be taken up to include non-canonical text genres, including Internet and hypermedia, in critical ways in schools. Critical literacy has something to say about the kind of misinformed attacks that are made against whole language and progressivist pedagogy in general. It can be positioned as a reasoned voice in the discussion.

I am not yet, or by nature, pessimistic about what might be done. Perhaps indifference is something that can be an asset when a self-conscious and organized group of critical practitioners are trying to get their collective foot in the door.

References

Baker, J. (1987) *Where the forest meets the sea.* New York: Greenwillow.

Chalkface Press Pty. Ltd., P.O. Box 23, Cottesloe, WA 6011 Australia.

Church, S. M. (1996). *The future of whole language: Reconstruction or self-destruction?* Portsmouth, NH: Heinemann.

Fairclough, N. (1992). *Critical language awareness.* London: Longman.

Luke, A. (1995a). Getting our hands dirty: Provisional politics in post-modern conditions. In P. Wexler & R. Smith (Eds.), *After postmodernism: Education, politics and identity* (pp. 83–97). London: Falmer.

Luke, A. (1995b). Text and discourse in education: An introduction to critical discourse analysis. In M. W. Apple (Ed.), *Review of educational research, no. 21* (pp. 20–46). Washington, DC: American Educational Research Association.

McLaren, P. (1994). *Life in schools: An introduction to critical pedagogy in the foundations of education.* 2nd ed. New York: Longman.

Newman, J. M. (1991). *Interwoven conversations: Learning and teaching through critical reflection.* Toronto: OISE.

Shor, I. (1992). *Empowering education: Critical teaching for social change.* Chicago: University of Chicago Press.

Simon, R. I. (1992). *Teaching against the grain: Texts for a pedagogy of possibility.* New York: Bergin & Garvey.

Wood, A. (1994). *Quick as a cricket.* New York: Scholastic.

CHAPTER EIGHT

The Quality of the Question: Probing Culture in Literature-Discussion Groups

CYNTHIA LEWIS
University of Iowa

This is a place in which you will be at least part of the time intrigued because of the quality of the question, not because the teacher wants you to be, and not because it's where you ought to be, and not because this is your task in life at this time, but because aren't stories wonderful?

JULIA DAVIS

In her comments, Julia Davis, the teacher whose fifth/sixth-grade classroom I studied for a year, uses the phrase *the quality of the question* to represent the class ethos she created in consort with her students—an ethos centered on the power of meaningful inquiry.[1] For her, *the quality of the question* was a metaphor that stood for meaning in life, and in this case, in literature.

In this chapter, I will offer vignettes from literature discussions in which Julia participated to show the particular kind of dialogue she invited her students to take up. I will also offer layers of reflection on these vignettes as I think about Julia's practice and question my own commentary. The school where Julia taught was situated in an older Midwestern neighborhood of mixed-income residents. Julia, who was in her fifth year of teaching at the time of this study, had returned to school in her forties to become a teacher, having previously earned a degree in philosophy, worked for a short time as a social worker, and spent time at home to raise her children. Speaking often of the important role that reading played in her own life, Julia had a strong commitment to literacy learning and teaching. The students in this class spent much of their reading time in one of three or four small groups, each reading and discussing a particular book related to a single theme. Students chose books from a wide range of literature about which their teacher presented book talks. Sometimes the group discussions were peer led, and at other times they included Julia. While the latter were influenced by the emphasis this school district placed on personal response, Julia often moved the discussions from the personal to the critical. Through the personal, students learned to immerse themselves in texts, whereas through the critical they began to distance themselves. Critical discussions in this class promoted a questioning stance toward textual ideologies and cultural assumptions.

Julia felt strongly about her role as an active member of literature discussion groups. Although she believed that children need time to construct knowledge together without the interference and control adults often impose, she also felt strongly that, as adults, teachers must offer children their knowledge and guidance. This view of the teacher's role stood in opposition to some of what she had learned in university classes, in current educational journals, and from district philosophy. Often, she felt, these sources promoted a "hands-off" approach that did not make sense to her. When Julia was part of the discussion group, the talk occasionally took on the interactional pattern of more traditional teacher-led talk, but the nature of the talk, I believe, was something quite different in that it invited readers to take up a critical stance toward text, one which led to the probing of cultural assumptions. In light of Carole Edelsky's call in this volume for a more critical whole language curriculum, I believe that the role Julia played in these literature discussion groups is worth examining.

Julia had a highly developed belief system about why literature is important to the lives of young people. Her words speak to her conviction that readers must adopt a critically engaged stance:

> Mostly that . . . we all own books in different ways depend-
> ing on where we are—the life we've lived. . . . I mean, even
> when we are sitting talking to one another and we know each
> other well, there is just always a filter between my brain and
> yours, and my life and yours . . . and I want kids to know
> there is no right interpretation, even about nonfiction. I want
> them to read with a little bit of doubt in their minds about
> anything they read . . . *a little skepticism, a little distance
> from it.* At the same time that I want them to own it, I want
> them to say, "Oh yeah, this is, this is one way of reading this
> right now." (emphasis is mine)

During another conversation:

> Imagining yourself having other lives gives you, it seems to
> me, more power over the kind of life you *do* lead . . . because
> often as you are reading a book and a character comes to a
> situation in which they must make a decision, if the character
> makes a decision that is very alien to you, you begin to weigh
> why you would have done what you would have done, and
> why the character did what they did. And in the character's
> life, you get to see how this turns out, at least hypothetically.

To Julia, then, reading literature involved *entering into the
text world, resisting text worlds, and examining one's immediate
world.* Considering Julia's beliefs about the meaning of literature,
her interest in adopting a critical stance is not surprising. When
readers enter a text, they make connections between life and text,
and when they resist the text or examine the immediate world,
they must push against textual ideology and probe cultural
assumptions. I don't mean to suggest that these probes always
emerged from a radical perspective. Instead, what Julia was after
was a certain habit of mind, a way of reading that included in its
repertoire the ability to distance oneself from the text as she herself does in the following example.

When responding to the book *Alanna: The First Adventure,*
a novel set in medieval times about a girl who disguises herself
as a boy in order to become a knight, Julia resisted the position
she felt the text promoted, one that equated feminism with traditional male roles. At one point in the book, the main character,
Alanna, worries that she will never be as good as even the least
able male. Julia told the students that this genuinely troubled

her, that she could not understand why Alanna would have so little self-worth. A female student responds that this was a time when women were not viewed as positively as even an average man, and therefore Alanna could not feel she was as good as a man. Julia invited the student to examine the immediate world in relation to the text world:

> Okay, you're living in a time when the average male will make roughly twice as much at what they do than the average female. Even though things have changed, there are things that are still fairly unequal today. Does that make you doubt your self-worth?

My initial response to Julia's comment was to want to push against it, to suggest that indeed a systemic lack of economic power does cause women, and others of oppressed economic classes, to question their self-worth. Often, in my conversations with Julia and in her conversations with her students, she represented the power of the individual as precariously balanced against the socially determined conditions that shape the individual. Later in this chapter, I include an exchange in which she questions her own desire to accent the individual. In this case, although her response does not key in to the effects of systemic inequality on self-worth, it did lead to a discussion about the ways in which medieval women may have had more financial stability, at least through marriage and inheritance, than women today. Thus, the students challenged prevailing assumptions about the current status of women and resisted the reading position promoted by the text.

In analyzing similar literature discussions in Julia's class, I will use the language of cultural theory as it has been applied to the teaching of English. According to Gilbert (1987), discussions should focus on "how 'personal experiences' are culturally constructed" (p. 249), and on why particular subject positions get validated in texts over others. Edelsky (1991) is concerned that whole language pedagogy may fail to acknowledge the political and cultural constitution of experience, but believes that teachers can bring cultural critique into the classroom by first building on the students' inquiries and interests. These suggestions call for an approach that sees texts as sites for "cultural conversations"

(Graff, 1987, p. 257). Such conversations would address the ways in which texts are culturally, historically, and politically constituted; they would include discussions of how one can make sense of the competing voices within a text (Bakhtin, 1981) and consider how one might find a place to stand within these competing subject positions.

Julia's own literary background did not include specific training in current theories about response to literature (either reader-response theories or cultural studies/critical theories), but she has been influenced by them nonetheless. Reader-oriented approaches were encouraged in the language arts/reading journals she read, the writing projects she took, and the district's language arts guidebooks. Responding to texts through one's personal experiences was promoted as what teachers and students ought to aspire to in a whole language classroom, and it was, indeed, one way that Julia encouraged students to respond to texts. In keeping with this view, Julia believed that reading literature involved entering the text world in ways that connect to one's personal life. She frequently invited students to relate what they read to their own experiences, to think about times when they might have felt the way a particular character felt. These invitations were often followed with a "What if . . ." question that encouraged students to imagine themselves into the lives of the characters.

However, other conditions in Julia's life—her educational background in philosophy, her family background, and her own reading experiences, for instance—predisposed her toward viewing literature from a more culturally oriented or critical position. Thus, Julia encouraged students to probe and, at times, resist the ways in which certain cultural assumptions and textual ideologies shaped their readings of texts and experience. The next two sections focus on how two reading positions—cultural critique and resistant reading—take shape in the discussion setting.

Cultural Critique

> JULIA: You know I thought about it, and I think the day that somebody says to me, "Okay, your job is just to get these books and give them to the kids, and you just quantify the

time, and you just analyze their . . . reading and writing samples," that's the day I will say I don't want to do that. . . .
And it's not because I think that I—this role I serve—is so
important; it's because of this feeling that . . . *asking
questions that you wouldn't automatically think of yourself
is important.* (emphasis is mine)

In the following two excerpts from discussions of *War
Comes to Willy Freeman* (Collier & Collier, 1983), Julia pursues
a question suggested by one student's comment, one which most
students in the group would not automatically think of as important. The main character of the book is Willy, an African
American girl who witnesses her father's death at the hands of
the British during the American Revolution. Her mother is taken
prisoner, and Willy disguises herself as a boy to go search for her.
The book group consists of James, Tyler, Andy, and Sam
(although Sam was absent for the two discussions from which
these excerpts were taken), all of whom were perceived by Julia
to be low- to middle-ability students. James, Tyler, and Sam were
perceived as such because they often did not complete their
work, and Andy because he lacked confidence and the willingness to take risks. *War Comes to Willy Freeman*, one of the
books read during a historical fiction unit, appealed to these students in part because other books in the themed unit were longer
and contained more difficult vocabulary. The discussion that follows is about a section of the book, quoted below, during which
Willy questions whether it really matters if she supports the
Americans or the British:

> And then I began to wonder: Why was I on the Americans'
> side, anyway? What had the Americans ever done for me,
> except keep me at the bottom of the pile? . . . There was
> Captain Ivers trying to put me back in slavery again, and
> nobody teaching me how to read or do sums, so's I couldn't
> even tell what town I was in without asking. And knowing I
> would have to take orders so long as I lived. Maybe in heaven
> black folks gave orders to white folks and women gave orders
> to men. (pp. 71–72)

Willy decides that it doesn't really matter what side she is on, but
nonetheless she considers herself American and would therefore

support the colonists' cause. This passage from the text is the subject of the following discussion exchange[2]:

JULIA: Do you have any sense that Willy is on one side or another, James?

JAMES: I think she is on the right side.

JULIA: Okay, why?

JAMES: Because that her dad fought for the army, that the American side freed her.

JULIA: Okay. Let's skip ahead to the end of the book. Pretty soon, you know, sooner or later we are going to finish this book. When we finish this book somebody is going to have won this war. What difference do you think that will have made to Willy's life?

JAMES: I don't know.

JULIA: Now she says before, because she is female and because she is black, she is going to be at the bottom . . . and people are going to be ruling no matter what. They are going to be white males. The men who are white and have land are going to be the ones who are calling the shots. If the British win, what do you think might happen to Willy?

JAMES: She might think that her mom died. I don't know.

JULIA: Do you think her mom might die if the British win?

JAMES: Uh.

TYLER: They'll be slaves together.

JULIA: Okay, they could be slaves again; her mom might die. Andy, what do you think?

ANDY: Well, I don't think they would be slaves again because all of the Americans might, like, be dead.

JULIA: Okay, they might be dead. If they're not slaves, they could be dead. Okay, what if the Americans win? What do you think's going to happen to Willy?

JAMES: All the slaves are going to be free?

JULIA: Okay, you think if, if we win this war all the slaves in the country are going to be free?

TYLER: No because, uh, I mean they're still black. I don't think that they'll free 'em. They'll still be slaves even after the war. Some of 'em will.

JULIA: Okay, James says the slaves will be free. And Tyler says there will still be slavery.

TYLER: Even after the war. And then Martin Luther King will come . . .

JULIA: And then he will free the slaves?

TYLER: Yeah.

JULIA: Martin Luther King will come and free the slaves.

TYLER: Yeah.

JULIA: How about you Andy?

ANDY: I think they will, um, keep 'em as slaves because like the war is over and it doesn't really matter when, if they . . . if they win the war, it will probably get . . . well . . . I mean you fought for us and we won so you are going to be a slave again or something.

JULIA: Okay, so you think that the people like Colonel Ledyard, who are in charge of the American side, are going to just use the services of the slaves in the war to fight and then the minute the war is over, they are going to go back to saying "Okay, too bad. You be slaves." Do we have any evidence for any of these in the book so far? Is there anything to make us think what you think? Is there any character, any event in the book so far, that makes you say "Yeah, that's what's going to happen, all right"?

In this exchange, Julia makes several moves characteristic of her performances during literature discussions. Shortly into the exchange, she asks students what difference the war's end will make on Willy's life, a question students wouldn't "automatically" ask on their own. She attempts to push students to think about the social and historical complexity of Willy's position, and Andy and Tyler eventually join in, despite the ahistorical reference to Martin Luther King Jr. to which Julia responds with some surprise, but chooses not to challenge.

One week later, the following exchange about *War* took place. Tyler starts by predicting that Willy will be free if she can get the legal papers that proclaim her freedom.

JULIA: Okay, so even in this situation . . . Tyler, you still believe in those papers' power? . . .

[Tyler asks Julia to help him identify a character's name.]

TYLER: Yeah, Colonel Ledyard. Captain Ivers, um, he said that he bought her before, um, Colonel Ledyard died. So, and, I don't know if he could, because don't, does, Colonel Ledyard still, um, own her, even after they made her free?

JULIA: Hmm. Okay. So you are asking, what I hear you asking is what does it mean to be a freed slave?

TYLER: Um-hmm.

JULIA: Um. From what, uh, from what you have read in the book, what do you think it means to be a freed slave?

Here, Julia "re-voices" Tyler's comments, presenting them in the form of a question she'd like the group to consider (O'Connor & Michaels, 1993). During our March interview, Julia explained to me why she didn't think she'd have the *War* group discuss the book on their own:

> Partly it's the feeling that maybe in . . . both in *April Morning* [Fast, 1961] and *War,* there are issues there that aren't kid's issues. . . . I mean when Tyler said, if Tyler had said "What does it mean to be a freed slave," at least I heard that question. Nobody else would have heard that question. . . . So in some ways maybe I'm talking myself into that I serve more of a purpose than I perceive myself as having served.

Julia saw her role both in terms of asking questions students wouldn't automatically ask on their own and hearing the questions of students that otherwise wouldn't be heard. The term *question,* for Julia, refers to that which is intriguing, confusing, or challenging. She lost patience with students who treated her questions as routine and authoritative, yet she used her authority to let them know that she expected more of a commitment. What follows is a continuation of the above discussion (after a break of several turns):

> JULIA: Now what does it mean to be a freed slave? Now let's think about this. . . . Mrs. Ledyard and Mrs. Ivers are free women. Willy and her mom were not free and have now been freed. They are freed slaves. When you say it means that they are free, are they exactly the same as Mrs. Ivers and Mrs. Ledyard now?
>
> ANDY: Not really as powerful /

JULIA: Okay. So . . . there is some difference between them and other free women. What difference do you see besides power? Or what makes the other free women powerful?

ANDY: They, maybe they were, like, born not to be slaves.

JULIA: Okay. They had been free all their lives. Do you think that would change the way you were?

. . .

TYLER: Um. What does it mean to be free?

JULIA: If Willy is free, what does that really mean?

JAMES: That she can do whatever she wants.

JULIA: Does it mean she can do whatever she wants?

JAMES: No.

JULIA: Why don't, why did you say no?

JAMES: I don't know. . . .

JULIA: It was just an answer? Okay, if Willy is a free person, what are the kinds of things she is going to be able to do that she can't do as a slave? Let's do that first.

JAMES: Go somewhere when she wants to.

JULIA: Exactly. She is not free. She can't change where she is if she is a slave. . . .

Julia begins by reviewing the characters and their roles, moving quickly to a question that asks students to consider the meaning of freedom from the perspectives of different characters. She wants them to understand that the concept of freedom is not black and white, that what most of us ordinarily believe about freedom is overly simplistic and in need of examination. Andy is beginning to understand something about the relationship between power and race. The above discussion continued under Julia's direction in an attempt to historically situate events in the text, yet point to the persistence of racism today:

JULIA: Are the circumstances of their lives [the women's lives] different? Is there a difference? Even if you are all free, are some people more free than other people? Andy, you said you thought so. What do you see as the difference? You saw Colonel Ledyard and Mrs. Ivers as being a lot more powerful. Do you know why?

ANDY: Because they are white.

JULIA: They are white. Um, what difference do you think that makes?

ANDY: Maybe because he is a Captain.

JULIA: Maybe because he is a Captain.

JAMES: They make more money.

JULIA: They have more money. He is a Captain. And you are right. Some of the status the women have is a result of their husbands' status. So some of the power they have is if they marry a powerful man they have more money and they are white. What other differences do you think being white makes? Let's say Colonel Ledyard's wife walks into a store. She wants to buy something. She doesn't have enough money to buy it and she says, "Oh, hold on to it for a minute, and I will go get some money." Do you think the store owner is going to do that?

ANDY: Maybe.

JULIA: Okay. Willy comes into the store. Do you think the store owner is just as likely to do that?

[They establish that the store owner might respond differently to Willy, and Julia asks Tyler to read from his journal. Julia makes a few comments on the journal before she's interrupted by Andy, who has a question.]

ANDY: Um, if the store owner was black, would that / ?

JULIA: Make a difference? What do you think?

[He thinks it probably wouldn't make much of a difference, but sounds unsure. Julia helps him to visualize the scene, first with a white customer, then black, and Andy decides that the black store owner would still trust that the white person could pay but would probably trust the black customer more than the white store owner did. Julia tries to explain why this might occur.]

JULIA: Just common experience. Just, this is a person who is in some way similar to me. I mean, these are huge generalizations. It would obviously depend on the people. . . . But one of the constraints of the time was that it was very difficult for black people to own anything. That is why Sam Francis [to whom the book refers] is so, is such a, a, character that you hear a lot about, because he was a very famous man and owned a very famous location during this war.

Julia's role in this discussion was to move students toward an examination of the relationship between power and race and the relative meanings of freedom. In addition, she historically situated the position of African Americans with regard to ownership before the American Revolution. While I believe that Julia's probes and responses during literature discussions worked to develop a critical awareness in students, I did find myself wanting to enter this discussion to comment upon the systemic nature of inequality, to point out that it is not just "common experience" but racism that keeps white store owners from serving black customers. However, Julia's comment came after an extended exchange about race issues, and she may well have felt that to further extend the discussion would have served her needs more than the needs of her students. Such is the problematic nature of discussions which highlight critical positions. Teachers must determine when to provide information and when to listen, when to probe further and when to let go.

It is clear that Julia took more turns than did her students in these *War* discussions, and her turns were lengthier. Furthermore, contrary to much that is written in educational literature about good discussion practices, the student responses volleyed back to her rather than building on one another: "I'm happiest when they just go off [building on each other's comments], but they don't do it very much when I am there," Julia explained. She recognized and accepted responsibility for her power in teacher-led groups, but wanted to find ways to make the talk more equitable: "I get to say when we start. I get to say when we finish. I mean, I'm the one who calls time." She attempted to decenter her own power by providing students with choices: They played a role in choosing the texts they would read in groups, decided as a group how many pages to read per night, and often kept a group agenda for discussion. Students also kept response journals that served as the starting point for the day's discussion. This strategy kept Julia from monopolizing and focusing on her questions and her agenda. In addition, there were opportunities for students to discuss books in peer-led groups without her participation. Julia felt that the historical-novels unit required more direction from her in terms of culturally and historically situating the texts, yet speculated that if she were to listen to the audiotapes of herself, she would be "horrified at the number of questions [she] asked."

Although she had reservations regarding her degree of involvement in literature groups, Julia had as many reservations about repeatedly leaving students to discuss on their own:

> What [teachers] say is terribly powerful with others. And I think all adults abdicate that role. I mean, most of the adults in their life abdicate that role and say, "You decide." Well, decide over or against what? And most cultures deliver with something for them to decide over or against by the time they are in sixth grade. And in our culture something has happened.

Despite her suggestion that contemporary American culture does not "deliver" what she believes to be important values, she was not naive about how her students were positioned within the larger culture. She purposely avoided reading a book by the series author R. L. Stine, for instance, although her female students loved Stine's books and repeatedly asked her to read one (not to the class but on her own):

> I kept promising I would read one of them, and I never did. . . . They are doing whatever task they need to do with that book all by themselves, and I suspect it's into aspects of the culture I don't want to support. And so I could maybe raise questions about those tasks.

Julia recognizes, here, that she could bring popular texts into the curriculum to make visible their discourses—naturalized views of violence and sexism, for instance. If I were teaching this class, I would have been very interested in having this discussion. In observing my own sons' growing interest in popular texts (music, books, and films) I had become as interested in their attraction to these texts as I was in my own discomfort with them. In this instance, I would have liked to listen for what Julia's students might have to say about the cultural work that reading popular fiction accomplished for them. For Julia, however, it felt more important to provide positive models:

> But I think adults serve that role of saying, "This is beautiful." Especially those subjective judgments. "This is good.

This is beautiful. This is just there . . ." we give meaning to kids for those terms by what we do and by what we model. And so I don't think we can lightly not do that.

At the end of another unit, one that focused on issues of individuality and conformity, the students' talk turned to despair over the state of the world. Each of the eight students in the group had read books in which conformity leads to evil and fascism. After a conversation about abuses of power, one student, Mackenzie, said that she thought "everybody human should die." Julia's reply is of interest in light of her vision of her role:

> It [this view] seems to abdicate the power that you have to change things, and I just have too much data that humans can make a powerful difference toward good—that we aren't always going to win. It's going to be messy, just as you've all decided that messy societies are perhaps preferable for their messiness . . . but if you are not going to be a player because you think you are going to fail, I am scared to death for the rest of us . . . I mean, I want you to think . . . it may not be possible for me to know at this point what the cost will be in human terms, but I want you to engage. I want you to be a player.

The ensuing discussion was long and philosophical, with the five girls contributing more than the three boys in the group. Julia addressed this gender issue, telling the group, "We cannot allow just Fifty percent of the human beings to be concerned about this stuff." One of the girls argued that one of the boys was concerned and that he *had* been talking: "You just really haven't listened because I hear him," she insisted. Julia told about a work of art she liked which showed a little boy looking vulnerable, wearing his pajamas that had the word "hulk" written across his chest: "I'm worried that that is what we do to males. We keep dressing them in these green hulk pajamas. . . . We tell them that they have to consider themselves to be powerful or not to exist," she added. The same girl said that males were like "frightened little kittens" now that females have more control. A few turns later, a student, Nikki, entered the conversation:

> I just never . . . realized why boys always act tough and we're never like that. I always just thought they were stupid or

[others laughed]. . . . All of a sudden, I realize it's just maybe how they were, how they were supposed to be in this society. I never, I never got that.

Julia took a turn to talk about the value of studying gender relations in other cultures. She talked about Margaret Mead and suggested that students might want to read *National Geographic* to learn more about that subject. Another student, Kate, entered the conversation next:

> Men are supposed to be powerful in our society. But then when they *do* do crimes like raping, I mean, then we look down on them. But we're sort of, our society is sort of encouraging that behavior. I mean, not like we are telling them to, but /

Julia continually pushed in the direction of cultural critique. Clearly, she saw her role in her students' lives as important, and literature discussions were times when she could have an effect on the way students viewed significant issues in their lives—a time when, in her words, *the quality of the question* mattered.

Sometimes the questions were ones that Julia asked herself and invited the students to help her answer. At the start of a discussion of *April Morning*, a book about the American Revolution narrated by a young boy whose brother was a Committeeman, Julia presented the students with a section that gave her trouble. The *April* group included six students perceived to be of middle to high ability. Julia referred to a section in which some of the men are talking about being more afraid of women than they are of God, and Julia asked the group to help her to understand how this could be true in a culture as sexist as this one was. Two female students made brief forays into the topic, with Nikki suggesting that women are feared because they are not really known. Mackenzie then built on Nikki's statement with a cultural critique:

> MACKENZIE: I think they don't know anything about women and so . . . that is why they are scared of them. And it's like . . . in Witch group [*The Witch on Blackbird Pond* (Speare, 1958)] how they are saying . . . if they don't know this one lady who

they think she is a witch, and they used to burn people because they said, "Well, this person is strange, so they are a witch." And so they [the men] are like, "Okay, we don't know anything about women, but all we do know is that we are supposed to be . . . in charge." . . . And so the women never get to explain themselves. . . . All they know is what their duties are. They don't really know much about each other. . . . So that is what I think.

JULIA: They just kind of fulfill roles, and because they are locked in these roles then you have to act out, you can only act out your role when you are in the presence of the opposite sex. Like that? Is that what you mean?

Here, Mackenzie engages in speculation with Julia about the structure of gender at the time and the ways in which that structure constrained social relations.

In another excerpt from the same *April* discussion, Julia directed students' attention to the systems that influence events which students attribute to individual choice. In the following excerpt, Nikki talks at length about what she sees as the theme of this book:

The main point of this book is that . . . this book is all about one choice that Adam made. And I was thinking about it and . . . you know every day you go through choices, and sometimes I think how can I go wrong, what if I would have said, "Yes, I want to do this and [go] with my dad to the store instead of staying home," you know. You think of all the things that would have happened . . . and he [Adam] made this one choice that really changed . . . his life completely. . . . He just said, "Okay, my mom wants me to stay, but you know I want to go to the war," and then all of the sudden he is in the war. And now . . . I mean he doesn't say this, but what I understand from what he is saying is "I want to go home." And if he wouldn't have signed the muster book, then he would have just been home right now doing whatever. . . . I kind of think of this book [as] just about choices—about how the committee is making choices, and about how he made choices. . . . I guess everything you do is kind of a choice.

Nikki is referring here to the decision made by the main character, sixteen-year-old Adam, to go into battle with his father. As the book progressed, Julia, who at first had told the students that war is not "a natural disaster," began to reconsider her perspective. What follows is an excerpt from a journal entry written by Julia. Because this was her first time reading *April*, she had decided to keep a journal along with her students, which she shared with them near the end of occasional discussion sessions. This is an excerpt from the journal entry she wrote after Adam's father died in battle:

> And now that the arguments are over, and the shots were fired and the family and friends are dead, this war seems for Adam exactly what I said it wasn't—a natural disaster. So Adam is stuck in the smokehouse with his grief and his fear, and it was as if it was the flood or earthquake in L.A. or something. This is something that has now happened and changed him forever. And originally I said war is a choice, and it was a choice they were making then, but now that it's come, it must feel for Adam and for everybody else just like Bob's death [a reference to Mackenzie's grandfather who had just died]. Any senseless death of someone you love and care about is just a disaster.

Although Julia is not explicit about the systems of domination at work which contribute to the decisions often attributed to "individual choice," she lets students in on her reflections as she revises her own thinking about the individual's role within a much larger system. When the group finished *April*, Julia asked the students to write about the book in any way that mattered to them. She referred to Nikki's thesis about important choices and said that this might be something Nikki would want to write about. Reflecting on her own thinking about the book and how that would impact her writing, she mentioned that she saw the choices as imposed upon by "external circumstances," that what seems to be "free choice" isn't free at all.

An important role that Julia played as a member of a literature discussion group was to perform a kind of cultural critique and encourage her students to consider why they believe what they believe. Julia also invited her students to view the text as a historical and social construction, and in so doing, to resist, at times, the pull of the story.

Resistant Readings

> Yevtushenko has this wonderful poem called "It is Wrong to
> Tell Lies to Children" . . . and the thesis of that poem is, it is
> wrong to tell children everything will turn out all right in the
> end. And, of course, that is very Russian, to not do that,
> right? And to say you can't count the cost. And I really think
> that is true—that they are hungry for, tell me a story . . . tell
> me something that will give me hope, that will help me make
> sense of my life. But do not tell me a lie. Do not tell me it will
> all be swell.

In this excerpt from an interview, Julia was responding to her
students' common complaint that children's books often had
unrealistically happy endings. Tyler told his group that he didn't
want *War Comes to Willy Freeman* to be perfect. When Julia
asked him what he meant since, after all, Willy's father had
already died and her mother had been taken away, Tyler said that
in *The Island of the Blue Dolphins* (O'Dell, 1960) everything was
too perfect, and he didn't want that to happen again. He wanted
action instead, he told her. Julia responded by making visible the
constructed nature of the text: "You are writing this book now.
What are you going to write next? You are in charge."

Another student, Steven, had a similar response to *April
Morning:* "I hope they all die," he said about the book's characters. When Julia expressed surprise and asked why, he told her, "I
want the good guys to die for once. In all the movies and books
all the good guys always win." Instead of underscoring the value
of the characters' lives, as I might have done, Julia again made
visible the constructed nature of texts. (The following exchange
includes Julia and several students.)

> JULIA: That's an interesting notion because the Greeks killed off
> all their heroes. It's a fine literary tradition to want the hero
> to die. It's the history of tragedy.
>
> MARK: It makes them seem more like a hero if they give their
> lives.
>
> JULIA: Ooh, ooh, now is that part of what you wanted?
>
> STEVEN: No, I just want them to die for once. . . because it's so
> *rare.*

JULIA: Not in real life, only in childhood books that /
STEVEN: Like in Cinderella.

In both of the preceding examples, the students, Tyler and Steven, perform resistant readings; that is, they read against the grain of the texts. If I were their teacher, I believe I would have responded more sympathetically to Tyler's desire for an imperfect ending than to Steven's more nihilistic desire for death, which I might have understood more as resistant behavior than resistant reading. Had I tried to squelch Steven's response, however, he may well have excluded himself from the conversation. Julia's response to Steven, on the other hand, served several purposes at once: First, it legitimized his contribution; second, it placed his contribution within a historical and cultural context, thus showing Steven that his wish for a character's death comes with a tradition and is rational; and third, it highlighted the constructed nature of texts, foregrounding their ideological functions (e.g., children's stories do not reflect reality but promote a certain version of reality). Her response suggests the malleability of texts, which are constructed and can be reconstructed by readers.

This sense of the constructed text was evident in the way Julia led discussions about *Where the Red Fern Grows* (Rawls, 1961) as well. Written in first-person narration, the book is a fictionalized memoir about the adventures and love shared by a boy and his two dogs. Most of Julia's students loved *Red Fern*, and entered the text world effortlessly. They talked about the book with their friends outside of reading time, and the girls cried whenever the dogs were endangered. It was not the sort of book that engendered doubt or resistance. For one discussion, Julia asked students to consider events in the book from a temporal perspective, deciding how those events were viewed when the story took place, compared with how they are viewed now. Julia's purpose was to invite students to question behavior which seems natural and acceptable in the text, actions such as chopping down a tree in order to catch a coon simply for the sport of hunting. Why might it have been acceptable to take this action at that time, but not acceptable now? Some of the students suggested that if today someone were to drive a nail through the fist of a live animal, as Billy did when he was trapping, the animal rights activists would try to stop this action, and David pointed out that no one would know about it if it happened way up in the mountains where the story took place. He continued with a comment that related the temporal change to a spatial one:

> DAVID: When you say it's now and it's then, you know? Well, the Ozark Mountains [where the story takes place] probably aren't as much as they were, you know. There are probably, like, houses.
>
> JULIA: I guess you're right. That's a good point. I should probably say not only just now and then but here and there. That's a good point, David. That, that, that sets of morality accrue to a place as well as a time. That's a real good point.

Although students were, for the most part, easily able to enter the text world of *Red Fern,* Julia's probes and responses moved students to situate the text socially, culturally, and historically, as well as to consider the constructed nature of Billy's life. Davies (1993b) discusses the need to deconstruct a text's "obviousness," what a text sets up as being natural or taken-for-granted. Davies argues that "teachers and students need to immerse themselves in text and distance themselves from that text at the same time" (p. 63).

Immersion and distance—a complicated positioning—is achieved by both David and Julia as illustrated by the following conversation. During one discussion of *April Morning,* Julia talked about a scene that struck her as being "absolutely real," and David responded:

> DAVID: I think that is what books are really about. It's just trying to write it real. . . . Books are just trying to convey a message to be real.
>
> JULIA: That's what books are about?
>
> DAVID: Yeah. That's all books are just supposed to, you are supposed to look at them and say, "This is real. This sounds real."
>
> JULIA: Really?
>
> DAVID: It's a story, but it sounds real.

JULIA: You know what I think of? I think of what we were doing in the sound stuff, when we were talking about a sound being a vibration.

DAVID: Yeah.

JULIA: You know, that there can be a sound over here and that vibration somehow reaches us.

DAVID: Uh huh.

JULIA: I think of that when I read books. . . . It's, it's almost as if it's resonance, you know. There is some string plucked in me. I know what that note sounds like. I know what this feels like. But I really love that experience. But also I turn to books for experiences I've never had—

DAVID: Yeah.

JULIA: —that I want to have.

DAVID: Yeah. And it's, it's supposed to just be like a book about a story that, like, something that happens to someone and you are that person.

JULIA: Uh huh.

DAVID: So like if I read this book and it's really, really real, I will feel like I am in the Revolutionary War as soldiers. It is like virtual reality.

JULIA: Did you do that?

DAVID: Um. Not really.

JULIA: It's better than virtual reality. Virtual reality doesn't use enough of *me*. There isn't enough *resonance* set up for me in virtual reality. I don't even like film for that reason. [David laughs.] How's that from the nonvisual teacher to the visual kid.

Despite Julia's claim of difference at the end of this conversation, she and David speak the same language when it comes to what literature means to them. Both Julia and he like to enter the text world—evidenced in their references to feeling the literature and living it—yet both retain some slight distance—the reality is virtual for David and resonant for Julia. Both accomplish what Smith (1992) refers to as "controlled surrender," a stance that combines both detached observation with involved identification, thus opening the way for a developing critical awareness.

I will end this chapter with an excerpt from a discussion that presents a crystallized performance of resistant reading. This took place during the individuality versus conformity unit I mentioned earlier, the one that included eight students. The students had all read books about societies where uniformity had become fascistic, books that promote individuality over uniformity, even when the latter is easier, less painful, or, in the case of *The Giver* (Lowry, 1993) more communitarian. The communities in each book strive for a sameness among people that leads to death or isolation for those who are different or refuse to conform. *The Giver* is the only book of the three that is about a community that is seductive for the first half of the book. Gradually, what seems like a utopian society reveals a dark underside. The two other books are about communities that are overwhelmingly evil: *Number the Stars* (Lowry, 1989), about the Nazi takeover of Denmark, and *A Wrinkle in Time* (L'Engle, 1962), about a planet that has been taken over by an evil force. The students who read each of these books were moved by them and, for many discussions, talked about the evil in each society.

In the exchange below, Julia moved in a different direction, encouraging students to resist the most accessible readings—those readings shaped not only by the ideology of the text, but by its constitution in, and their own positions as early adolescents living in, an individualistic society. Thus, she asked the group to think about ways in which the communities in their books are better or worse than aspects of our society. Answering how they are worse, Nikki offered the first response in one word—"sameness." Julia used that word as the starting point for a resistant reading in the discussion that follows:

> JULIA: Okay, now think about inequity in terms of, think about in our society, inequity in terms of education, inequities in terms of educational opportunities, in terms of economic opportunities, in terms of, um, those kinds of things. Do you ever view the unequalness, the unsameness about our culture as being a problem?
>
> [Kate, a fifth grader, talks at length about the need for everyone to go to school and how some don't take it seriously enough.]

JULIA: So we said that sameness is not a good thing, by and large, in these societies. But now Kate is saying, "Well, except I'd like to see everybody go to school." So these are places where we value sameness, and Kate values sameness in education.

[Most of the students comment on the education issue, after which Julia asks for other positive outcomes of sameness.]

NIKKI: Like in *The Giver*, they take pills so you can't, so you can't really fall in love with anyone, right? It controls your hormones, right? So it's kind of good that you don't look different, because . . . I notice some people have really big deals about looks, and I think it . . . can be a big problem for somebody, you know. And looks aren't really an issue if you have sameness, you know.

[Julia, Lisa, and Nikki take several turns on this subject. Then Lisa continues.]

LISA: Yeah, but it's good and bad because you can't fall in love with the person you want to fall in love with.

KATE: But, if you've never experienced love, then you wouldn't really know the difference.

NIKKI: Yeah, but it's still bad. I mean—

KATE: We think it's bad, but they probably don't notice it, because they never even felt it.

[After several more turns on this topic, Julia invites Jason into the conversation. He had read *Number the Stars*.]

JULIA: Jason, how about you?. . . We hardly think of . . . Europe under Hitler as a utopian society, but in fact it was a real attempt on the part of the Germans to reform society in a way that would be good for them. And that is connected to what Nikki said. . . . They [*The Giver* group] were all having an argument about how society ought to be, and Nikki had an insight. She said, "I realized I designed a society that was good for me." And so Hitler's Germany was a design for the good of Aryan Germany. What are, can you see anything that was good about Germany in those days?

JASON: Hmm. No.

JULIA: What about some of the problems that you see in, what problems do you see in Denmark under Hitler?

JASON: The Nazis will come to your house and look for Jews and take them away.

[Julia relates this to search and seizure without a warrant, about which Mackenzie and David each take a turn. Kate then talks about how difficult it is to think of positive things about what happened in Nazi Germany because now *we are all looking through the eyes of the Jews.*]

JULIA: You raise a very interesting point. Um, especially because as we do history in this country, we tend to ascribe all of World War II to Hitler, to one person. And, in fact, World War II could not possibly have happened if it only had been the idea of one person. It was not only an idea that was palatable to an enormous number of Germans, it was palatable to an enormous number of Europeans, and plenty of Americans as well. And so you have to ask yourself . . . why did they buy it? Why did this uneducated demagogue get up there and have millions of people following him.

[Mackenzie says that she knew why because she had studied Hitler for an independent project. She shares what she had learned about the Jews as scapegoats.]

DAVID: It wasn't just then that no one liked Jews. They had always had . . . a bad reputation. Like there were ghettos and there were ( ).

JULIA: Um hmm. In fact, there were expulsions from entire countries. And 1492 is famous in Jewish history because all of the Jews were expelled from the country of Spain at the same time that Christopher Columbus set out. That's true. This is a long, long history of prejudice. . . .

In this exchange, Julia leads the students in a discussion that makes available to them another way of reading their texts. Most of them, having fully entered the worlds of their texts, had embraced the message conveyed therein that individuality is critical—a message that is reinforced in their music, in other books, among friends, and in the larger culture. They had spent a good deal of time during previous discussions talking about the evils of a society that demands conformity, but this time, Julia wanted to make another way of reading available for her students. Most of the group tried on this alternative perspective.

The difficulty of this kind of pedagogy lies in the ease with which it can tip the balance toward teacher-directed practice. Yet the role of the English/language arts teacher has long been ambiguous in that the teacher is cautioned to lead without squelching individual freedom. Gemma Moss (1989; 1995), who writes about critical theories related to literacy teaching, points out that a critical pedagogy is no less ideologically based than a humanistic pedagogy. She argues that as educators we need to acknowledge that we want students to read texts in certain ways because we hope to influence the sort of people our students will become.

When I reread the above exchange between Julia and her students, I think about the sort of people I want those students to become, and I consider ways to help them understand more about the economic and political conditions that made the Holocaust possible. Indeed, I think that this was what Julia was after when she implicated the United States and all of Europe, indirectly inviting her students to focus on political struggles among countries rather than the struggle between good and evil among individuals. Perhaps I would have wanted to focus more on the structures that created and supported the ideology Julia refers to when she asks why the Holocaust was possible, but Julia was the one making the difficult moment-to-moment decisions, not me. Mackenzie jumped in wanting to share what she had learned about Jews as scapegoats for a weak economy, and Julia went with the moment. After David adds what he knows, Julia frames his comments with earlier history, but does not fully contextualize that history. Again, the problematic nature of critical teaching rears its head, with teachers like Julia continuously negotiating the nature and degree of their involvement.

Why Do We Believe What We Believe?

Literature discussions in which Julia participated often probed dominant belief systems in an effort to examine hidden assumptions, and students were encouraged to view the text as a historical and social construction. Teachers can serve an important function in literature groups, as Julia did, by situating texts and engendering cultural conversations. Her tendency to lead discussions that probed widely held assumptions and her focus on the text as a constructed artifact opened up roles for literature that students did not often take up on their own. Understanding the ways a text promotes a familiar and unquestioned discourse—the discourse of individuality, for instance, in *The Giver*—and learning to read against the grain, to examine or resist as well as to enter the text world, provides students with another role that literature can serve. This role, exemplified by the underlying question of discussion groups that included Julia—"Why do we believe what we believe?"—is essential if we view the development of a critical social awareness to be an important function of schooling.

Peer-led literature groups without teacher participation offer certain advantages. Findings from my larger study suggest that they can serve as hybrid communities in which students borrow from the culture of the classroom as well as from youth culture, thus using linguistic constructions and interpretive norms appropriate to both spheres. However, the move to decenter authority in student-led environments is not enough if what we are after is a critically democratic stance, not only because the inequities of the larger culture are reproduced in the classroom, but also because allowing students to choose texts and responses will not challenge familiar and comfortable discourses (Lewis, 1997). Thus, young girls left to their own devices may consistently choose to read books that promote desire as it has been constructed within a patriarchal ideology, and young boys may choose horror books which promote the discourse of violence, often directed against women. Davies (1993a, p. 157) argues for the important role of the teacher in providing a forum for critique in the classroom:

> If the language used in classroom text and talk is treated as transparent, it is more likely to become the reader's language through which they fashion the world and themselves. If the metaphors, images, and storylines through which characters are created are not themselves understood as constitutive, the reader cannot turn a critical gaze on that constitutive process.

The teacher's role, according to this scheme, is to teach students to read in search of that constitutive process. While I would not want to suggest that critically engaged reading is the only kind of reading worth promoting in school, I would suggest that this is an important role of literature that is largely overlooked in school. I envision a role for literature instruction in the classroom that encourages students to "listen" for the multiple voices in texts as they read, those that are promoted by the text as well as those that are silenced.

Notes

1. This work is part of a larger study that examines the nature of social contexts and interactions as they shape the literary culture of a classroom. All the names used in this chapter are pseudonyms out of concern for student anonymity.

2. The following conventions are used in the presentation of transcripts: [text] indicates descriptive text added to clarify elements of the transcript; *text* indicates emphasis; ( ) indicates unintelligible words; . . . indicates extracts edited out of the transcript; / indicates interrupted or dropped utterances. In the interest of clarity, repeated use of the word *like* is omitted from transcripts.

References

Bakhtin, M. M. (1981). *The dialogic imagination: Four essays.* (C. Emerson & M. Holquist, Trans.). Austin: University of Texas Press.

Collier, J. L., & Collier, C. (1983). *War comes to Willy Freeman.* New York: Dell.

Davies, B. (1993a). Beyond dualism and towards multiple subjectivities. In L. K. Christian-Smith (Ed.), *Texts of desire: Essays on fiction, femininity and schooling* (pp. 145–173). Washington, DC: Falmer

Davies, B. (1993b). *Shards of glass: Children reading and writing beyond gendered identities.* Cresskill, NJ: Hampton.

Edelsky, C. (1991). *With literacy and justice for all: Rethinking the social in language and education.* New York: Falmer.

Fast, H. (1961). *April morning.* New York: Bantam.

Gilbert, P. (1987). Post reader-response: The deconstructive critique. In B. Corcoran & E. Evans (Eds.), *Readers, texts, teachers* (pp. 234–250). Upper Montclair, NJ: Boynton/Cook.

Graff, G. (1987). *Professing literature: An institutional history.* Chicago: University of Chicago Press.

L'Engle, M. (1962). *A wrinkle in time.* New York: Dell.

Lewis, C. (1997). The social drama of literature discussions in a fifth/sixth-grade classroom. *Research in the Teaching of English, 31*(2), 162–204.

Lowry, L. (1989). *Number the stars.* Boston: Houghton Mifflin.

Lowry, L. (1993). *The giver.* Boston: Houghton Mifflin.

Moss, G. (1989). *Un/Popular fictions.* London: Virago.

Moss, G. (1995). Rewriting reading. In J. Holland, M. Blair, with S. Sheldon (Eds.), *Debates and issues in feminist research and pedagogy: A reader* (pp. 157–168). Clevedon, Avon, England: Open University.

O'Connor, M. C., & Michaels, S. (1993). Aligning academic task and participation status through revoicing: Analysis of classroom discourse strategy. *Anthropology and Education, 24*(4), 318–335.

O'Dell, S. (1960). *The island of the blue dolphins.* Boston: Houghton Mifflin.

Pierce, T. (1983). *Alanna: The first adventure.* New York: Knopf.

Rawls, W. (1961). *Where the red fern grows.* New York: Bantam.

Smith, M.W. (1992). Submission versus control in literary transactions. In J. Many & C. Cox (Eds.), *Reader stance and literary understanding: Exploring the theories, research, and practice* (pp. 143–160). Norwood, NJ: Ablex.

Speare, E. G. (1958). *The witch of Blackbird Pond.* Boston: Houghton Mifflin.

CHAPTER NINE

Third Class Is More than a Cruise-Ship Ticket

BEVERLY BUSCHING
University of South Carolina at Columbia

BETTY SLESINGER
Educational Consultant, Corvallis, Oregon

K im and Erika arrived in seventh-grade homeroom on a chilly winter morning, filled with concern about students in Michigan who were facing a blizzard without coats. They galvanized students and parents to collect and clean more than twenty winter jackets. As the box of coats was taped and addressed, it was gratifying to see these children, mostly all "haves" living comfortable and protected lives, so involved in activism. Although their glimpses of poverty were mostly secondhand, when they bumped up against a need, some of them were ready to act. We were glad that they had come to view their classroom as a place where they could act on their concerns, but we wanted them to go further.

We wanted the students to uncover the structure of society that creates the conditions of deprivation. We wanted them to think about why deprivation happens. We wanted them to raise questions about their society. If they investigated the underlying structure of society, we reasoned, more thoughtful opinions and activism would emerge. We knew that this was a lot to ask, but we still thought that it was important to try. If we really believed in a participatory democracy, shouldn't a middle school classroom be preparing students for it? If students don't understand how a society works, how can they work for its betterment?

Betty's language arts classroom is in a large middle school in a rapidly growing suburban area of the South. Beverly is a professor at nearby University of South Carolina. We are both part of an active circle of colleagues in our area who keep in touch through our local TAWL group, the Midlands Writing Project, and teacher-research meetings. We have collaborated as researchers in Betty's classrooms for more than five years. During the past few years we have worked together with her students to expand an authoring approach into humanities studies,[1] and now we are working to make the classroom more of an operating democracy. As the changes in the classroom have grown and deepened, so have our professional relationship, our collaborative writing, and our friendship.

Inquiry, topic immersion, portfolios, student choice, and student collaboration are now essentials in this classroom, and topics range all over the world and into students' own lives. Students regularly write and speak to real audiences. We have been pleased to see the stronger student engagement, even from marginal students, and the connected understandings that develop when topics are pursued in depth through student questions. Students have enjoyed being collaborators in creating some of the structures for learning in this classroom, and have a sense of pride in themselves as learners—a sense of respect for self and a collective sense of pride about their seventh-grade unit.

Inspired by the growing national conversation about democratic values and education (Ayers, 1993; Edelsky, 1994; Giroux, 1992), we decided to see what we could do to move Betty's literature and writing curriculum toward more critical analysis of society here and now, in the United States. We realized that students had done serious work looking critically at historical conditions such as the Holocaust, but they knew little about their own country. We wanted students to engage with the real and troubling issues of democracy in our times—issues of participation, access, privilege, rights, and responsibilities. This did not mean abandoning all required curriculum and texts. It meant selecting and supplementing in different ways. It meant raising different questions about literature and giving students access to the social conditions that surround a novel or story. It meant turning the eyes of their journals away from themselves and toward the world after the first nine weeks. We wanted each new text selection, journal assignment, or unit of work to move students further in their questioning—and perhaps understanding—of the social forces that shape civic life.

As this year progressed, students did move toward a critical stance, but slowly. For both of us, this was new territory, and we were feeling our way. Betty wondered if she would be criticized for "going too far" into controversial issues. The feeling of not being as well-prepared as usual made many days uncomfortable. Despite these anxieties, it was exciting to see a class focus emerge. The students were drawn to issues surrounding our society's dispossessed citizens. In this chapter we will focus on our year's experiment by sharing three engagements with literature— first, a discussion early in the year that revealed to us the yawning gap in the students' understanding, followed by a reading that was a breakthrough. Then we will share conversations and projects from a novel study that led students to investigate and question how society works.

"The Secret Lion": Issues Inaccessible to Students

A critical incident for us as curriculum planners was a discussion of one of the Junior Great Books stories, "The Secret Lion" (Rios, 1992). It was early in the year, and Betty was excited about the developing ability of one reading class to formulate their own questions and control their own book discussions through rotating leaders. She had spent some time modeling and analyzing different kinds of questions, and students had reflected on the kinds of questions that helped them probe into the books more deeply. Beverly was visiting on this day, in order to see a student-led discussion, in particular, of a story that dealt with issues of unequal access to the benefits of society through the lives of culturally and economically marginalized Chicano families. We wanted to see what the students would do with it.

It was gratifying to watch the students asking deeply probing questions and dealing earnestly with them—questions that included recognition of the metaphorical role of the title, the golf-course setting, and the golf ball itself. But after a few minutes, we were startled to watch the discussion dwindle. It became evident that in order to interpret the ironical message of the story, one would have to bring to it an already developed understanding of the causes and consequences of extreme poverty and cultural isolation. "Why didn't they [the Chicano boys in the story] know what a golf course was?" had obvious answers for us, but we watched students offering rather pitiful explanations: "The boys may be younger than we think. My cousin is in a middle school but he's only in fifth grade." "Maybe they don't watch sports on TV." Like many other Junior Great Books stories, the subtext was implied, not provided, and the students just did not have information or experience to bring to bear on it. Yes, they recognized the signs of being poor, but poverty seemed to be an individual family problem, not a societal one.

We shouldn't have been so surprised. Our society is good at hiding this information from children. Betty recollected going to the "hills" of her high school town with friends and thinking that all the Italian families lived in their crowded small houses because they liked being close to each other and were happy talking and cooking together. Beverly remembered growing up in the all-white suburbs of Dallas in the 1950s. She had no inkling of the racial and economic segregation that permeated this city. When her church youth group met with a black youth group from across the city, even this small gesture was too much for the church elders, who forbade the youth to continue the meetings. Of course, our school learning never dealt with all these differences. Our understandings are still growing slowly many years afterward.

The "Secret Lion" discussion strengthened our resolve, and it also turned our focus toward economic inequities. How does a life of poverty restrict people's participation in society and their access to its benefits? Complex layers of causes and conditions are involved, and we knew that canned generalizations would not do. We did not want to force a didactic interpretation—our interpretation—on the students. Just telling about problems would not be effective either. Students were already expert at ignoring the evening news. We needed for them to "encounter" issues so that they could "see" economic inequity happening and care about the outcomes.

Last year we had seen that the extended study of World War II, and the Holocaust stirred strong feelings about cruelty and persecution, which carried over into school and community issues. Extended immersion in fiction and factual sources worked together so that history *mattered*. But it was easier to study the Holocaust than American poverty. Resources on World War II were plentiful, and other teachers were available for consultation. No one else in our area was working on this. We also still worried about parental objections. While we were still wondering about the next step, the way opened naturally.

The *Titanic* Text Set: A Breakthrough

The students were reading about the *Titanic* disaster,[2] with several different selections from different points of view—survivor, victim, and rescuer. A film clip added a dramatic visualization of the context, and the dress of the passengers helped the students ground the event in the historical period. A *Read Magazine* docudrama ("The *Titanic*," 1995) that described the tragic fate of an emigrant family from third-class accommodations became a pivotal reading for this class. The docudrama followed the family on the night of the collision: After being kept below for many hours without any information, they and other steerage passengers fight their way to the main deck. First-class passengers are already filling the lifeboats. Although the father wins a place in a lifeboat for the mother and youngest two children, she refuses to separate the large family, and they all face the end together.

The class was horrified. Could this have been true? Were people really treated this way? A selection from the log of the rescue ship *Carpathia* in *Read* corroborated the unequal treatment of passengers according to class of accommodation, and other texts dramatically portrayed the sense of privilege claimed by wealthy passengers. Caroline waved her hand over the hubbub, and called out, "What I want to know is this, Mrs. Slesinger—Would *we* have been *third* class?" When Betty replied, "I'm not sure, but I know we wouldn't have been *first* class," the reality of social class as a sorting mechanism began to set in. The film clip was still vivid in their minds—steerage passengers clutching bundles as they waited on the dock, and the Vanderbilts with their fur coats, nursemaids, and carts full of trunks. Now they really cared about what happened. A healthy commotion filled the room, and they agreed to debate issues such as these: Did first class deserve the right to use the lifeboats? Was the captain of the *Titanic* at fault?

The metaphor of "third class" emerged as a way to talk about poverty, prejudice, and injustice. While students had understood that money was a pervasive determinant in our society as far as "things" and lifestyle, they had not considered that the poor did not have access to the same freedoms and rights as the rich and powerful. They had not realized that social position can limit one's safety, one's well-being, and one's choices. In December, when they read *A Christmas Carol* (1992), the social conditions of Victorian London jumped off the page, and it became much more than a popular holiday tale.

When the Stars Begin to Fall: The Reality of Cultural Hostility

The students' concerns about economic injustice led Betty to choose their next shared novel, *When the Stars Begin to Fall* (Collier, 1986), about a family that is economically marginal and thus outcast. The selection of this novel is a good example of how planning occurs when a teacher is strongly committed to an instructional focus. This novel was among the choices designated for seventh grade and available in class sets, but Betty was not acquainted with it. While browsing in the book room for a novel that addressed societal issues, Betty remembered that it had caught the interest of a few students in another class who had read it as an individual choice. The words "community" and "carpet factory" on the back cover blurb reminded her of a carpet factory near the school that had raised a controversy about chemical pollution, and so she took it home to review. We have found that when an issue emerges as important, sources that will stimulate further study will be found. After all, if the issue is important to society, others will be writing and talking about it.

Like radio waves, sources are around us; we just have to be tuned in to them.

The societal and economic context of poverty is accessible to young readers in *When the Stars Begin to Fall*. It was just what we needed to engage students in sorting out the complexity of individual and societal forces. Family dysfunction, environmental community activism, stereotyping, economic oppression, and exploitation are all intertwined in the personal development of the young hero, Harry White. Through the eyes of Harry and his sister, students could identify with marginalized points of view of the world and see how personal values are part of a cultural and economic context. The novel was a natural next step on the students' journey.

The White family are outcasts in their isolated, economically depressed town, living in a run-down farmhouse with a littered yard. Refusing to take a regular job ("I will not be a slave"), Mr. White ekes out a subsistence living for his family by doing odd jobs and by other activities which are probably illegal. The mother, while loving, is in a chronic state of depression and inactivity. Harry's older sister lets boys in her high school class sexually exploit her. The family is labeled as "trash" by the rest of the community and is treated as such. To escape from his family and the ostracism of neighbors, Harry spends his free time hiking alone in the woods. After he spots some suspicious effluent in the river adjacent to the local carpet factory, Harry is determined to prove it is pollution, both to contribute to the life of the town and to redeem his family in the eyes of others. While he eventually is successful in gathering evidence, the carpet factory, as the main employer in town, holds the town officials hostage. There is no Lone Ranger ending. Harry is threatened, forced to suppress his findings, and must console himself with the prospects of joining the Air Force and leaving his town and family when he graduates.

As they read, students raised questions in their notebooks, focusing on interesting issues and uncertainties, and then discussed/answered them in small groups. Both the suspenseful action and the social issues captured their imagination. As their thinking grew, they had insights into what made Harry worthy of respect despite his outward deviation from the norm. On the day that the class gathered for a full literature discussion circle at the end of the book, questions taken from their journals were the basis for the intense conversation that followed. As in past literature circles, two students led with questions, with Betty and Beverly sitting outside the circle as occasional contributors.

Allie opens the discussion with an attempt to characterize the complexity of Harry's character: "We think he's different, [but] he doesn't want people to think his family is different. He's the only one trying to do everything. He's the only one that cares." The acquiescence of the rest of the family to their outcast status bothers and puzzles the students. Chad's query "Why doesn't the rest of his family care about what people think about them?" elicits a rash of inconclusive explanations that leads the group to their real concern: How can people call other people such an ugly word as *trash*?

Ley is adamant when he interjects, "I don't think a person can really *be* trash. I mean they might be a little weird or might be crazy or something. Trash is something you throw away. Everyone has something good about them, so nobody can be trash! They could have some bad qualities, be, like a little dirty, maybe steal, and something like that, but nobody is trash." The group is very intent, hunched and leaning forward over their desks. Many nod in agreement, and others are poised to jump in. Zac begins to list all the ways the White family is outside the community. The students know very well what makes people outcasts. Many others chime in and the topic veers onto stealing and bad reputations, how people judge you by your house, and a disagreement over whether Harry and his sister would have been better off if they had been placed in a foster home.

Amy will not allow the initial discussion of "trash" to be dropped. Two more times she brings the group back to reinforce Zac's point about judging people by outward characteristics: "People can act 'trash-ee,' like if they are mean to other people or they do things like steal or deal drugs to get money, but no one *is* trash. . . ." After a pause, she launches into a new concern about labeling others. She knows and disapproves of labeling people by materialistic criteria. She and Allie try to express subtle cultural differences, for instance, that in some cultures the ideal is to live without things, not making an impact on the earth, and in other cultures, many relatives and sometimes the whole village help raise its children. These girls are aware that dissimilar societies operate differently.

Ley continues the distinction that seems to be so important to the students, saying most emphatically, with nods of agreement from the others: "It's what they *do* that makes themselves become trash. Trash isn't what they *have*, it's what they *do*." Now many other students jump in to defend the White children and how they couldn't help smelling when they had no washing machine and their water cut off, and a depressed mother who didn't cook or clean for them. Christina, who knows someone in depression, comes to the mother's defense: "Maybe she knew her kids were miserable, but she didn't think she could do anything about it so she just sat around." Emily adds her insight about the difficulties of getting out of a bad relationship: "Maybe before she married, she had her own good life, or he might have said, 'I'll beat you if you get a divorce.'"

The discussion continued, intense and provocative. This book allowed students to speculate upon causes of behavior, both psychological and societal. At the end of the discussion, a question was raised about why Collier would have written this book, and a student answered, "So students could have the kind of discussion we've been having. So people will talk about these things."

During the novel reading, students' journal entries and finished writing paralleled Harry's interest in community issues, and even pushed them into activism on a small scale. For this nine weeks, students' journals were their eyes on the world. They wrote about problems they thought were important in their school, neighborhoods, town, or state. They began bringing articles and shared them along with the classroom copy of the newspaper. "I think everyone will be interested in this," said Lindsay about an article on homelessness. Issue-based discussions actually competed with Spirit Week. Several students got hooked on an issue. Irena and Kimberly got their parents to take them to a Ronald McDonald home to learn more about how they serve sick children and their families. They wrote letters about it, and created a brochure later in the year. Lance brought news of Dr. Kevorkian's trial as it unfolded in the newspaper, and students questioned the popular media's antagonism toward the doctor. Jillian kept promoting teachers and police officers as role models over arrogant sports stars and entertainers. Richard and Kim were able to question Rosa Parks online, and after this personal connection was made, they followed with greater interest news articles and specials featuring black history. Students began to have identities as concerned citizens, not just athletes or joksters. The class got a reputation, as well, and an eighth-grade student came to Betty to borrow their materials on child labor!

From the discussions about issues, students identified a problem they perceived to be important. They conducted surveys to gather more information, and then they communicated in writing their results to someone who needed to be aware of the problem and might be able to effect change. Kim wrote to the assistant superintendent of the district about including more multiracial emphasis in the curriculum. When she did not receive a prompt reply, she drafted a sharper second letter; a reply came soon after. Patrick's findings on the condition of school bathrooms and E. J.'s complaint about support for intramurals versus junior varsity basketball were published in the school newspaper. Emily's criticism of unsanitary food handling in a local fast-food restaurant received a rewarding reply—a promise to correct the conditions. Once they had educated themselves and had uncovered disturbing information, the students felt powerful enough to seek answers from officialdom. In Amy's letter to the president about preserving rainforests, shown below, it is evident that she sees herself as having passed beyond the stage of popularized opinions. She feels herself to be a serious citizen who investigates and then acts:

Dear President Clinton,

When you read the next sentence, you may come to the conclusion that I am just another "save the worlder" but I'm not. I am, though, concerned with the preservation of the earth, its wilderness, and its resources. I am most especially concerned about the rainforests and the survival of raptors.

One of the many places that existing raptors live and migrate to is the Arctic Wildlife Refuge in Alaska. I would like to thank you for vetoing the plan to drill for oil in the Arctic Wildlife Refuge.

At this time, I would like to bring up a letter that you may not remember as you wrote it about two years ago. Mrs. Slesinger's Language Arts Extension class wrote to you while you were running for office asking you why you would like to be the next President of the United States. (Your response is the second letter enclosed in the envelope.) In your third reason, you stated that "I will protect the environment, especially the rainforests, the wetlands, and the Arctic Refuge."

You have fulfilled the part about protecting the Arctic Refuge, but it's time to do something about the rainforests. A rainforest is a treasure chest of plant and animal life. Most people think of treasure chests as being full of gold and precious stones. Let's pretend for a moment that a treasure chest could contain a rainforest too. For every acre of land taken from the treasure chest containing a rainforest, subtract at least $90,000 worth of gold and precious stones from the second chest. Pretty soon, both chests will be empty and we will have nothing left on which to survive.

Deforestation is not only harming the plants and animals that live there, it is also harming us. For example, one of the breeds of monkey that is going extinct due to deforestation could be carrying the only virus or bacteria in the world that could cure AIDS or cancer. If the monkeys go extinct, then we will have no way to cure AIDS or cancer, diseases that every day kill hundreds of thousands of people across the world.

In writing this letter, I hoped to encourage you to try to stop at least some of the deforestation that is going on in South America alone. But I also wrote to point out a fact that you may already know. The group of people who are largely responsible for deforestation are the poor, uneducated residents of South America who log for survival. My point is that if the impoverished Latin Americans were given an education, then they would stop logging for a living and find a job.

I realize that you have no control over what South Americans choose to do with their countries, but I also have a suggestion. There are, more likely than not, educators in the Peace Corps that can speak several languages (including Spanish) who would be more than willing to establish a school or training program in some of the poorer towns and cities. Therefore the man logging would have a chance to get an education and stop cutting the rainforest down.

I wold like to thank you once again for vetoing the plan that would have allowed drilling in the Arctic Wildlife Refuge. And in closing, I would like to simply state that my letter will have some, at least minor effects on stopping deforestation.

> Sincerely,
> Amy Summerford
> Grade 7

At the same time that students were watching issues in the world, Betty planned some role-playing activities to extend students' analysis of the controlling forces in *When the Stars Began to Fall*. Although the discussion excerpted above demonstrates that some students saw the economic structures that created oppression, others were not so involved. To give everyone a chance to think through questions of authorship and power, Betty asked pairs of students to get inside the head of the author, James Lincoln Collier, and write a letter seeking a publisher for his manuscript. Who gives voice to other peoples' lives and what their purposes are is a central question of democratic life. Betty thought that the students needed more than an ephemeral statement in a discussion to address this question. Here is one savvy letter, written by a group of students, that reached back to the concepts of "third class" and "trash," and demonstrated an awareness of Collier's intent to educate others about injustice and prejudice. Note also the realistic awareness of the finances of publishing!

Dear Publisher,

I would like you to deeply consider the text for my new novel. I don't think that it will be one of those books that will only sell a few copies. I think it will sell a lot. The reason I say this is because I think people in our society need to know what it is like to be considered "trash." I think that the topic for this book will intrigue many readers and let them know more about being "trash."

Another good reason that this book will do well is because it will appeal to many schools. Many schools have families just like the Whites and it would be a good idea for their other students to learn just what it is like to be "third class."

I think it will be worth giving me a good contract because I think this book will do great!

Sincerely,
James Collier

Students also revisited social status and its relationship to the treatment of others. They had lively discussions as they did some written role-playing of these various status positions. Small groups drafted a set of written documents as if they were characters from the book doing their jobs—a memo from the factory president to employees about Harry as a trespasser, a report by a social worker on the decision of foster care for the White children, entries in the newspaper editor's logbook, and so forth. The discussions while creating these documents gave students opportunities to understand better the viewpoints that led characters to act as they did. The following excerpts from Christina's group show that the students thought about rather subtle prejudices. It is sad to recognize that twelve-year-olds are so skilled at imitating not only the voice but the nuances of meaning as the adult characters express contempt and disdain for the poor, as we can see in this memo:

Timber Falls Factory Memo
To: Security Officers
From: James Tyler, Pres. of Timber Falls Carpet Factory

We have had a bit of trouble with the White boy from Mountain Pass Road. He seems to be a nosey brat. He says he comes to the river area to bird watch, but I doubt it. Just keep an eye on the factory grounds and don't let him trick you. He's a good liar. It runs in the family, I guess.

We were surprised that the students could see into the burden of the newspaper editor's compromised life, as in these two entries in his daily log:

- if they charge Harry, I would have to print story on this pollution
- wish I had as much guts as the kid—river would have been clean five years ago if I did. . . .

They could also set aside their own empathetic feelings to capture the chilling professional stance of the social worker:

Department of Social Services Report

After a complete investigation, DSS declares that the Whites have an unsuitable living environment for their two children, Helen and Harry. The social worker and I were very disappointed in that living environment because it did not offer what children their ages need to have. The most important thing was it was not a clean and sanitary way of living. Nothing in their house was clean and almost everything had fungus growing on it. . . .

The other reason I am filing a complaint and asking that the children go into foster care or live with a relative is because the parents do not watch over their kids very well. They have demonstrated this by giving them unfit living conditions and by abusing their children. . . .

The students understood all too well how parents judge others on the basis of assigned status and rumored reputation, not on a personal evaluation of individual integrity. In imagined conversations between Harry's friend and parents, they envisioned the parents' disdainful rejection of the boys' friendship, and even more painful, Harry's awareness of his rejection: "Your parents aren't going to let me spend the night at your house. Think about it for a minute."

Reflections

This has been a year of risk taking and exploration for us, and we have been energized by our discoveries. Our concern about parental objections was never realized. Parents were surprisingly supportive. We think that their support was greatly influenced by the way that Betty began the year. The first unit immersed students in memoir, family history, and personal journals. This unit was, in a sense, a celebration of the students' families and their values. Parents came several times to watch students present their autobiographical projects. As they listened to their children trace family history, including tragedies and challenges, parents obviously felt proud of their families and their children's work. Perhaps, having been affirmed by Betty's program at the beginning of the year, parents were less mistrustful when controversial issues entered the classroom door.

When students value themselves, they can more easily value others. This first unit created community and trust among many of the students, and this trustful atmosphere was a key element in the open discussions, and also, perhaps, in the caring that students extended to others.

Another reason for parent support may have been that when literature study took students into societal critique, controversies emerged through the students' own active learning strategies. For the most part, students themselves collected the background information that revealed inequities. Opinions expressed in the classroom were primarily those of the students, and Betty worked to support the free exchange of ideas.

What if a student had "freely expressed" an oppressor stance? This did not happen, but we think that since the focus was on finding the real people behind the face of poverty and prejudice, and describing the social forces that create poverty, such a stance would have met with disapproval from other students. Of course, Betty did not bring just any resources into the classroom for students to choose from; rather, those that she thought sensitively presented some realities of inequality.

What do we know now that we did not know a year ago? We have learned that it is both worthwhile and workable to have an overarching year's theme that is democracy-based. Students did move from empathy for individual problems to awareness of societal constraints and injustices. As Betty said:

> To start kids on critically examining their society, you have to fuel feelings of empathy. If you can show ways that injustices create problems, you can probably elicit their concern and involvement. First by helping them notice inequities that exist, and later moving students to consider causes and changes.

We found that students needed rich and extensive engagements before they had meaningful insights. A one-shot exposure is never enough. The forceful letters that the students wrote were a result of many weeks of journal writing, discussion, and surveys. The empathetic role-playing emerged from extensive talk and literature responses. Although adolescents can't be expected to deal with a steady diet of social ills, we were gratified to find that students retained their interest as the curriculum revisited economic issues throughout the year. Some students became so involved in an individual concern that they returned to it time and time again as they made choices for speeches, debates, plays, editorials and other writing. Lyndsey, for example, wrote this moving poem later in the year for another class:

On The Streets

I walk through your streets everyday,
but you seem to pass me by.
I turn every corner you do,
but you don't even notice I'm there.
I speak the same language you do,
but you treat me like a foreigner.
I look and act just like you,
but you don't even care.

I'm no different from the rest,
just I have no place to go.
All I want is a friend,
but you treat me so low.
We're supposed to be brother and sister,
but you treat me like a stranger.
The same guy died for all our sins,
and he was born in a manger.

Why am I called different?
Is it the clothes that I wear?
You seem to always ignore me.
Like I am never there.
Even if you're cold and hungry,
you have a place to go.
When I get cold and hungry,
I have to sleep in the snow.

You think you have nothing.
But take a look at me.
Your world is like a paradise.

> You even have a TV.
> Maybe when we realize,
> how much there is to share,
> we'll find too much in common,
> to pretend it isn't there.

LYNDSEY PLYLER
GRADE 7

Yet, along with the meaningful moments we have featured in this chapter, the inconsistencies of adolescent thought still operated, just as they do in the larger society. There were groans when they heard that they had to send their survey results to an appropriate audience. There were kids who reveled in resolving their fiction writing with scenes of extreme violence. Along with thoughtful journal entries on problems of the world such as low minimum wages were dismissive messages like "In my life, however, I don't care about that stuff. I mostly care about music." There were still cliques in the team, racially and socially. One day when Betty asked why it was easy to sympathize with characters in their reading, but so much harder to change how we act toward people in our real lives, a solemn quiet fell over the room. No one had an answer, but they were caught by the question, just as we have been.

Note

1. The planning and activities of this approach are described in more detail in Slesinger & Busching (1995) and Busching & Slesinger (1995).

2. The study of the *Titanic* preceded by several years the Hollywood movie *Titanic*.

References

Ayers, W. (1993). *To teach: The journey of a teacher*. New York: Teachers College Press.

Ballard, R. D. (1988). *Exploring the* Titanic. (P. Crean, Ed.). Ontario: Madison.

Busching, B. A., & Slesinger, B. A. (1995). Authentic questions: What do they look like? Where do they lead? *Language Arts, 72*(5), pp. 341–351.

Collier, J. L. (1986). *When the stars begin to fall.* New York: Dell.

Dickens, C. (1992). A Christmas carol. In *Junior great books: Series 7.* Chicago: Great Books Foundation.

Edelsky, C. (1994). Education for democracy. *Language Arts, 71*(4), pp. 252–257.

Giroux, H. (1992). Educational leadership and the crisis of democratic government. *Educational Researcher, 21*(4), pp. 4–11.

Rios, A. (1992). The secret lion. In *Junior great books: Series 7.* Chicago: Great Books Foundation.

Slesinger, B. A., & Busching, B. A. (1995). Practicing democracy through student-centered inquiry. *Middle School Journal, 26*(5), pp. 50–56.

The *Titanic:* Lure and lore. (1995). *Read Magazine, 44*(11), pp. 16–21.

When the great ship went down. (1995). *Read Magazine, 44*(11), pp. 4–5.

CHAPTER TEN

Critical Literacy: Teaching Reading, Writing, and Outrage

LINDA M. CHRISTENSEN
Portland, Oregon, Public Schools

From history to literature to language, my teachers' choices informed me to lower my expectations. I knew that the people who changed history were great men—Columbus, Washington, Lincoln. Because no one like me or my family was included in the curriculum, I learned I wasn't important, my family wasn't important, and I shouldn't expect too much. The women who made a difference were ordained by God, like Joan of Arc, or sewed their way to fame, like Betsy Ross. I clung to those few women and claimed them as my guides. I never heard of Fannie Lou Hamer or Frida Kahlo until I started teaching.

I was from a working-class family. My mother, the eighth child out of twelve, was the first to finish high school. My father only finished grade school. I was the fourth child in my family and the first to attend college. We didn't talk right. We said "chimley" and "the-ater." We confused our verbs. In the ninth grade, Mrs. Delaney asked me to stand in front of my English class and pronounce words like "beige," or "baj," as we said. I was an example of how not to talk. I became ashamed of myself and my family.

It wasn't until I studied the history of the English language that I realized there might have been a reason, other than stupidity, laziness, or ignorance, for the way my family pronounced words and used verb tenses. And I was angry that I hadn't been taught that history, that I'd been allowed, in fact, *made,* to feel ashamed of my home language.

Today I am outraged by the experience. And I want my students to be outraged when they encounter texts, museums, commercials, classes, and rules that hide or disguise a social reality that glorifies one race, one culture, one social class, one gender, or one language, without acknowledging the historical context that gave it dominance. I want to teach a critical literacy that equips students to "read" power relationships at the same time that it imparts academic skills.

As a high school English teacher, I attempt to make my literacy work—in a predominately African American, working-class neighborhood—a sustained argument against inequality and injustice. My high school is currently scheduled to be reconstituted because of our low test scores. Of the 2,200 neighborhood students who could attend our school, only 950 do; the rest transfer to other schools districtwide. The majority of students who enter "Jeff" have not passed the eighth-grade tests in reading and writing. I write this because these numbers "say" something about my school and the state of the students who enter the building. But those scores do not tell the truth about the intelligence and ability of my students.

I use critical literacy in all three of the classes I typically teach. "Contemporary Literature and Society" and "Writing for Publication" are both untracked senior English classes that meet daily for eighty minutes, one during the fall semester and one during the spring semester. "Literature and U.S. History," an untracked eighty-minute block class I teach for the entire year, carries junior English and U.S. history credit. I typically teach the standard three-class daily load under Jefferson's block schedule, which means two sections of literature and U.S. history and one each of the senior classes. These courses carry standard English and/or history credit, so I must still follow all of the official guidelines and "standards" hoops set up outside of my classroom as I do my critical-literacy work. This term I have thirty-five students in my senior class and thirty-eight in my junior class.

Some might say that the role of language arts teachers is to teach reading, writing, and language and that we should not be worrying about issues like injustice or racism. But I would respond that the teaching of literacy is political. Any piece of literature my students pick up—from cartoons to children's books to the literature we read in class—legitimates what Chilean writer Ariel Dorfman (1983, p. 7) calls a "social blueprint" about what it means to be men, women, poor, people of color, gay, or straight. And that vision is political—whether it portrays the status quo or argues for a reorganization of society.

How and when I "correct" students' language and writing is also political. If I do not teach students that the standard language in this country, or any country, is not based on the "best" language but on the language that the powerful, the ruling class, developed, then every time I "correct" their home language I am condemning it as wrong, as incorrect, as "nonstandard." If I fail to make that social blueprint transparent, I endorse it.

No subject in school, including literature, composition, and the study of language, is "value-free," as Ira Shor points out in *A Pedagogy for Liberation* (Shor & Freire, 1987). Too often, "[t]hese falsely neutral curricula train students to observe things without judging, to see the world from the official consensus, to carry out orders without questioning, as if the given society is fixed and fine" (p. 12).

Teachers must draw students into what Brazilian educator Paulo Freire described as a "critical dialogue about a text or a moment of society . . . to reveal it, unveil it, see its reasons for being like it is, the political and historical context of the material" (Shor & Freire, 1987, p. 13). But beyond illumination, students must use the tools of critical literacy to dismantle the half-truths, inaccuracies, and lies that strangle their conceptions about themselves and others. They must use the tools of critical literacy to expose, to talk back to, to remedy any act of injustice or intolerance that they witness.

What Is Critical Literacy?

Several years ago, I attended a literature workshop at which we read a chapter from Olive Ann Burns's novel *Cold Sassy Tree* (1984). The workshop was wonderful, full of useful techniques to engage students in literature: a tea party, text rendering, writing from our own lives, using an innocent narrator as Burns does. Great methodology. And ones I use with almost every unit I teach. But the entire workshop ignored the issues of race, class, and gender that run like a sewer through the novel—from the "linthead" factory workers, to the African Americans who work as kitchen help, to the treatment of women. The workshop explored none of this.

For too many years of my teaching career, I also ignored the social text. I thought it meant talking about setting. I had not been taught anything different. Saying that the novel was set in the South during such and such a period was enough. But it is not enough. Not questioning why the lintheads and the African Americans in the novel were treated differently or not exploring the time Grandpa blamed Grandma for not bearing him a son—this allows readers to silently accept these practices as just. Young women internalize the idea that they must be beautiful and bear sons to be loved. Working-class students learn that it is their fault if they are poor like the lintheads in the novel. When I taught literature without examining the social and historical framework, I condoned the social text students absorbed.

Critical literacy does explore the social and historical framework. It moves beyond a description of society and into an interrogation of it. Why were the lintheads poor? Why weren't they accepted by the middle class? In a society that has so much, why do some starve while others get fat? Why do women have to be beautiful to be loved? Critical literacy questions the basic assumptions of our society.

In each unit of study I use the same basic format: (1) a question that provokes the examination of historical, literary, and social "texts"; (2) the study and involvement of students' lives; (3) the reading of a variety of texts, ranging from novels to historical documents, to first-person narratives, to movies, speakers, role-plays, and field trips; and (4) a final project that opens the possibility for students to *act* on their knowledge. Critical literacy is big and messy. It combines the reading and writing of poetry, fiction, essay, historical documents and statistics, lots of discussions, read-arounds, days of writing, responding, and revising of student work.

This kind of work takes time. We cannot race through a half-dozen novels. I am forced to make difficult choices about what I include and what I leave out. Often, one novel will provide the center, or core, and I will surround it with other texts, role-plays, videos, improvisations, museum visits, or speakers.

The Question

In my "Contemporary Literature and Society" classes, we are exploring the question, "Is language political?" Why language? Because language is about power. And critical literacy is about "reading" and uncovering power relationships in the world. Whose language or dialect has power? Whose does not? Why not? What happens if someone has a Spanish or Vietnamese accent? A British accent? How does language benefit some and hurt others? Through the study of language, students look behind the Wizard of Oz machinery that ranks some languages as standard and others as substandard. We ask, whose papers get corrected for language errors and whose enter correct? How might that affect their feelings about themselves? Their language? Their family? We ask, who scores high on SATs and who doesn't? We stop pretending that grades, achievement, and high test scores are only based on a meritocracy in which everyone starts out equal. We look at how some privileges, like high SATs, might look as if they are earned, but have really been inherited on the basis of social class or race or gender. We look at pieces of literature, we read studies, and we examine our own lives as we search for answers to the question "Is language political?"

We also look at how language is embedded in culture. Language is not just about subjects and verbs; it is about music, dance, family relationships; it is about how we view the present and the future. We read Jack Weatherford's (1991) study of native languages. What might a language full of nouns tell us about a culture? How about a language full of verbs? A language with no past tense? No future tense? A language with no word for "read" or "write?" A language with two hundred words for snow? A language with six words for love?

Students' Lives at the Center

Critical literacy is embedded in students' lives just as deeply as the students' lives are embedded in this society. To teach students to read and write and think critically about "the word and the world," as Freire phrases it, means to engage them in a study of their lives in relation to the larger society. Why is it important for students to write about their lives? Why is it part of critical literacy? Why is it necessary to include student lives when studying a unit on language? Because in critical literacy, their lives are part of the text of the class. Their experience with language helps us to understand how society creates hierarchies that rank some languages as "standard" and others as "substandard"; some as "educated," others as "ignorant."

Bringing in students' language is more than a feel-good gesture; it is more than erasing the shame that comes when one's language is considered inferior. What Lois Yamanaka writes about Pidgin, I could have written about my home language and many of my students could write about their linguistic heritage—from Ebonics to Spanish to Vietnamese:

> But Pidgin, written and published Pidgin, is the evidence of the integrity of the language. What was once an indication of belonging to a particular community has become a way of validating the individuals within this community. It is impossible to ban the *sound* of one's memory. Ours is a history of coercion that alienated an entire community of Pidgin speakers. To refuse, to neglect or forfeit, the direction of the language that a voice pursues is to manipulate the person away from the self. (Yamanaka, undated)

As we discuss language and culture, the students write pieces about themselves, their homes, their family sayings, their language. We do what Yamanaka urges. We remember our homes without censoring. We read, for example, George Ella Lyon's (1996) poem "Where I'm from." We note how Lyon's poem includes details from her life—lists of items cluttering her house, a counting of the trees and bushes in her neighborhood, sayings from her family, the names of family members, the memories of foods they ate together. I encourage students to use their "home language" as they write. The following excerpts are from student poems which Lyons' piece provoked:

> I am from bobby pins, doo rags, and wide tooth combs.
> I am from prayer plants that lift their stems
> and rejoice every night.
>
> I am from chocolate cakes and deviled eggs
> from older cousins and hand-me-downs
> to "shut ups" and "sit downs"
>
> I am from Genesis to Exodus,
> Leviticus, too.
> church to church, pew to pew

I am from a huge family tree that begins with dust
and ends with me.

ORETHA STOREY

I am from the little brown house
in the city streets.
I'm from a street
that is much, much too tough.

I am from a neighborhood
where the crack heads roam free.
The police never seem to harass them,
but they always harass me.

CANDACE BROADNAX

I am from dust, beaches and shells,
the coconut tree hanging over my house.
I am from a big belly man
and black haired woman.
I am from an island in the Pacific.
I am from Victoria and Scott's branch,
breadfruit and coconut,
the hand my grandfather cut off
when he tried to get a coconut from the tree.

DIOVINA THOMAS

I am from old pictures
and hand sewn quilts.
I am from the Yerba Buena
to the old walnut tree that is no more.

I am from carne con chile
to queso con tortillas.
I am from farmers and ancient Indians
to the frijoles and sopa
they ate.

LURDES SANDOVAL

I am from awapuhi ginger,
sweet fields of sugar cane,
green bananas.

I am from warm rain cascading over
taro leaf umbrellas,
crouching beneath the shield of kalo.

I am from poke, brie cheese, mango, and raspberries,
from Maruitte
and Aunty Nani.

I am from Moore and Cackley
from sardines and haupia.
From Mirana's lip Djavan split
to the shrunken belly
my grandmother could not cure.

DJAMILA MOORE

I am from Aztlán
where many battles and wars were fought.
I am from the strength and courage of the Aztecs
who died for our freedom.
I am from traditions and customs
from *posadas* and *quinceañeras*
to *día de la muerte* and *buena suerte*.

I am from the blood of my ancestors,
the dreams of my grandmother,
the faith of my mother,
and the pride of my culture.

I am from the survivors.

ALEJANDRO VIDALES

I am from the land that struggles
for freedom.
I am from the rice field, water buffaloes
and cows.
I am from the place where
    Blood floats like rivers
    Innocent souls are trapped

under the ground
Dead bodies haven't yet been buried.
A beautiful barn becomes
a cemetery.

It wasn't supposed to be like this.

I am from the place I hold
now only a memory.
I am from a family with hearts like stones.

—CANG DAO

Why is it important to have students writing about their lives? Why is this a part of critical literacy? As Lois Yamanaka says, "With language rests culture. To sever the language from the mouth is to sever the ties to homes and relatives, family gatherings, foods prepared and eaten, relationships to friends and neighbors. Cultural identity is utterly akin to linguistic identity" (undated). Bringing students' languages, ancestors, and sayings from their homes into the classroom validates their language, their culture, and their history as topics worthy of study. It says they count; their language is part of a history that most language textbooks ignore, or worse, label as "incorrect." Speaking their languages and telling their stories breaks the pattern of silence and shame that correction without historical and linguistic context breeds. How else can we understand our society and our world if we don't bring in the lives of the people who are living it?

Reading the Word and the World

During this unit we read literature from diverse perspectives: *Wild Meat and Bully Burgers* by Lois Ann Yamanaka (1966), about the politics of Pidgin in Hawai'i; *Pygmalion* by George Bernard Shaw (1914/1951), about the politics of English in England; "How to Tame a Wild Tongue" by Gloria Anzaldúa (1987) and "Achievement of Desire" by Richard Rodriguez (1982), about the politics of English for people whose home language is Spanish. We also read segments of *Brothers and Sisters* by Bebe Moore Campbell (1994), *Talkin' and Testifyin'* by Geneva Smitherman (1997), the

Ebonics issue of *Rethinking Schools* (see Perry & Delpit, 1997). We read these pieces, talk back to them, examine how the characters feel about themselves, their families, culture, and race. As they read, I ask students to take notes on their readings, to think about why one language is standard while the rest struggle under labels of "lazy," "incompetent," or "broken," to think about whose languages are in those categories and whose are not. I encourage students to "talk back" to these readings, to imagine they are in a conversation with the writer.

For example, when responding to Geneva Smitherman's article, "Black English/Ebonics: What It Be Like?" (1998), Kesha wrote, "I used to think that Ebonics meant we couldn't speak proper English, that we were dumb. I'm glad we learned the true history." Later, reading the same piece, she noted, "Reading these articles and watching the video [the video segment "Black on White" in McCrum, Cran, & MacNeil (1986)] made me realize that the words I speak and the way I speak came from my African people. I felt pride." Ebony wrote, "People don't understand Ebonics, so they call it 'ghetto' or 'slang.' They need to learn the history." Saqualla noted, "A lot of us who speak Ebonics are ashamed of our talk because the society we live in expects something different, looks down on us." Responding to the quote "Attitudes shape expectations and a teacher's expectations shape performance," Niambi wrote, "This is so true. A kid can tell if they are being treated as if they are stupid, and many times feel they must be if a teacher says they are."

Our discussions of these articles and pieces of literature spark heated debates. After reading Richard Rodriguez's "Achievement of Desire," students argue about the need to leave their culture and language behind in order to succeed. They compare Rodriguez to Esther in *Brothers and Sisters,* people who move up, "act white," and leave their culture and their people behind. Students ask: Should Lakeesia, a young mother with a desire to be a bank clerk and get off welfare, get the job even if she speaks "nonstandard English"? How much are we willing to change in order to get ahead? Is speaking Standard English acting white? Does everyone have to code switch on the job? Kesha asks, "Why we always gotta be the ones who have to change?" Goldie asks, "Why can't we be the Standard?" and Masta asks, "Who made the Standard? Who died and made them the standard makers anyway?"

I also nudge them to see if any of the characters' lives parallel the struggles they face. When students read a book that is as foreign to their lives as Shaw's *Pygmalion*, one of the ways they can engage in the reading is by finding similarities in their own lives, linking Eliza's Doolittle's struggle with English in England and the world of my student, José, who crossed the border with his grandmother and a coyote when he was five years old. Even noncritical reading theory acknowledges that students must be engaged with a text in order to read it.

Later, when students write critical essays on one or more of the texts we've read during our unit on the "Politics of Language," they write about their lives as well. Alejandro and Hecmarie compare their difficulties learning English when they came to the United States and the taunts they faced with Eliza's attempts to learn "proper" English. As Alejandro writes in his literary essay:

> When I came to this country and started school, it was a new experience. When I arrived in my classroom all the kids stared at me. I had hair like the white kids, but I was darker than them. I was not black though. I was in between.
>
> I was constantly made fun of because of my accent. It seemed funny to my classmates and all the stereotypes in the cartoons would make them say stuff to me like *"Arriba! Arriba!"* This really aggravated me. Like Liza [Doolittle from *Pygmalion*]. I wanted to be respected for who I was. If it meant changing, I was willing to do it. I had to teach people who I was and make them respect me. In the process, I had to beat up a couple of kids. But even though I changed, I remembered where I came from. Liza didn't.

Denedra compares the disruptive role of alcoholism in Eliza's life with the abuse of alcohol in hers. Djamila and Jason discuss the difficulty of going "home" that both Eliza and Richard Rodriguez experience after they've become educated and their struggles to belong in two communities: Hawai'ian/mainland for Djamila and urban African American/suburban African American for Jason.

Writing the World

Creating a critical-literacy classroom still means teaching students to read and write. But instead of only asking students to write essays that demonstrate a close reading of a novel or engaging in a literary evaluation of the text, critical literacy creates spaces for students to tackle larger social issues that have urgent meaning in their lives.

As Deshawn demonstrates in the opening to his essay, these pieces can reflect the struggles students deal with daily:

> I was born black, raised black, and I live black. But now that I have achieved a job outside the general blackness, some say I'm white because of the language I choose to speak at work. Have I put my culture behind me in order to succeed?

Kaanan wrote his essay to an audience of teachers. He came alive to the study of Ebonics and its ensuing struggles in Oakland, California. He began to understand that his problems with spelling, grammar, and writing might have been influenced by home language. But he also came to see that if his teachers understood more about his "home language," they might have helped him more:

> Teachers should be able to teach students Ebonics if they want. People need to accept it. Ebonics is going to be here forever. You can't take a whole language and get rid of it. Teachers who don't know about Ebonics should learn about it so they can build better relationships with kids. Teachers would understand what kids are talking about when they speak Ebonics.
>
> When I went to school, teachers didn't really teach me how to spell or put sentences together right. They just said sound it out, so I would spell it the way I heard it at home. Everybody around me at home spoke Ebonics, so when I sounded it out, it sounded like home and it got marked wrong. When I wrote something like, "My brother he got in trouble last night," I was marked wrong. Instead of showing me how speakers of Ebonics sometimes use both a name and a pronoun but in "Standard English" only one is used, I got marked wrong. So when my teachers graded my papers, they would either put a lot of corrections on my papers or just give me a bad grade. They didn't know where I was coming from.
>
> People are going to speak and write how they hear things from home. Kids should be able to get taught both, but just know when to speak "proper" and when not to. Like when they go to a job interview, they should speak proper, but when they are at home, they should speak Ebonics. Teachers should teach kids when and where to speak Ebonics.

> I feel you can't take a part of someone's history and heritage away from them. In school they teach us about a lot of stuff that never happened, like when they say that Christopher Columbus discovered American. They might as well teach kids something that's real, like Ebonics, and help kids out.

Moving beyond Classroom Walls

When students are "steeped" in evidence from one of the units, they begin to write. I want them to turn their anger, their hurt, their rage into words that might affect other people. We talk about potential audiences and outlets—from parents, to teens, to corporations. Students have written pamphlets for parents to "teach" them about how to use cartoons and videos carefully with their children, articles about anorexia for middle school girls. Khalilah wrote a piece about the politics of color. Joe sent his cartoon essay off to *Essence* magazine because he wanted African American males to take note of how they are "dissed" in cartoons. Tammy wrote about the prejudice against "fat" people in our society. In our whole language classrooms, audience should not be a "pretend someone" out there. We need to find ways for our students to express their real concerns about the world.

Sometimes their writing addresses the outrage that comes when they understand that they do not need to feel the pain or shame that their "secret education" drilled into them. During the follow-up to our unit on the politics of language, students read a chapter from David Owen's book *None of the Above* (1985) called "The Cult of Mental Measurement." In this essay, Owens describes the racist past of the SATs and also points out how race continues to be a factor in these kinds of standardized tests today. Students are outraged by their discoveries. A few years ago, Frank rallied the class to go on strike and refuse to take the SATs. After a long debate, the class decided that their strike might hurt them more than it would hurt the Educational Testing Service. Several students vowed that they would not apply to any school that used the SATs as an entrance requirement.

But we did find a way to demystify the tests and use our knowledge to teach others about our outrage. I asked students to analyze each of the verbal sections of the SATs. We examined the instructions, the language, the "objectives" of each section. We looked at how the language and culture of the SATs reflected the world of upper-class society. After examining each section and taking the tests a few times, I asked students to construct their own tests using the culture, content and vocabulary of our school. A sample is reproduced in Figure 1 on the following page.[1]

After students complete the test and our unit on language, we take our tests and knowledge up to Ruth Hubbard's education classes at Lewis and Clark College. Sometimes we find other professors at local universities who welcome my students in as teachers for a day. My students "give" the preservice teachers the JAT and ask them to imagine that it is a high-stakes test that will determine their future—what college they get into, scholarships, and so on. After the tests, students discuss the issue of testing and language. In this way, my students have a real audience whose future teaching practice will hopefully be enlightened by their work. They see that what they learn in school can make a difference in the world, and so can they.

Language arts teachers need to explore more than the best practices, the newest techniques in our profession; we need to explore and question the content as well. Too often, the work of critical literacy is seen as necessary in inner-city schools or in schools where students of color represent the majority of the student body, but it is deemed unnecessary in schools where the majority of students are of European descent. I would argue that critical literacy is an emergency in these schools as well. How else are students who have only been exposed to the status quo going to recognize and resist injustice? Students must learn to identify not only how their own lives are affected by our society, but also how other people's lives are distorted or maligned by the media and by historical, literary, and linguistic inaccuracy.

Notes

1. Not all of these fit exactly the prototypical SAT question. The point is to get students to understand the relationship among tests, culture, privilege, and meritocracy. This is just one vehicle for learning that lesson. Answers: (1) The "correct" answer according to Jefferson students is (d). Tony is the award given for plays. At Jefferson the

---

JAT

Jefferson Achievement Test

Each question below consists of a related pair of words or phrases, followed by four lettered pairs of words or phrases. Select the lettered pair that *best* expresses a relationship similar to that expressed in the original pair.

1. Tony: Play::

   (a) Broadway : Annie
   (b) Oscar : Tom Hanks
   (c) Brandon : Soccer
   (d) Howard Cherry : sports

2. New Growth : Perm ::

   (a) press : straight
   (b) weave : long
   (c) corn row : braid
   (d) nails : fill

3. Ranfal : Lowrider ::

   (a) Ben Davis : shirt
   (b) Mexico : cold
   (c) Mexican : brown
   (d) Cuete : gun

4. *Red Beans and Rice* : Play ::

   (a) corn and tortillas : run
   (b) song : dance
   (c) mozzarella : cheese
   (d) sonata : musical

5. Dancebelt : Boxers ::

   (a) shoes : socks
   (b) student : teacher
   (c) leotard : leg warmers
   (d) prison : freedom

6. Hater : Jealous ::

   (a) love : fighter
   (b) peacemaker : unrest
   (c) gangsta : ruthless
   (d) fighter : chaos

FIGURE 1. *JAT student-constructed test.*

Howard Cherry is awarded for excellence in sports. (2) The "correct" answer is (d). When hair gets "new growth," it needs a perm. When nails get new growth, they need a fill. (3) The "correct" answer is (a). A ranfal is a type of lowrider. Ben Davis is a type of shirt. (4) The correct answer is (c). *Red Beans and Rice* is the name of a play. Mozzarella is a kind of cheese. (5) The "correct" answer is (d). A dancebelt is worn by a male dancer to keep his "privates" in place. Boxers are loose-fitting underwear; thus, the difference between a prison and freedom. (6) The "correct" answer is (c). A hater is a person who is jealous. A gansta is a person who is ruthless.

References

Anzaldúa, G. (1987). How to tame a wild tongue. In *Borderlands/La frontera: The new mestiza* (pp. 53–64). San Francisco: Spinsters/ Aunt Lute.

Burns, O. (1984). *Cold sassy tree.* New York: Dell.

Campbell B. M. (1994). *Brothers and sisters.* New York: Putnam.

Dorfman, A. (1983). *The empire's old clothes: What the Lone Ranger, Babar, and other innocent heroes do to our minds.* New York: Pantheon.

Lyon, G. E. (1996). Where I'm from. In J. Blum, B. Holman, & M. Pellington (Comps.), *The United States of poetry* (p. 24). New York: Abrams.

McCrum, R., Cran, W., & MacNeil, R. (1986). *The story of English.* Chicago: Films Inc. 9 videocassettes (60 min. ea.).

Perry, T., & Delpit, L. (Eds.). (1997). The real Ebonics debate: Power, language, and the education of African-American children. Special issue of *Rethinking Schools, 12* (1).

Owen, D. (1985). *None of the above: Behind the myth of scholastic aptitude.* Boston: Houghton Mifflin.

Rodriguez, R. (1982). *Hunger of memory: The education of Richard Rodriguez.* Boston: Godine.

Shaw, G. B. (1914/1951). *Pygmalion: A play in five acts.* Harmondsworth, England: Penguin.

Shor, I., & Freire, P. (1987). *A pedagogy for liberation: Dialogues on transforming education.* South Hadley, MA: Bergin & Garvey.

Smitherman, G. (1997). *Talkin' and testifyin': The language of black America.* Rpt. ed. Boston: Houghton Mifflin.

Yamanaka, L. (undated). The politics of Pidgin. Promotional material. New York: Farrar, Straus & Giroux.

Yamanaka, L. (1996). *Wild meat and bully burgers.* New York: Farrar, Straus & Giroux.

Weatherford, J. (1991). "Americanization of the English language." In *Native Roots: How the Indians Enriched America* (pp. 195–213). New York: Crown Publishers.

Recommended Sources

Baca, J. S. (1995). So Mexicans are taking jobs from Americans. In J. Daniels (Ed.), *Letters to America: Contemporary American poetry on race* (p. 29). Detroit: Wayne State University Press.

Crawford, J. (1992). *Hold your tongue: Bilingualism and the politics of English only.* Reading, MA: Addison-Wesley.

Dunbar, P. L. (1994). We wear the mask. *In Search of Color Everywhere* (p. 72). New York: Stewart, Tabori, & Chang.

Espada, M. (Ed.). (1994). *Poetry like bread: Poets of the political imagination from Curbstone Press.* Willimantic, CT: Curbstone Press.

Jordan, J. (1988). Nobody mean more to me than you and the future life of Willie Jordan. *Harvard Educational Review, 58*(3), pp. 363–374.

McDaniel, W. E. (1994). Who said we all have to talk alike? In L. King (Ed.), *Hear my voice: A multicultural anthology of literature from the United States* (p. 7). Menlo Park, CA: Addison-Wesley.

Walker, A. (1982). *The color purple.* New York: Washington Square.

CHAPTER ELEVEN

Schooling for Gangs: When School Oppression Contributes to Gang Formations

RAMÓN A. SERRANO
St. Cloud State University

Violence is increasing in the United States. Gangs have contributed to this outbreak of violence which has claimed the lives of many innocent children. As an educator and ex–gang member myself, I believe that blame for this increase in violence and for the growth of gangs cannot be placed solely on society's victims. We educators may point to "family values" and the glorification of violence in the media, but seldom do we look at our own practices as a major contributor to the growth of student gangs. Our expectations, especially toward those who live in low-socioeconomic communities, can help to either challenge the present situation or reproduce it.

Educators' low expectations of lower-class students is a fundamental problem which affects the lives of the very students they have been entrusted to educate. Teachers' low expectations for students extends to students' parents; the parents are also looked upon as not cooperating responsibly in the education of their children. But lower-class parents are indeed concerned with their children's education. According to research conducted by Darder (1991):

> Public education has been the only legitimate hope for escape from poverty for the majority of people of color. Contrary to the prevailing stereotypical notion that parents of color prevent their children from engaging successfully in educational pursuits, many of these parents actively encourage, urge, support, and struggle for their children to get an education. (p. 1)

In this chapter I will *not* be describing any of my actual holistic, critical work with students, teachers, and the community, because that work was blocked by a school district's action and inaction. Instead, I will describe my plan for that holistic, critical educational work on and with gangs. But first, I will describe my own experience as a youth in getting into and out of a gang, followed by my recent observations of the practices in one school that were intended (but failed) to reduce gang activity.

Schooled toward the Path to Gangs

My mother's biggest struggle in life had always been for her children to receive the education she could not have. When she lost her mother at an early age, she was taken out of school and put in charge of raising her brothers and sisters. My father, on the other hand, made it through college, but when he and my mother immigrated to the United States in search of a better life, they were confronted with the harsh realities of racism. While my father was a bright, well-educated man, he soon learned that his biggest problem in finding a job came down to the color of his skin. Unable to find a good job, he found himself working in a factory; he realized that many opportunities in this land of so-called opportunities were only open to a privileged group destined to inherit the skills necessary to succeed in life. Unfortunately, he also found out that his children were not a part of that group and would not receive an education which would help them develop to their full potential.

As a student in the New York public school system, I was always considered a good student. Every school year, as I recall, I would start off in one group and then be transferred to a more advanced group. This may seem like a wonderful thing and it was—until I reached ninth grade. That was the year my problems began. At the school I attended there were several ninth-grade groups ranked from the best to the worst. The higher the group number, the more at-risk you were considered. Students in the higher ninth-grade groups were often called "the losers," and they were treated as such by many teachers and administrators. This tracking process in my school was "heavily mediated by teacher expectations" (Darder 1991, p. 17), expectations which included considerations of students' personal characteristics as well as the social context where the students came from, the teachers' own pedagogical theories (which many times were based on a deficit orientation), and teachers' personal understandings and experiences with community building (Darder, 1991).

I started my ninth-grade experience in group 9-5; after being there a couple of months I was transferred to 9-2, a "better" group. I was never told why, but I can remember that my first day of class was a nightmare. I was told by my teacher that on Monday I was to report to the counselor's office and that he would escort me to my new classroom. That Monday morning I reported to his office and was escorted to what was supposed to be my new classroom, but in reality it turned out to be my own living hell. I can still remember with pain when the first thing that happened was that an argument broke out between my new teacher and my counselor. It began because my new teacher could not accept that a Puerto Rican would be placed in his classroom. He argued that someone must have made a mistake because the "Puerto Ricans in this school [do] not have the brains it [takes] to be placed so far ahead." In my defense, my counselor replied that "maybe he is different and we should give him a chance." Here we see two examples of the deficit orientation at work—tracking by skin color and ethnicity, and explaining "exceptions." This deficit orientation not only produces such practices, it also leads to a pedagogy of exclusion that limits and silences the voices of students (Macedo, 1994).

After a couple of minutes my new teacher agreed to the situation and told me where to sit. He *did* give me a chance, but the chance he gave me was more of a punishment than an opportunity to prove myself. That day (remember, it was still my first day), he asked me to solve a math problem on the board. I was unable to solve it because I really did not understand the problem and told him so. After I told him I did not know the answer, he looked at me, and then turned to the class and said, "It looks like someone did not eat their Goya beans this morning" (Goya is a brand name which is very popular among Puerto Ricans in New York). With this comment the class (which happened to be all

Anglos) began to laugh. I felt really bad and just went to my seat and looked at him, wishing he would drop dead on the spot. This episode was the start of two weeks of anguish which ended with me throwing a chair at him and then being suspended for two weeks. What caused me to go to such an extreme was that during a confrontation in which he called me stupid, I replied that I knew two languages and he only knew one. At that point he turned and made a remark about my mother, which in my culture is something you do not do unless you are willing to accept the possibility of physical violence occurring. Upon hearing this I was so enraged that I picked up a chair and tossed it in his direction. I guess this was the opportunity he had been waiting for, and I handed it to him on a silver platter.

My parents never found out about this situation because I was able to intercept the mail and keep it from them. Meanwhile, during my suspension I hung out in the hallways of the school. This is where I had my first encounter with members of a local gang. I talked to some of the people I met about what had happened. In their view I had done the right thing because the teacher should never have said anything about my mother. As I talked about my own actions in rejecting the teacher's authority and the "decorum" of the classroom, I gained acceptance into a culture that would later embrace me as one of their own. I felt like one of them because I was treated like one of them. During my two-week suspension I learned ways of getting in and out of the school building without ever getting caught. It was a fascinating time. What I learned from the people I met made me feel important and superior to other students. It was a new sense of power and control which I had never before experienced.

When my two-week suspension was up, I reported to the office and waited until someone came for me. I remember thinking it would be good to get back into my old classroom where I knew everyone and everyone knew me. After sitting there for a while I was called into the assistant principal's office, where he lectured me for about twenty minutes. He then got up and told me to follow him to class. We started down the hall. Once we were in front of the stairs, I was surprised that instead of going up to the second floor, we actually headed down to the basement classrooms. I told him that my classroom was upstairs, hoping he had been mistaken, but he looked at me and said that my new classroom was downstairs. We finally arrived and I met my new teacher. He had a sort of noncaring look; later, I found out he really did not care about teaching us. I sat down, looked around, and found that many of the faces surrounding me were familiar; they were my friends from the halls.

I adapted quickly to the environment of the class. My new friends were teaching me the ropes and assuring me that the teacher did not care if we were there or not. One of the first things I can remember was my friends' disrespect toward their teachers. During one conversation, I remember asking a friend why nobody cared about what happened in class. He told me that "no one cared because we are considered kind of crazy and hopeless" and that the only teachers who were there were the ones who "sucked and did not give a damn about us." I later found this to be true. The teachers who taught us were the worst in the school; they just lectured and never allowed us to ask the questions that we felt were important. The most common answer I remember receiving was "that's the way it is." Our classes were usually boring and full of disruptions. Clearly, we were there to listen and not ask questions, especially questions which were meaningful to our lives. When we asked questions about issues like sex, drugs, and injustice, the answers were always reduced to simple-minded clichés. In other words, we were being schooled to become semiliterate in the sense that while we could read the words around us, we were not taught to read the world (Macedo, 1994). We weren't helped to make connections between what was presented in our textbooks and the social and political realities in which we lived.

We were experiencing a situation similar to that found in a study on silencing by Michelle Fine (1987). Fine refers to silencing as a process in which schools avoid discussions that name tensions relevant to students' lives. One example of silencing, or what Fine refers to as "not naming," happened frequently in my school, especially when problems between gangs surfaced. Teachers never wanted to discuss these problems because they felt that it would make things worse. It was as if they felt that if they ignored the problems, they would go away. In reality, however, the problem was not *discussing* gangs; it was *not* discussing that made it worse.

As time continued, I began to lose interest in class and became more disruptive. I was fulfilling the expectation of my teachers without realizing I was falling into a vicious cycle that would make it hard for me to succeed. The more negative feelings I perceived from my teachers, the more disruptive I became. I then began to hang around more gang members until I was finally invited to become part of one. It was here that I finally felt like someone and wanted everyone (except for my parents) to know who and what I was. During this time I basically lived a double life. Away from school I acted differently, but in school I became increasingly disruptive, getting into more trouble and more fights. The only thing I had in my favor was that I always managed to do well on tests—tests which were developed by our teachers, who had such low expectations for us that the tests were so simple they were a joke.

The following year, things got worse. When I first read Jonathan Kozol's (1991) *Savage Inequalities,* I felt as if he were describing the high school I went to. The lack of space, the lack of commitment, and the lack of consideration he described brought back painful memories of my high school years. Throughout high school I continued to get involved in gang activities, but as hard as I tried to change, the environment I was in would not allow me to make changes in my life. I was at a point where I felt that my own sense of power and possibilities was sliding downward; I knew that I had to do something to change this, but the harder I tried, the harder it became. There were several occasions when I attempted to go to class, only to be met by my teachers' refusal to accept that I was there to participate. In their eyes I was already labeled as a "troublemaker" who was there to disrupt the class and make life miserable for them. This refusal to accept me as a changed person frustrated me and helped push me deeper into a world that seemed hopeless and full of violence. On other occasions my attempts to change were met by peer pressure which reminded me that I was one of them and that the school administration had it in for me. My friends made it clear, by using the examples of my previous attempts to change, that my word would not be trusted and I would always be seen as a loser and a troublemaker. Because of my failure to change, I found myself no longer contemplating going to college; I figured I'd just finish up and go to work in a factory somewhere. What made matters worse was a conversation I had with one of the school counselors, in which she told me that my best alternative was to learn a trade like repairing cars. According to her, there were a lot of Puerto Ricans who were very good mechanics because "it runs in your blood."

Throughout my high school experience, there was only one teacher who made a difference. He was young, from the ghettos, and not well liked by some of the senior teachers. He was a teacher who talked with us, not just to us. He was open to having discussions and shared many of his personal experiences, which happened to be very similar to ours. He pushed us hard and was not afraid of "telling it as it is." He got me to begin questioning my actions and involvement with gangs, and I finally began to see some hope. The first thing I had to decide was whether it was worth being in a gang and how I was going to get out.

Taking the Path to Freedom

One day the opportunity arrived, and I immediately took advantage of it. My parents had been talking about returning to Puerto Rico in about a year, and I saw this as an opportunity to change my life completely. My sister and her husband had left first, to buy a piece of land in Puerto Rico and build a house. I managed to convince my parents that I should be sent ahead because I could stay with my sister, finish my last year of high school there, and learn how to read and write Spanish.

Going to school in Puerto Rico was a real cultural shock for me. The first big difference was the attitudes of my new peers. In New York, all we talked about was graduating and getting a job, but in Puerto Rico, all I heard were my peers talking about graduating and going on to college. At first, this was a real shock; over time, though, I began to embrace that goal myself and found myself working hard on learning to read and write Spanish so that I could join many of my new peers in their dreams of a better life.

During that last year in high school, my attitude toward school changed completely. I credit this change to my teachers and the way they taught. They were open and had us participating in a lot of discussions. They addressed our questions, and they were not afraid of naming things as they were. They also helped me personally by being willing to listen to my stories and to talk about them with me. They would take time from their lunch hour to sit down and help me with my Spanish, which helped change my perceptions of teachers. The caring environment the teachers in Puerto Rico provided was very different from the environment I had experienced in New York. It was there in Puerto Rico that I finally began to see hope again and the opportunity to become someone. It was there that I discovered that I had always had the potential to get to where I am today and to help others see that they also have the potential to succeed in life.

Sharing My Experiences to Help Others

As I look back on my life, I think about how many of my peers in New York really could have been able to make it. We all had something in common back then and that was that schooling was not preparing us to live a productive life. Today I work preparing future teachers at a medium-size university in the Midwest. The town I work and live in has just over 58,000 residents. Being close to a large city, our town now has gangs that have filtered in, causing concern for those who are willing to see it. During the past year and a half, groups of youths have begun to get together as gang "wannabes." They are not yet causing great problems, but the potential for trouble is there. If the community and school administration do not address these problems immediately, I fear things will get worse. An important part of addressing these problems will be to do two things: (1) call on those like myself who "escaped" gang membership and succeeded, and (2) put aside an attitude common in school bureaucracies that administrators with no special training and no firsthand knowledge of gangs will know how to handle these problems themselves.

During the 1996–97 school year, I received a call from one of my colleagues, asking me to attend a meeting between school officials and a couple of gang members who had gotten into a fight at the high school. I said I would be happy to attend and reported the following day to the district offices. There, members of both gangs, one a totally Asian group and the other group composed of a few Latinos, African Americans, and Anglos, were seated across from one another. The meeting began. Members from each gang were interviewed separately in a conference room. I sat in on one of the interviews. The conference room was very intimidating. In the middle of the room, there were a microphone and a videorecorder pointed right at the student. During the general meeting and the interviews, the administrators talked to the youths as if they were in first grade. There was no dialogue whatsoever with them. The administrators were asking these gang members to promise that they would never fight again. Of course, in that intimidating and dehumanizing setting, the youths agreed. The peace lasted for about a week, and then they were back fighting again.

After this meeting, the administrators asked me if I had any suggestions and if I was pleased with how they had handled the situation. I explained that I felt very uncomfortable with the whole procedure and that I felt that nothing was really accomplished. I explained that just talking at these youths was not going to resolve anything because they needed to be heard and heard by someone with credibility, someone who had been in their shoes.

It was at this point that I offered to help, an offer that was never accepted because, as I heard and surmised, the administrators thought they knew how to handle these problems. My offer was that if they were interested, I could put together a discussion panel consisting of a few of my colleagues and students who were ex-gang members, and we would work with the situation. The administrators' response was positive on the surface. However, the entire school year went by, and I never heard another word from them. Meanwhile, the gang situation has continued to grow.

During a conversation I had with some of the members of both gangs a couple of weeks after the meeting at the school, I learned that not very much had changed from when I was in school. These students expressed some of what I felt when I was their age. Some of the issues they brought up were that they were always treated like little kids, that they were excluded from a lot of school activities, and that teachers never wanted to listen to what they had to say. They also felt that when they had something to say about what was being taught, they were often cut out of the discussion because they were talking about personal experiences or opinions and not about facts. This was especially a concern of the Asian gang members. One of them explained how he was asked to leave the room because his views on the Vietnam War were different than those presented in class. This type of censorship is what Macedo (1994) refers to as the "stupidification process," by which big lies are produced on the basis of misrepresentation and the withholding of historical truths. Our conversation continued, and the more we talked, the more these students opened up. It was as if they were venting all their anger with the situation at school.

I asked them what led them to form or join gangs in the first place. Their response was interesting; they indicated that at first they just hung around together because they felt comfortable with each other. Shortly after that their peers, teachers, and administrators began calling them a "gang." Since they were getting blamed for things that they didn't do and for an organization that they didn't really have, they decided to form a real gang so that they could protect each other. Some of the minority gang members who were present also felt that they were treated unfairly by teachers; they felt that they were looked down upon and even treated as if they were idiots. I also asked about classroom conditions in general. The students all indicated that school "sucked," that it was boring, and that they could not wait to get out and go somewhere else. They named a couple of teachers who, in their view, were considered "cool" because they treated the gang members/wannabes well and made their classes interesting. They also indicated that the only teachers who would listen to them were the "cool" ones.

During our discussion I noticed that members of both "opposing" gangs agreed on a lot of the issues we were talking about. Contrary to what had happened weeks ago, there was no pointing of fingers or blaming of each other. It was an open dialogue in which they demonstrated that they could talk to each other with respect. This open dialogue would have been a good start had the school taken me up on my offer.

Schooling for Inclusion and Responsibility

After my dialogues with these students, I sat down and began to develop a plan that would help the school become more inclusive and at the same time help these youths regain their voices. Unfortunately, my plan was never implemented, and the school never contacted me again. I have been led to believe that the administrators felt they were in control of the situation furthermore, and that they were not interested in pursuing an offer from a former gang member. My plan of intervention was to help members of both gangs critically examine what they were doing and how they were falling into the trap of playing out other people's expectations. Although it was never implemented, I present it here as a possibility for critically and holistically engaging students, teachers, university personnel, and the wider community.

The intervention plan consisted of seven "projects" which focused on community, student, and teacher involvement. These were: a discussion panel to explore existing problems in the school; community involvement activities; a guest-speaker forum; a mediation council; a support group; a film-critique club; and finally, teacher workshops. The main purpose of this plan was to get everyone involved at some level, while giving students who were directly affected a level of ownership that would permit them to be active participants in resolving problems.

Discussion Panel

The members of this panel would be my colleagues and students from the university who at one point were gang members. It is crucial that those who have "been there" would play this major "consultant" role. The function of the discussion panel would be to help open a dialogue, explore what students felt about their situation, and, crucially, allow students to see that they could change and succeed outside a gang. The discussion panel would also give students the opportunity to ask questions and listen to the different stories members of the panel would share with them. My plan was to make this a sort of retreat in which we would spend a half day or possibly a full day talking with students.

Community Involvement

At a later stage, with help from the community, we would have had students get involved in community activities. These activities could include helping in shelters, at school, or working with different organizations in the community. The goal here would be not only to get students involved with the community, but also to get the community involved with them, including employing some of the youths.

Guest-Speaker Forum

I have started a guest-speaker forum in my university. This forum is known as the Institute of Critical Pedagogy and Children's Rights. The objective of this institute is to develop a forum that will serve the university, the community, and other higher education institutions in the area. The institute has presented national speakers addressing issues that affect critical pedagogy and children's rights and the representations/misrepresentations found in the media and popular films. The issues presented and discussed are aimed at enticing the general public and students to attend and participate in the institute. Within the plan, the focus would have been to interest gang members in attending activities of the institute and to help them form a branch institute at their own school. Some of the local speakers presenting in the institute would have included people from different social organizations, ex-gang members, convicts from the prison, and potential employers from the community.

Mediation Council

This council would have been composed of students, faculty, and members of the community. At first, the sponsor would have been The Institute of Critical Pedagogy and Children's Rights. The reason for this would be to convince students that the mediation council was not just another school-sponsored program to keep them quiet. Community members and teachers would have been included because there are individuals in these categories who are truly concerned with the problems of these youths but who do not have a forum in which to work with them. This council would have provided the forum needed without causing the distrust a school-sponsored program would have elicited. The aim would have been to help the mediation council become a self-governing body sponsored by different youth organizations. Members of the council would have been able to examine and address issues of concern to all. It would have been a forum in which students could have vented problems affecting the school or their own community.

The members of the council would also have been elected by student members who, presumably, would select people who they felt would understand their problems and work toward developing real solutions. Council meetings would have taken place at a neutral location such as a community center, city council meeting facilities, or other public meeting sites.

Support Group

A support group would have been developed similar to other groups such as Alcoholics Anonymous and Narcotics Anonymous. Its purpose would have been to support students as they try to change their lives. This would have been a group in which students could share what was going on in their lives with others who understood their problems. The support group could have also helped students discuss problems such as drugs, alcohol abuse, and teen pregnancy. It would have provided a setting in which students could share and seek support from other peers who had experienced the same problems.

Film-Critique Club

This club would have been developed to allow students to view and critique popular films and the ways in which they (mis)represent youth. The club format would have given students an opportunity to discuss stereotypes, racism, sexism, and the glorification of negative behaviors in the media. Along with their own critiques, students would also have read critiques by other view-ers and writers. Films such as *Pulp Fiction, Kids,* and *Born to Kill* are just a few of the films that would have been discussed from a critical perspective. These discussions would have allowed stu-dents to see the injustice that the media can do to different social groups and how these (mis)representations have affected their own lives because of who they are and where they come from.

Initially, the film club would have been sponsored by the Institute of Critical Pedagogy and Children's Rights. Here stu-dents would have had a space where they could speak freely about what they are seeing in the media about themselves. The rationale for the institute sponsoring this club in its beginning stages is to ensure that critiques would be from a critical perspec-tive. Currently, the school sponsors a film club but its activities are limited to rating movies (one star to four). This form of "cri-tiquing" does not engage students in a critical process in which they are able to share personal experiences, but rather, limits and silences stories that can rupture the (mis)representations seen in films. I also wanted to invite teachers who would be willing to participate in this club and to help them, along with their stu-dents, to discuss more than just whether a film is good or bad; to help them examine the content for issues that stereotype and (mis)represent the realities of our daily lives.

Teacher Workshops

With the help of my colleagues, I was planning to deliver a series of workshops to help teachers understand the importance of showing that they care about their students and of exploring signs of caring and not caring. The workshops would have also helped teachers to understand the importance of students' voices in the learning process. Such tools as the inquiry process, the writing process, live social studies projects, and so forth would have been presented so that teachers could see the benefits of using these instead of relying solely on textbooks.

We would have also worked with teachers on issues of cen-sorship. As I said earlier, some of the Vietnamese students had a different perception of the Vietnam War, but were never allowed to share that view. My daughter had a similar experience. She has a nonmainstream take on the relationship between Puerto Rico and the United States, but she has not been allowed to share it in class. Within the workshops we would have stressed the importance of becoming more open-minded, and rather than censoring something because it is not in the text or does not represent a popular view, we would have worked on how to take it up from a critical perspective. By "critical perspective," I am referring to going beyond what is written, allowing questions and personal experience to surface, and finding and trying to investigate contradictions. In other words, students would have been allowed and encouraged to become investigative reporters, using the inquiry process as a purposeful tool in finding the truth. This is what Freire and Macedo (1987) refer to as "reading the word and the world." In general, the workshops would have been offered to help teachers rather than to tell them what to do. Follow-up and support would have been one of the primary goals of these workshops.

Conclusion

Whether in the future I will be able to put this plan into effect in my community or elsewhere will depend on the willingness of a school district to receive help from someone who has "been there and done that." The issue is plain and simple—either we critically examine our own practices or we will continue to reproduce injustice again and again. It is time for educators to stop blaming the victims and to ask ourselves how we have contributed to the formations of gangs. We need to ask questions such as "What makes some teachers 'cool'?" And "What are some teachers doing that makes a real difference in the lives of students?"

The answer to eliminating a school's contribution to increasing gang membership may be simple: We need to care about and respect our students, their families, and their lives. Then again, it may be very hard: We need to turn to those whom we haven't usually respected in the past—gang members and former gang members—for expertise in just how to carry out such a humane agenda.

References

Darder, A. (1991). *Culture and power in the classroom: A critical foundation for bicultural education.* New York: Bergin & Garvey.

Fine, M. (1987). Silencing in public schools. *Language Arts, 64*(2), 157–174.

Freire, P., & Macedo, D. (1987). *Literacy: Reading the word and the world.* South Hadley, MA: Bergin & Garvey.

Kozol, J. (1991). *Savage inequalities: Children in America's schools.* New York: Crown.

Macedo, D. (1994). *Literacies of power: What Americans are not allowed to know.* Boulder, CO: Westview Press.

CHAPTER TWELVE

Probing the Invisible Life of Schools

BILL BIGELOW

Franklin High School, Portland, Oregon

B ecause students are rarely invited to reflect critically on their own schooling, they are taught to accept inequality as normal. Textbooks and school curricula fail to encourage students to ask an assortment of critical questions: Which social groups pushed for the particular kinds of schools that we take for granted today, and why? How does ethnic background, race, class, or gender contribute to the character of the schooling one receives? Who benefits from "ability grouping" and the myriad special programs in school districts? What are the mechanisms by which students are classified and sorted? How do students resist school's regimentation, and how effective is that resistance? When have students banded together to reflect on the character of their schooling and to work for greater equity?

These and other critical questions may be taken up in the occasional sociology class, but most students will never be encouraged to consider them. According to a recently published critique of high school U.S. history texts, none of the books reviewed prompts students to think critically about the history or politics of education (Loewen, 1995). What underlying lesson do students learn when they leave high school after thirteen years of schooling without ever being asked to question the institution within which they've spent so many thousands of hours? Probably that their role in society is to perform the work they're assigned, within the context it's assigned, and not to wonder whether any of this is right or fair or worthwhile. Inequity grows nicely in this soil of suppressed doubt, of unasked questions.

Several years ago my partner, Linda Christensen, and I began teaching a unit on the history and sociology of schooling. We stumbled into it. A friend of ours, Michele Miller, asked if she could bring her classes, from a more privileged suburban school south of Portland, to Jefferson High School, located in a working class, predominantly African American neighborhood. In exchange, Michele offered to host our students. We accepted her offer and decided to make the trip to the school in the wealthier community a centerpiece of a larger inquiry on the nature of public schooling. Over the years, we've added and subtracted pieces of this curriculum, but it has remained a vital component of the history and literature courses we've taught both together and separately. We've described several of these lessons in other articles (Bigelow, 1990; Bigelow, 1994b; Christensen, 1989), but I offer here an overview of a number of the activities in the unit. It is a high school class, but our approach could be adapted to lower grades. What follows is a sketch of the unit.

The Hidden Curriculum

We introduce the concept of a "hidden curriculum"—the values, habits, and beliefs that are imparted to students through the way schools are structured and through the routines of school life (see Giroux, 1983, Chapter 2 for an extended discussion of the "hidden curriculum"). The Chilean writer Ariel Dorfman (1983) uses the term "secret education" to describe the deep but unacknowledged messages in children's literature; it is also a useful expression for describing the beneath-the-surface totality of school life. With students, we brainstorm aspects of the explicit and hidden curricula at Jefferson, and analyze the "secret education" in one classroom described in the first few pages of David Storey's novel *Radcliffe* (1963).

The excerpt we use describes a teacher who singles out a working-class student for humiliation as she tries to elicit "correct" answers about why buildings are constructed with slanted roofs and tall chimneys—"Just you stand there a moment, *Vic*, and let me see you paying attention and listening" (Storey, 1963, p. 12). The other youngsters in class sit passively as the teacher uses Victor to show the unpleasant consequences of failing to answer her questions satisfactorily. As we introduce the piece, we ask our students to consider what the nine-year-olds in the class are learning, not about roofs and chimneys, but about authority and power, where knowledge comes from and what constitutes valuable knowledge, decision making, resistance and solidarity—people's capacity to stand up for one another. Before we discuss the reading, we ask students to write an interior monologue—the inner thoughts—of one of the characters in the story; or to imagine that they are nine-year-olds in the classroom described, and to write from their own, imagined points of view; or to write as if they are immigrant children whose first language is not English.

Jennifer, a student who dropped in and out of school throughout the year, wrote hers as a dialogue between Victor and his mother. She portrays a Victor both compliant and critical:

> "So son, what did you do at school today?"
> He thought, I was separated from the others, humiliated. I wanted to stand up for myself but couldn't. Why didn't anyone else help me? Why do teachers always have to be like this? I'll try my best, maybe I'll try more. I'm not good for anything but to listen to another. I just don't want to get in trouble.
> "Mom, I did my work, and had a good day at school."

Afterward, as students read aloud these thought portraits, the patterns of deep learning in the classroom begin to emerge. Before we discuss these, we ask students to take a few minutes to write a summary of what they see as the "secret education" occurring in this class. This may sound like write-this, write-that teaching, but I've found that asking students to collect thoughts on paper prior to talking about a topic democratizes discussion—not all students are equally glib and able to call out thoughts the moment a question is asked.

I am always amazed at the diversity of student response when we begin to ask the class to think deeply about processes of schooling. Some students tend to focus on the powerlessness of the nine-year-olds in the *Radcliffe* class, others on the competition between students promoted by the teacher. Forest's "secret education" summary blended his long experience as a student with his interpretation of the classroom dynamics described in the short reading; it was simultaneously pithy and extensive:

Hidden Curriculum

Never question

Plot against or compete with your peers

Resistance is futile

Hate authority, but always fear it

Knowledge comes naturally

Some people will always be better than you

Tonia wrote that "The students learn to keep their feelings to themselves. They learn to live with their fears." And in response to my asking what students *weren't* learning in this classroom, she wrote that the students are "learning to not stand up for themselves. These students are also learning to not stick together as a big group and solve problems." I wanted my students to see "not learning" as a verb—that curriculum can be both a presence and an absence, and what is *not* taught can be as significant as what *is* taught.

Experiences of Inequality

Sometimes we follow these initial discussions of the hidden curriculum by asking students to think of instances in their school lives when they experienced inequality or unfairness—either as victim or beneficiary—and to write these up as first-person narratives. Other times, we've asked students to write about positive learning experiences, either in or out of school. These stories contribute to a yearlong "grassroots literature," as Ira Shor and Paulo Freire (1987) propose, that allows students to know and appreciate each other's experiences. We ask them to share their writings in read-arounds—Linda and I write and share as well— and to listen for patterns that recur throughout the stories, to read the "collective text" of the class.

One year, before the inequality read-around, we asked students to listen for what the hidden curriculum taught about authority, decision making, equality, and making change. Daniel, then an eleventh grader, marched down the list:

Schools teach children to bow down to authority and that no matter what, all authority is correct and you must listen to them. . . . Schools teach kids that the kids can't make decisions in the world, that all the decisions are made for them in what they learn and how to act. . .The schools teach children that no one is equal to another, that there is always someone who is better than you, no matter what you do to change that. . . . Schools teach kids that they can't make any change . . . any changes that are made will be by the teacher and only the person in authority; you don't have a say.

A pretty grim picture, but an accurate and astute reading of the collective text created by the class members. (By the way, although Forest and Daniel arrived at similar insights, they were students during different years.)

Explaining Discouraging Realities

One might argue that to unearth and to publicly acknowledge this cynicism also reinforces it. This is a potential hazard of any classroom examination of injustice. It is important to nudge students beyond description to attempt to *explain* the discouraging realities they uncover. Who decided that the school day would be regimented by bells? Who decided that students would be slotted into "advanced" and "remedial" classes? Who decided how power would be distributed among the different members of a school community? And more important: Why? Strategies (and hope) for change can come only from careful diagnosis of the problems.

Through role-playing, we engage students in probing the social realities of the early twentieth century that led schools to adopt standardized testing, tracking, and a civics/history curriculum of flag-waving indoctrination (Bigelow, 1994b). Students portray Hungarian immigrants, corporate executives, members of the middle class, black activists, and Industrial Workers of the World organizers and respond to an energetic superintendent committed to bringing the typical Northern "Central City" into the modern world. For example, he proposes administering intelligence tests to "scientifically" sort students into four tracks: feeble-minded, dull, average, and superior—categories suggested by an influential educator of the time. In their roles, students examine an actual test developed by Stanford University in 1920 to measure students' scholastic aptitudes. "Sirloin is a cut of: beef, mutton, pork, veal," asks one question. Exactly what kind of intelligence is measured by a question like that? The role-playing exposes students to the underlying politics of early-twentieth-century school reform. In the face of huge enrollment increases, especially of immigrants and working-class children, schools were engineered to reproduce social class hierarchies—not to further social equality, but to guard against it. Compulsory mass education gave an appearance of equal opportunity, but there was nothing equal about the education encountered by different groups of students in stratified tracks.

We also look at a typical teacher's contract from 1923 (Apple, 1988), which regulates every inch of a female teacher's life. For example, the contract enjoins an instructor "not to loiter downtown in ice cream stores," and requires her "to wear at least two petticoats," and "not to wear dresses more than two inches above the ankles" (pp. 73–74). This was part of an ethos of decorum and regimentation, but it is also worth considering the impact of gender on the "scientific" sorting of students. Could it be that the virtually all-male school hierarchy could not trust women teachers to adequately slot students into the appropriate feeble-minded, dull, average, and superior tracks? As the century wore on, fewer and fewer males could be found in the classroom. What impact did this feminization of the educational workforce have on school structure? How was it connected to decades of low teacher salaries?

Testing as a Sorting Mechanism

We also probe the role of testing as a sorting mechanism of students and as an allocator—and justifier—of unequal distribution of educational resources. An excerpt from Chapter 9, "The Cult of Mental Measurement," in David Owens's *None of the Above* (1985) is a bit difficult, but it prompts students to think critically about the meritocratic rationale of the first Scholastic Aptitude Tests, and provides some startling background about the individuals who developed them. For example, Carl Campbell Brigham, father of the SAT, was a passionate racist who worried about an "alarming" increase in people of mixed race, and called for an end to the "infiltration of white blood into the Negro." He once published an article in *Eugenical News,* a journal that later reprinted Adolf Hitler's "Text of the German Sterilization Statute."

In a "talk back" journal, students select quotes to respond to from the article in Owen's book. Sekou chose the following:

> In a nation without dukes or princes, "native capacity" provided the basis for a sort of alternative aristocracy. Intelligence tests gave the nation's privileged a scientific sounding justification for the advantages they enjoyed. The wealthy lived in nice houses because they were smart; the poor were hungry because they were stupid. American society was just after all. (Owen, 1985, p. 180)

Sekou responded:

> This quote jumped out at me, not only because of its content, but because of the fact that, although it's written in the past tense, if you were to go through and change it to be in the present tense, it could be readily applied to today's society. When written out like this, people tend to consciously object to it. But unconsciously, I think people tend to accept it as the way of life. . . .

Linda and I administer parts of a contemporary SAT test to students, both to build their skills in taking tests like these, but also to critique the tests' legitimacy. Some of the items resemble the 1920 sirloin question on the Stanford test: "Heirloom is to inheritance as . . ." and "oarsman is to regatta as. . . ." Whose knowledge is this? What does answering these questions correctly have to do with succeeding in college? How can we account for SAT scores correlating more closely with family income than with future success in college?

Connecting to Students' Lives

Throughout the unit we want to weave together history, contemporary society, and students' lives. We ask people in class to recall a personal test-taking experience and to write it up as a

story. Feelings about tests are often close to the surface for students, and they rarely have difficulty thinking of something to
write about. Again, after the read-around we ask people to analyze the "collective text" they've created. Cam wrote: "Tests
seem to just stack ourselves against others. 'How do I measure
up?' 'They're smarter than me!' You feel low or high, insecure or
too secure, not confident or too much confidence. . . . Sometimes
people just feel completely worthless and empty . . ." Tara noted
that "it seemed as if just because someone told us we were
dumb, we became dumb." Kimberly wrote that "The test made
me feel as if I wasn't as smart as I thought I was. . . . [T]hese tests
are designed to make people feel bad about themselves." And
Christine, a student who had spent much of her school life in
low tracks, noticed that students in class had never thought critically about the psychological effects of the tests themselves: "No
one really thought of the test and what its powers are."

We had shared with students a 1920 survey (Chapman,
1988, p. 126) indicating that young people's expectations were
simply too high; the economy of the time offered mostly farm
labor and industrial jobs, but almost all students wanted professional and creative jobs. According to William Proctor, author of
the study, tests and proper guidance counseling would lower students' employment aspirations: "For their own best good and the
best good of the nation a great many of them should be directed
toward the agricultural, mechanical, and industrial fields" (p.
126). This quote frames students' diminished sense of self as an
intended and necessary attitude adjustment—an adjustment
required by the economy's incapacity to provide creative, fulfilling jobs for all its citizens.

Considering Class

Comparing the curriculum at Jefferson—both hidden and
explicit—with those at schools serving different social populations is an important part of the unit. Some years we've read
excerpts from an article by Jean Anyon (1980). For example,
Anyon found that in schools serving predominantly working-class
communities, "work" means following the steps of a procedure

and "rules" are steps to follow. However, in "affluent professional" schools, "work" means creative activity carried out independently. Students from affluent homes are continually asked to express and apply ideas and concepts.

We ask students to keep a log of the "hidden curricula" in their classes. Which of the schools described by Anyon best correspond to Jefferson? We are careful to emphasize that we do not want students to use the names of specific teachers; this is not a "let's rag on Mr. or Ms. So-and-so" assignment. And we also ask students to analyze our own class; inevitably all classes impart lessons that teachers are unaware of. And students consistently make incisive, sometimes troubling, observations about our class. In preparation for their research, we discuss the kinds of things they should look for that might indicate something important about the hidden curricula of their classes. Here are some questions we've raised during past years: How are the desks arranged? Who does most of the talking? How are students made to feel either important or unimportant? What kinds of questions are asked: thought and analysis questions or memory questions? Do students seem to be encouraged to think critically or to accept school and society as they are? Is most of the work individual or group? Do some classrooms appear to have better equipment or facilities than other classrooms? How can we account for this? What ways do you see students resisting (e.g., skipping class, talking, being rude, not paying attention)? Some students make classroom maps, others tell stories, or some jot quotes from various class sessions.

Monique noted the ways in which she was made to feel important and unimportant during one week at Jefferson:

Unimportant

1. By telling us that they have already received their diploma and that we have ours to get.
2. "Shut up."
3. Saying you should have learned this years ago.
4. "I shouldn't have to go over the same thing more than twice for this group."
5. "You need me more than I need you, so listen up."
6. "Pay attention or don't come back into this classroom."

7. "Don't make me write a referral."
8. "I'm busy right now. I'll get to you in a minute."

Important

1. When they encourage students to speak out in class.
2. Help students for a long time, one on one.
3. When they are understanding about other pressing obligations concerning schoolwork.
4. When they submit a student's name for an award.
5. When they put a professional, businesslike attitude back into their pockets.

For some students, this assignment uncovers great bitterness and raises difficult ethical questions for us as teachers. J. wrote:

In sixth period my teacher again plays favorites. He sometimes follows girls, especially good looking ones. . . . You may get a better grade if you shake your butt in front of the teacher, or say or do something to stroke his ego. Many of the females who realize that he is overly friendly and that this may affect their grade positively accept this. And thus are accepting the whole connotation that women are sex objects and it is fine to use this to our advantage. We don't have to use any of our intellect when we can use our bodies. This is where the sick ideas of society today are introduced.

Once we encourage students to examine their own school lives through a critical lens of justice, it is hard to predict where it will lead. What is our responsibility as teachers when we receive a paper like this? A vital aspect of the unit, which I'll touch on in a moment, is to prompt students themselves to ask: What is to be done?

This student detective work on the school's hidden curriculum obviously does not need to be limited to teacher behaviors. Students can engage in a broader "equity check" of the school: Is there tracking? What kinds of assessments are used to place people? Do the ethnic backgrounds of the teachers match those of the students? Which classes or programs get the best equipment? Do some programs have special privileges, like more field trips, *how about the social curriculum?*

or smaller class sizes? One year, my ninth graders surveyed students on their attitudes about justice in the school.

Firsthand Comparisons of Schools in Richer and Poorer Communities

Nonetheless the theoretical proposition in Jean Anyon's article still lingers: Does the nature of the curriculum at Jefferson have something to do with the social class of the community that the school serves? We travel to the wealthier suburb—let's call it Oakwood—to test this out for ourselves. Students carry with them the same questions (listed above) that they used to analyze the hidden curriculum at Jefferson. Over the years, we have traveled to several different "Oakwoods," but wherever we go students are consistently astonished by the numerous differences between these more elite schools and Jefferson. About Oakwood, Nicole wrote:

> The school smelled clean. That was the first impression it made on me and several other people standing by me. . . . The desks being arranged in their sterile rows seemed to reinforce the idea that the student's mind is a clean chalkboard that needs to be filled with information. . . . Overall, I liked the quieter bells, bigger lockers, and better equipment. I also though got the impression from the hidden curriculum and attitudes of the kids that they knew they are and will become the "beautiful" people of our generation.

It was hard not to notice the quieter bells. The bells at Jeff are the loudest of any school I've ever been in. Their volume seems to underscore a hoped-for order and discipline—and have surely damaged my ears at least as much as Grateful Dead concerts.

In preparation for discussion after our return from Oakwood, we asked students to write two summary paragraphs that might begin: "At Oakwood, students are being trained for . . ." and "At Jefferson, students are being trained for . . ." Dyan wrote:

> At [Oakwood], the students are being prepared to be bosses and in positions of high pay. This was seen in the way they

regarded the rules. . . . For instance, a student walked in a little late and he was not penalized at all—in fact, the teacher
didn't even look at him. Also students would leave their classrooms to retrieve a book from their locker and wouldn't take
a pass. Simple rules, but complex messages. By not being
penalized, the administrators and staff were saying, "It's your
life, your responsibility. One day you'll be the head of a corporation— we're getting you prepared for that now."

At Jefferson, the hidden curriculum is different. We're
learning to give way to authority and *be* bossed rather than be
a boss. This is demonstrated by our tardy policy, required hall
passes, and again classroom structure. Quantity not quality is
important for many teachers here. Ditto after ditto is passed
out in hopes that by repetition and rote memorization we'll be
able to take our place in the "working world" efficiently.

I tend to think that Dyan was overly harsh on Jefferson, and
perhaps too influenced by the lack of ambiguity and nuance in
Jean Anyon's analysis. It has always seemed to me that for a variety of reasons, Jefferson is a good deal more contradictory than
Dyan indicated. On the other hand, I've never been a student
there; she has.

Class and Race

Last year, Linda and I used the powerful poem "Two Women"
(in Bigelow et al., 1994, pp. 112–113) as a prompt for students
to write about the sharp class and race differences they perceived
between Oakwood and Jefferson. It is a dialogue poem between
two Chilean women—one wealthy, one working-class—who
experience life very differently:

> I am a woman whose man wore silk suits,
> who constantly watched his weight.
>
> *I am a woman whose man wore tattered
> clothing, whose heart was constantly
> strangled by hunger.*

The back-and-forth structure of the poem allows students a
way to imagine and express some of the implications of the different kinds of school experiences at Oakwood and Jefferson.

Hope and Action

Riding home on the bus from Oakwood, Rochelle, an eleventh grader, turned to me with a disgusted look: "Have you ever thought that you shouldn't do this unit with juniors? You know, *we* still have to come back here next year." What did we expect these eleventh graders to do with their new critical awareness? Was it just academic? Did we expect them to spontaneously rise in revolution against the school? We didn't sufficiently appreciate how disempowering it can feel when knowledge is not linked to action, critique not linked to transformation.

In recent years, we've made more effort to encourage students to reflect on how they can *act* upon their new awareness. Last year we asked students to draft proposals that they might choose to present to the administration or site council, recommending a concrete change at Jefferson. In all honesty, most of these were not very good. From the beginning of the year, the class was fractured along lines of race, class, sexual orientation, musical taste, speech patterns, athletic pursuits, senses of humor . . . you name it. They were all deeply concerned about issues of justice, albeit in different ways and for different reasons. But Linda and I waged a constant, usually less-than-successful, struggle to get them to take themselves seriously as people who could make a difference.

Out of our history and politics of schooling unit, one student, a young woman who midway through the year came out to the class as a lesbian, wrote an eloquent appeal to the administration. It began:

> We have classes, clubs, and organizations for African Americans, Hispanics, Asians, Native Americans and many other oppressed groups; but there is one group that was forgotten. They have been oppressed throughout all of history, used as kindling to burn people at the stake. They are the "Queers," "Dykes," "Faggots," "Queens," "Butches," and "Fairies." Where are their clubs to support them and their needs? Where is a class dedicated to the history of homosexuals? Why have they been forgotten?

In a deeply personal paper dripping with pain and rage, she argues for more curriculum addressing gay and lesbian issues and for a gay and lesbian club. She returned to Jefferson for this, her senior year, and with administrative tolerance, if not approval, organized her club, which continues to meet regularly.

Students in my U.S. history class last year preempted the proposal writing with direct action. In a lesson which called for students to discuss, without teacher involvement, problems in the school and possible solutions, class members decided that the school's no-hat rule best symbolized their powerlessness. So they decided to call for a one-day student boycott of the no-hat rule. I had agreed to say nothing during the discussion and kept my promise as they turned the classroom into an organizing center. Together, they wrote a short leaflet:

> We're tired of bowing down and taking our hats off to please the administration. So this Wednesday, June 1st, fight back and stand your ground by boycotting the hat rule. Don't have no fear, and on Wednesday wear your head gear. Hats, shower caps, do rags and Kangos. If you don't control what you wear, what do you control? It's time students take power.

One student volunteered his uncle's printing press; other students volunteered for leafleting brigades.

Abolition of the hat rule did not seem to me like the most significant school reform that students could secure. But I was inspired by the intensity of their engagement, how careful they were to involve everyone in class, and how seriously they took themselves. The final assignment of the year in my U.S. history class asked students to write about what or who in U.S. history made them feel hopeful about the future. Jeremy wrote in part:

> The class actually left me with more hope than I had when I entered. I learned about several ways of resisting, and actually practiced resisting, organizing, and protesting, and made a difference thru our non violent demonstration. We have developed leadership skills in here, and that is something we can use on jobs, in other classes, and in our community. It is important to know that you can make a difference thru non violence, and if everyone knew that, then there wouldn't be riots, and wars. Slaves resisted, soldiers in the Vietnam War resisted, and we resisted. And everyone made a difference. [The Vietnam reference is to the U.S. soldiers who refused, at great personal risk, to participate in the My Lai massacre.]

Jeremy is African American; he knows all too well that his hat protest does not rank with the struggles of black slaves. However, we need to respect his list. He draws hope from both the history as well as his own accomplishment. The challenge for me as a teacher is to continue to search for curricula that can at the same time impart critical knowledge and a sense of hope for the future.

My attempt here is not to sketch out a curriculum on the politics of schooling and to say, "Here, teach it like Linda and I taught it." My aim is more limited. I want to suggest that it is a "basic skill" for students to reflect critically on issues of schools, equity, and social justice. When we neglect to invite students to critique their own school lives, we necessarily teach them habits of not-thinking and not-questioning—we teach them to be morally numb to their immediate surroundings.

If we are serious about educating students for democracy, then such an education needs to reach beyond teaching about the three branches of government or how a bill becomes a law. We need to equip students to enter society as *subjects,* as individuals who look around at the social architecture and ask why is it like this; who benefits and who suffers; and what will it take to make it better for everyone? Studying an institution with which they're intimately familiar seems a good place to start.

References

Anyon, J. (1980). Social class and the hidden curriculum of work. *Journal of Education, 162*(1), pp. 67–92.

Apple, M. W. (1988). *Teachers and texts: A political economy of class and gender relations in education.* New York: Routledge.

Bigelow, B. (1990). Inside the classroom: Social vision and critical pedagogy. *Teachers College Record, 91*, pp. 437–448.

Bigelow, B. (1994a). Getting off the track. In B. Bigelow, et al. (Eds.), *Rethinking our classrooms: Teaching for equity and justice* (pp. 58–65). Milwaukee: Rethinking Schools.

Bigelow, B. (1994b). Testing, tracking, and toeing the line: A role play on the origins of the modern high school. In B. Bigelow, et al.

(Eds.), *Rethinking our classrooms: Teaching for equity and justice* (pp. 117–125). Milwaukee: Rethinking Schools.

Bigelow, B., Christensen, L., Karp, S., Miner, B. & Peterson, B. (Eds.). (1994). *Rethinking our classrooms: Teaching for equity and justice.* Milwaukee: Rethinking Schools.

Chapman, P. D. (1988). *Schools as sorters: Lewis M. Terman, applied psychology, and the intelligence testing movement, 1890–1930.* New York: New York University Press.

Christensen, L. M. (1989). Writing the word and the world. *English Journal, 78*(2), pp. 14–18.

Dorfman, A. (1983). *The empire's old clothes: What the Lone Ranger, Babar, and other innocent heroes do to our minds.* New York: Pantheon.

Giroux, H. A. (1983). *Theory and resistance in education: A pedagogy for the opposition.* South Hadley, MA: Bergin & Garvey.

Loewen, J. W. (1995). *Lies my teacher told me: Everything your American history textbook got wrong.* New York: New Press.

Owen, D. (1985) *None of the above: Behind the myth of scholastic aptitude.* Boston: Houghton Mifflin.

Shor, I., & Freire, P. (1987). *A pedagogy for liberation: Dialogues on transforming education.* South Hadley, MA: Bergin & Garvey.

Storey, D. (1963). *Radcliffe.* New York: Avon.

CHAPTER THIRTEEN

Stories of a Liberatory Pedagogy

REBECCA JARVIS

Eastern Arizona College, Thatcher, Arizona

M any students at community colleges lead extraordinarily harried lives; some are attending school at great sacrifice. To those already overburdened, the time commitments required by a composition class are substantial. As a community college composition instructor, I often wonder if what we're doing in my classes matters much, if these one or two courses can make any difference in students' educations or lives. Some critical theorists and feminists assert that liberatory pedagogies can make a difference in helping to enable students to work toward creating and actively participating in a democracy. In this paper, I describe and problematize some of my efforts to work toward these ends in my first-year college composition courses. As critical pedagogues usually do, I want to emphasize that I am not posing these practices as a prescriptive model for others to follow. Rather, I am describing my current practices, what Elizabeth Ellsworth (1989) calls "situational pedagogy," which change each time I teach.

Like the Australian feminist researcher Bronwyn Davies (1993), I find joy in reading feminist novels. Both Davies and I have found that such stories help us to envision what feminist theories might actually look like and to question our current ways of thinking and acting; they may even make possible a "different living and telling" of our lives (p. 152). Likewise, others' stories of actual classroom practices have helped me to question my own practices and to envision new possibilities; I add to these stories.

Questioning My Assumptions and Authority

Crucial to my pedagogy is an ongoing effort to make conscious and explicit my assumptions and goals in teaching. Calls for teachers to examine their own positioning abound in discussions of feminist poststructural pedagogy. These researchers believe that examining positioning and subjectivity can help lead to an understanding of both how we are constructed and how, individually and collectively, we may oppress, be oppressed, and exercise agency. As a start at this, I include on my first-semester composition course syllabi the following statement of my assumptions and goals for the courses (English 101 and 102; see Figure 1).

Ideally, being as open as possible about my assumptions will encourage students to think critically about their own and other faculty members' and courses' politics, debunking notions of objectivity. However, when I have discussed these assumptions and goals with my classes at the beginning of the semester, I have been met with understandably blank stares and bored silence. Initially, most students are mystified or even alienated by this section on my syllabus, and thus my attempting to be explicit and honest about my beliefs may actually create a more hierarchical gap between us. As we come back to these concepts repeatedly, by the end of the semester, we have learned more about these ideas through sharing our perspectives. And articulating my assumptions in language that avoids jargon—a demanding task—has taught me much about my teaching and assumptions. However, I am constantly reminded that nothing is essentially liberating.

As I attempt to explore my assumptions, I am particularly concerned with my beliefs about authority in teaching. Issues of authority are much discussed in feminist, critical, and whole language pedagogies, sometimes under the label of student-centered versus teacher-centered debates. During my first few years teaching college composition, I tried to move away from what Gay Fawcett (1992) calls "big desk" or teacher-centered metaphors of education. After reading the work of compositionists such as Peter Elbow (1973) and of feminists such as Pam Annas (1985)

Assumptions

My convictions about language and education guide my choices of activities for the semester. In addition to learning about the obvious course content—such as persuasive writing and comma usage—in school, we are also subtly influenced by various ways of thinking and being. At the beginning of the semester, I think it's beneficial for students to have a general idea what convictions about language and education their instructors embrace. I do not ask you to agree with my assumptions, now or at the end of the semester, but I do expect that you will come to understand them.

1. Education is political. By this, I mean that what goes on in schools is intimately connected with power. Within classrooms, we can act in ways that support democratic freedom or in ways that reproduce oppression. In all my teaching, I try to work against world-views I see as oppressive, such as racism, sexism, and classism.
2. Language, both written and spoken, is crucial in school interactions as it helps sustain and create relationships and knowledge. Our language can support democratic potential or reproduce oppression. In a class such as this, in which our focus is on language itself, exploring the ways language is connected with power is appropriate. Better understanding of the interactions between language and power may allow us to choose more consciously how we use language to empower and disempower.
3. I don't perceive my job in this class as primarily one of filling students with knowledge which they will regurgitate back to me at appropriate moments. Certainly I have expertise in my field, but I also recognize that students bring much valuable knowledge to the classroom. In addition to learning from traditional authorities (textbooks, library sources, and your instructor), you will help create knowledge through sharing your stories, doing primary research, and analyzing aspects of your life. Your processes of writing and reading and sharing writing will receive as much emphasis as will your final products, such as papers.
4. Standard English is just one dialect among many beautiful and expressive dialects of English; all dialects follow rules and have communicative power. In fact, calling one particular dialect used by certain groups of people "standard" is a way of asserting the power of those who speak it. However, because the ability to

continued on next page

FIGURE 1. *Statement of assumptions and goals from syllabus.*

Figure 1 continued

---

speak and write standard English is crucial to academic success in most of this nation's colleges and universities and in many careers, the conventions that we will focus on are those of standard English and college-level writing, or what writing teachers often call "academic discourse."

5. Reading and writing are best improved by actually reading, writing, revising, and discussing our work within a community of other writers and readers. While lecturing and disconnected exercises may have uses in education, we don't improve our literacy by listening to someone else talk about it or through filling in blanks on a worksheet. Thus, in this class, we will do much writing and reading and sharing of our writing; I hope that some of the work we do will have purpose and meaning outside this classroom.

Goals

1. To begin to explore connections between literacy and power by investigating the roles language plays in our own and others' freedoms and oppressions;

2. To explore differing images of writers and conceptions of writing, and to experience one version of these: writing and reading as social processes;

3. To develop processes for writing that enable us to successfully tackle any writing we wish to accomplish, even after this course has long passed;

4. To improve competency in using written standard English grammar and punctuation and other conventions of academic discourse; to be aware of political implications of using or flouting these conventions; and

5. To write and revise a series of papers using a variety of rhetorical strategies, using these strategies to fit personal or group writing purposes and voices.[1]

---

and Carol Gilligan (1982), I hoped that a more student-centered curriculum might reduce the alienation many students, including myself, have felt in college classrooms. The whole language and feminist beliefs I still adhere to require that students have the opportunity to read and write about subjects that matter to them.

However, I vacillate about the amount of control I give students over topic choice because, when they choose topics, critical thinking rarely seems to result. As adults, most of us have been so well trained to accept the status quo that we simply replicate hegemonic thinking. And I am sincere in my use of "we" here: with students working on a wide variety of topics, it is difficult for me to find the time and intellectual ability to encourage critical approaches. For example, recently in one of my classes, a highly motivated, articulate student read and wrote about study skills, hoping to find methods that would help her teenage son improve his learning and grades in his high school math class. For my assignment, modeled on a common one described by Wayne Booth (1983, pp. 71–72), she wrote a persuasive letter to her son, describing and asking him to test the methods she believed held the most possibility for helping him. He agreed, and they were proud to report that on his next test, he was awarded a B instead of the F's he had been receiving. Certainly, this assignment held meaning outside the classroom and was not an empty writing exercise; she believes that this was an empowering assignment. However, only after the semester, as I reflected on her description of the experience, did I consider the ways in which I might have done more. Along with giving her space in class to explore issues important to her, I wish I had encouraged a critique of an educational system that requires failure, a critique which would lay blame on tracking, overcrowded classrooms, kill-and-drill teaching approaches that make math seem tangential to a teenager's life, and an inequitable society—instead of accepting uncritically her blaming herself and her son.

Only rarely do students' topic choices and critical thinking seem to coincide. Last spring, a young male athlete superficially researched the topic of acquaintance rape, then wrote a tirade against women who accuse men of date rape. The other members of his peer group were three outspoken, assertive women accustomed to razzing the young man at any opportunity (they called their writing group "three women and a baby"). When he read his paper to them, these women clearly articulated the reasons his paper struck them as superficial and offensive. After reading my response to the next draft of his paper, which was poorly written and researched and which offended me by saying that rape was sometimes a woman's fault, he asked to talk with me after class. He started our discussion by saying, "You probably think I'm a jerk, a twenty-year-old kid"; then as we talked, he repeatedly said that he was working with this topic because he honestly wanted to understand more about date rape. Because of his sincerity, I tried to put aside my indignation at his attitude toward rape and listened quietly as he continued talking. He went on to explain that he had a double personal interest in the topic: several years previously, his then fourteen-year-old sister had been gang raped, and recently his girlfriend's best friend had accused several of his friends, athletes at a university, of date rape. Not only was the topic of crucial interest to him but also to his family and friends. As the first member of his family to attend college, he shared his work with them. He said they had worked together to make sense of my comments on his paper, and that, although now he "wasn't angry anymore," they still had questions, both about his paper and about date rape. We talked for an emotional hour and a half, after which time he went late to a football practice and I late to a university class on literacy and gender.

Because of experiences in our class, I believe this young man, who saw himself as a representative of his family and friends in working to understand acquaintance rape, began to think critically about his topic: to question his—and our society's—assumptions about violence against women being women's responsibility, and to examine his assumptions about sexuality and women's and men's roles. I learned more sensitivity toward the anguish that can underlie sexism. A number of factors combined to give us a liberatory experience: the student's sincere desire to learn about the topic he had chosen, our willingness to share and listen to each others' stories, my knowledge of the subject, his responsibility to and support from his family and girlfriend, a strong peer-writing group, and the time and space to talk. But most of the time, circumstances are not so ideal, and I have neither the time[2] nor the expertise to teach critically the many topics that interest my students.

So, who should choose topics? I do not have an answer. Every semester I agonize over the question of whether to use my authority to choose broad topics which I hope I have the expertise to teach critically and which I believe may have liberatory potential, or to allow the majority of the class to vote on topics, "democratically" choosing for all students, or to allow individuals and/or small groups to work on topics of their choice.

Unlike some feminist and whole language teachers, I do not attempt to diminish or disguise my use of authority. However, I do try to clarify for myself the times when teacher-centeredness is crucial, asking myself these questions: First, should I work to persuade students to see the world through the socioconstructivist lens that underlies my beliefs about language and social relationships? I believe so: I use my authority in selecting assignments and discussion topics toward these ends, because for me these theories offer great promise for democracy. Second, should I push students to recognize inequity, such as classism and sexism and racism, in others' and their own lives? Education for democracy requires this. However, I recognize that this use of my authority can be coercive, and that I may not insist that students agree with me or base my evaluations and caring on whether or not they learn to think like I do. The "extraordinary balancing act" this requires is easier in theory than in praxis (Davies, 1993, p. 63).

For example, last spring in one of my class's on-line bulletin boards, a white, male student, just back from a spring-break trip to Germany, wrote a long tirade against what he called the "illegal immigrant problem," specifically complaining about undocumented Mexican workers. I waited a few days for someone to rebut his arguments, but only white students wrote on the issue, all agreeing with him. Disturbed by what I saw as racism and fearing that his insensitivity to the Hispanic students in the class was contributing to their silence, I posted a short rebuttal using the pen name students recognize as mine.[3] The result was complete silence about the topic for several weeks. I felt like I was in a no-win situation: Either I was silent during the racist discussions and thus complicitous in them, or I participated, squashing potentially liberatory discussion of the topic. Finally, that same student asked me if I would be offended if he researched and wrote about immigration for one of his papers. Shocked at his use of "offended" and with the rest of the class eavesdropping, I tried to explain to him the conflicts I faced between encouraging students to disagree with me and, through my own silence, seeming to endorse attitudes I see as racist and thus possibly silencing other class members. I am not sure that he had any clue as to what I was talking about, and my subsequent interactions with him and other students researching the subject seemed only to entrench racism. No student in the class ever spoke, either orally or online, against the immigrant bashing. Using my authority to open up discussions and to provide space for diverse and even conflictive voices is intensely challenging. As Davies (1993) asserts, "To do this we need to find a way of constituting authority not as an end to discussion but as a way of providing multiple voices whose speaking can begin the conversation" (p. 63).

Positioning in Schooling

In addition to critically questioning my assumptions and authority, I encourage students to examine their own and others' positioning. Throughout the semester, I attempt to debunk transmission or banking narratives of education, in which students' knowledge and experience are valued less than official knowledges. As Ira Shor (1992) suggests, a pattern I rely on consists of asking students to brainstorm about a topic and then to share the knowledge thus created—before we read the text, before I present any additional materials, and sometimes instead of the text and supplements. For example, as part of a unit on narrative writing, in the following assignment I ask students to observe and describe storytelling practices in their own communities:

Storytelling Observation
To begin this assignment, I'd like you to listen carefully to stories. For example, you might listen to friends, family members, or co-workers tell stories; you might observe a story in a favorite TV show or movie; you might reminisce about or reread some of your favorite written stories. Then, think and write about what makes these stories good or what makes you like a story. What qualities do these stories seem to have

in common? What differences do you notice? What do people do to get and keep your attention? What seem to be the main parts of the stories and how are these parts organized?

Comparing our responses with this assignment encourages students to recognize cultural differences in storytelling and to approach critically the limited ideas on storytelling and good writing in our text. This assignment often leads into a discussion of definitions of good writing, in which students explore the gaps between texts they enjoy reading and what they have been taught in school as being "good" writing.

We also explore the common myths that the nontraditional paths many community college students create as they attend college are not as respectable as more linear paths, and that school failure—community college failure in particular—is solely students' responsibility. Few community college students are familiar with theories of what Burton Clark (1961) calls the "cooling-out" process, whereby students' aspirations are gently lowered while their belief in the openness and meritocracy of the American dream is sustained. All community college students should be aware of debates surrounding students' astronomical attrition rates and low numbers of transfers to four-year colleges and universities. Although failure and cooling out occur at all levels of higher education, some critical theorists argue that these processes are most powerful at community colleges— partly just because the students are at a community college. Several often-quoted studies argue that community college students are much less likely to finish a bachelor's degree than students at a four-year college or university, even when such things as background and test scores are taken into account (Brint & Karabel, 1989, pp. 236–237; Griffith & Connor, 1994, p. 127). However, community college faculty members Marlene Griffith and Ann Connor critique such dire predictions, arguing convincingly that we don't really know how many community college students actually do finish bachelor's degrees. What we do know, they assert, is that many community college students' educational paths do not follow a straight line from high school to college to work. Regardless of how powerful its effects, like Brint and Karabel, I believe that this cooling out process does exist and should not be covert, but rather should be visible to all students.

The chance to compare stories might help alleviate the embarrassment many students feel about what Griffith and Connor call the "zigzag" nature of their educational paths. Examination of causes of stopping out[4] and returning to school might also encourage students to recognize how common these patterns are and to see societal influences rather than internalizing all the blame. Certainly, experiences students have in classrooms and in seeking academic counseling contribute to the cooling out of their dreams and to their zigzagging educational paths.

It is essential that both students and faculty critically examine how students choose and are channeled into transfer or terminal programs and how and when they stop out and/or return to school. Students should be encouraged to examine critically the factors that lead them to make such decisions; faculty should examine carefully their own part in exclusion through racism, classism, and sexism. For example, students who fail first-year composition several times because of a lack of facility with standard English and the conventions of academic discourse may be encouraged by these failures to select a terminal program. However, if these students are encouraged to critique the need for standard English while being given extra assistance in mastering these conventions, they might feel more free to make a decision on the basis of their own situations rather than on exclusion by others.

But in encouraging this critique of our educational system, I am cautious. Several years ago, in a wonderful summer evening class, I shared some of my concerns about community college attrition with my class of mostly middle-aged working adults. In the resulting discussion, a number of the older students in the class attested passionately to the difficulties and problems resulting from starting school as a part-time community college student. Just as class was almost over, a young, articulate, intelligent woman of color sitting attentively in the front row of class burst out as she shoved her books into her bag and stormed out of the class, "So what's the point anyway? Why should I even bother trying?" I and the other members of the class murmured some lame you-can-do-it type comments; I was stunned. She punctuated her point with erratic attendance over the next few weeks. Although she eventually did achieve well in the course, I was guilt-ridden over how that discussion had affected students.

Now, as we discuss these issues, I ask students to consider what a possible re-visioning of our educational system might look like, and how, individually and collectively, we might effect change. Most critical pedagogues talk about showing students examples of people successfully bringing about change through collectively organizing against hegemonic practices. Stories of people collectively working for change in education might help us to become hopeful and active. Still, this trying to encourage hope and agency is sometimes difficult for me, as I am not always convinced myself that such hopefulness is warranted and that the necessary educational and social reforms can occur within the current political climate.

Identifying problems that we can work collectively to solve through reading and writing would be ideal. Ira Shor (1987, pp. 162–163) tells an inspiring story of his classes examining hamburgers from the school cafeteria, and, in one class, organizing to demand more nutritious lunch fare. However, the diversity in my community college classes often makes finding common goals unfeasible, even for small groups of students. As I have already discussed, I hesitate in imposing common topics, even when students have suggested the topics and voted to select the ones we will explore. Not everyone will find a discussion of hamburgers empowering; in fact, many of my students have never even been in our school cafeteria. I am as uncomfortable with choosing or letting the class vote on what Paulo Freire calls "generative topics" as I am with the lack of critical thinking that often results from personal topic choices. Even though I may see a generative topic as crucial to their lives and many students may find it passably interesting, allowing me or the majority of students to control the topics for others denies the diversity of my students.

Another way I attempt to make the often-invisible process of positioning in education more visible is to work with students in creating what William Bigelow and Linda Christensen call "collective texts" (Bigelow, 1990, p. 438). I have asked students to share stories of schooling, such as worst and best teachers, times they experienced prejudice or acted in a prejudicial way, and struggles and sacrifices that have been required of them as they go to school. To help make visible underlying assumptions about education and the roles our assumptions play in students' experiences in schools, I have developed a group assignment on "Metaphors of Education," which usually provokes critical discussion about the appropriateness and efficacy of these metaphors (see the Appendix for this assignment). Open discussion of the conflicts associated with grading, especially with grading writing, can also encourage students to see school failure as a social phenomenon and to critique this practice.

We also explore the dominant narratives of composition instruction in students' previous schooling and in our district. About halfway through the semester, I give students a copy of our district-mandated course description, outline, and competencies; these materials encourage a skills-based, fragmented, product-centered curriculum. As a class, we discuss how these materials might encourage instructors to structure their courses in ways much different from my course. It is common for as many as a third of my students to be repeating English 101 for a second or third or fourth time. Their experiences in other courses, combined with students' stories of previous schooling, allow them to discuss our course critically, if they have space in class to do so. Some already frustrated students usually assert that they would prefer a "banking" type course in which I simply teach rules they memorize and illustrate in simplistic five-paragraph essays, without all the so-called deep thinking and painful revision my course entails. Others, probably for a variety of motives, defend the course I am teaching. Regardless of how they feel about my pedagogy, I hope these dialogues encourage students to link the problems they have in courses to social and pedagogical issues, rather than simply internalizing blame for failure individually.

We also critique the master narratives promoted by our text, *Strategies for Successful Writing* (Reinking, Hart, & von der Osten, 1993). This text, like many college composition texts, includes a long section on logic, including discussion of logical fallacies; the powerful use of pathos, empathy and ethos receive much less emphasis. And although narrative and descriptive writing are two of the modes described, neither the discussions of these modes nor the sample essays mention the genres of journal, diary, or personal letter writing. Instead, journal writing is relegated to the realm of freewriting—not *real* writing; personal letters are not mentioned. The idea that narratives are a simple form of writing which students need to move beyond and that exposition, argument, and analysis are more intellectually complex than narrative are common academic (mis)conceptions that our text promotes. As many feminists have argued, presenting these genres of writing as less intellectual and less important than other genres is a political move which denigrates forms of writing often associated with women. Making visible prejudices against the emotional and subjective and examining the roles pathos and storytelling play in students' lives may help them begin to question these biases and even to approach other coursework critically.

Sharing with my classes another conflict that I face, attempting both to value nonstandard dialects and to teach standard English, can also help raise students' consciousness about language and power. In class, I emphasize that all dialects of English follow systematic rules, that each is equally capable of expressing complex and poetic ideas, and that decisions about dialects are political. Linda Christensen (1994) argues that, with our students, we need to ask "who makes the rules, who enforces the rules, who benefits from the rules, who loses from the rules, who uses the rules to keep some in and keep others out" (p. 145). Asking students to describe and then evaluate from a critical standpoint their experiences learning (or not learning) standard English can be powerful. As a young man concluded in our online bulletin board, "Our constitution should really read, 'All men are created equal, as long as you don't sound stupid when you talk.'" After reading Christensen's essay "Whose Standard? Teaching Standard English," one woman wrote in big letters at the bottom of her response to the article, "Why didn't I hear this before when I needed it?" Despite sometimes impassioned discussions of these issues, many students still believe that their home dialects are "Bad English" and that my job is to imbue them with "Good English" (Lemke, 1990, p. 163).

The solution for liberatory pedagogues is to attempt to teach standard English and a critical attitude toward it, while also valuing other dialects. I am not sure this is possible because the bias toward standard English is so strong in academe, and, because for many students and for myself, this means overcoming attitudes inculcated over years of schooling. I sometimes feel like a hypocrite in such discussions of dialect, because when I grade students on grammar and mechanics, as I am required to do, it is on their use of standard English, not on their use of diverse dialects and conventions.

Stories of people working collectively for language change might come from the trend toward eliminating overtly sexist language, the de-emphasis on conventions in online communication, or the changes that some nurse practitioners are making in the power relations in doctor-patient discourse. The idea is to show students possibilities for hope and change; all this while also teaching survival skills in standard English and academic discourse. A difficult prospect.

Positioning outside Schooling

In addition to critiquing some of the master narratives of education and composition instruction, I continually look for ways to encourage students to examine how they are positioned and how they position others in their writing. For example, I ask students to explore who they present themselves as in the narrative writing they do early in the course through writing prompts such as this:

Examining Ethos in Narratives

A. As we've discussed, we all have contradictory aspects to our personalities. For example, we may sometimes want to be independent and sometimes to depend on others; sometimes we act as leaders or nonconformists, sometimes as followers or conformists; sometimes we are crazy or reckless, sometimes sensible and careful. Think about and describe aspects of your personality that seem contradictory to you.

B. Which aspects of your personality have you chosen to emphasize in your narrative writing in this class? Give some examples
of your ethos.

C. What might be behind your choices to present yourself in the
ways that you have? Do your choices support or fit into cultural stereotypes about the normal or appropriate behavior of
different groups of people, such as women, men, mothers,
fathers, teenagers, newlyweds, students, employees, or racial,
ethnic, or religious groups? Do your choices violate stereotypes? What might underlie your choices of ethos?

D. How is the personality or ethos you emphasize in your online
writing different from and similar to that which you've done
for the in-class essays? If you were writing for people or situations other than those in this class—for example, for a friend
or an employer or in a diary—how might your ethos differ?
How might other aspects of your writing differ?

Beginning with a description of themselves and with a discussion of the many-sided, even contradictory voices that compose
poststructural concepts of identity, students explore why they
have emphasized particular voices in their writing. In one class,
after a number of students promoted an authentic voice theory of
self, asserting that they were simply writing to express their *true*
selves, several began to explore how their public and even private
identities are constructed. For example, one woman wrote:

> In my narratives, my main character usually has the most
> power. My main character has the most control because I
> have the control over him/her. When I write, I usually write
> about the way that I want things to be, because for once, I
> have the power. I believe that life has a lot of very unwanted
> aspects, and so in my writing I either throw out those aspects,
> or I get rid of them while I write. When I write, the world
> around me is lost, and MY world comes alive.

Another option is to have students explicitly write about
power, and race, class, and gender after having shared stories
with each other. Here are examples of two such writing prompts:

> Examine power and status in the relationships you describe
> in two or more of your narratives or electronic forum (ef)
> entries, or in other experiences you haven't written about

yet. Most of these relationships will be between people, but some may also be between people and things such as schools or government or workplaces or the media, or between people and things such as books, clothing, or cars. Describe briefly the relationships you want to focus on. Who is powerful in the relationships? Who is usually in control? Why? Are different groups of people represented in your narratives? How do these groups stand in relation to other groups in your narratives and ef writing? In society in general, do these groups have relationships that are different from those in your writing? Does your power or that of others change? Why? What are some possible generalizations about power and your relationships to it that you could make on the basis of your descriptions? What effects might language have on these relationships?

Examine gender, race, and social class in two or more of your narratives or ef entries or in other experiences you haven't written about. What effects might race, class, gender or other things that affect power/powerlessness have on your experiences or on your relationships? For example, have you suffered or been discriminated against because of who you are or because of others' stereotypes? Do you have extra status or privileges that you might not have otherwise? Are you sometimes in control in situations and, in other situations, not in control? What are some possible generalizations you could make about gender, race, or social class or other aspects of power?

Doing this writing on our computer bulletin board system (ef), where students can read each others' writing but are anonymous to each other, helps demystify these ideas and provokes some intriguing discussion. For example, in a class last spring, a young white woman proclaimed,

> I . . . believe that race is not important, unless you are talking about your culture. . . . I have never discriminated against anyone, therefore I have never been discriminated against. As for social classes, who needs them—Yeah, so what some people have a lot of money and some people don't.

I was pleased that this comment provoked a storm of stories about discrimination on the basis of class, race, gender, body size, job status, and athletic abilities; two female students were even brave enough to broach the subject of homophobia.

However fascinating the responses to these prompts, many students initially approach them perfunctorily, dreading doing another of my weird assignments. Their attitude is much different in other types of writing. One type of writing we always do includes assignments such as "describe a memorable experience" or "create a metaphor for your life." Through feminist pedagogy such as that based on the work of Carol Gilligan (1982) and Mary Belenky and her colleagues (1986), I can justify these assignments. Allowing students to tell stories of what is important to them is a way of validating their experiences and knowledge and is also a way of allowing space for trust and friendship to develop. However, with such stories there are two problems: first is the potential for perpetuating prejudice such as racism and sexism. Simply celebrating individual stories may conserve the status quo without recognizing the liberatory potential of narratives. As Roger Simon (1992) states,

> How can one avoid the conservatism inherent in simply celebrating personal experience and confirming that which people already know? In other words, how can we acknowledge previous experience as legitimate content and challenge it at the same time? How do we encourage student "voices" while simultaneously encouraging the interrogation of such voices? (pp. 61–62)

Asking students to analyze or critique stories of personal experience or doing it myself can be problematic for a number of reasons, which leads us to the second problem, the potential for valuing analysis over narrative, which I discussed earlier. When applied to students' narratives, emphasis on analysis and logic can have powerful personal meaning. Elizabeth Ellsworth (1989) explains:

> As Barbara Christian has written, ". . . what I write and how I write is done in order to save my own life. And I mean that literally. For me literature is a way of knowing that I am not hallucinating, that whatever I feel/know *is*." . . . It is inappropriate to respond to such words by subjecting them to

rationalist debates about their validity. Words spoken for survival come already validated in a radically different arena of proof and carry no option or luxury of choice. (p. 302)

I believe we may sometimes be able to solve both of these problems the same way—by backing off. Resisting oppressive practices in education may at times mean that we are not critical or analytical, and that we avoid saying, "well, but . . ." in response to students' ideas and stories. As Geoffrey Chase (1990) asserts, there are times when "perhaps we need just to say yes" to students' experiences and work to understand them rather than broaden or critique their perspectives (p. 29). For many community college students, acceptance and validation of their narratives is a new experience; the sharing of these stories may encourage rethinking stereotypes more powerfully than any analysis could.

Thus, despite the prejudice (sexism, racism, classism, ableism, homophobia, etc.) and promotion of common cultural myths often evident in students' narratives, I neither critique nor analyze these aspects of their stories. However, I do ask students to anonymously share narratives with their peers online and then to compare their stories, looking for common themes and types of stories. Here are several prompts I've used:

> On the electronic forum, briefly summarize each of the first four in-class essays you wrote. Then, after most students have written their entries, go back and read through them. What issues seem to be important to students in the class? What themes do you see in these narratives? What do some of them seem to have in common? What differences strike you as being important? What comments or questions about our society—for example, our workplaces, our educational systems, or our relationships—do you have after reading these descriptions?

> For people in this class, what makes an experience memorable? What seems to give us joy? pain? knowledge?

> Do any of your stories describe romantic relationships or close friendships? In your descriptions of these relationships, what aspects did you emphasize? How does what you emphasized compare with others' descriptions?

Examine the narratives and descriptions you've read in *Strategies* (our textbook). What does the textbook say about whose lives are important enough to be written about? Hypothesize about what the editors of this text think people or lives should be like. How does what seems to matter to them compare with who and what you and your classmates have chosen to write about?

As they write in response to these prompts, students sometimes also begin to explore how their experiences, perceptions, and selves are constructed and positioned. Sometimes wonderful insights appear during creation of such collective texts. For example, after reading other students' descriptions of themselves and of some of their memorable events, one student wrote: "I am surprised that Race and Ethnicity matters so much to so many people. I never thought it mattered much." That such an important realization came not through any analysis guided by me, but through "uncritically" and "unproblematically" (Simon, 1992, p. 124; Ellsworth, 1989, p. 302) shared stories leads me to question assertions that individual stories must be analyzed and critiqued. Sharing the stories and having time to reread and compare them may be more powerfully consciousness-raising than any analysis I can guide students in.

I do encourage students to examine their positioning through modeling this process, looking at class texts, the media, familiar and new arguments, and well-known stories. For example, we have fun comparing traditional and Disney renditions of fairy tales to feminist fairy tales such as Babette Cole's *Princess Smartypants* (1986) and *Prince Cinders* (1987) and the Merseyside Fairy Story Collective's (1986) re-visioning of *Snow White*. Disrupting what Bronwyn Davies calls cultural "obviousnesses" in myths such as *Cinderella* and *Snow White* may encourage students to take a similar revisionist approach toward their own cultural narratives and may encourage them "to make the unthinkable thinkable" (Davies, 1993, p. 11).

This examination of positioning is time-consuming and often difficult, partly because it sometimes involves making both students and myself uncomfortable. I occasionally find myself ignoring opportunities because I am uneasy about discomfiting or embarrassing students. For example, in posts in which students introduced their pen-name personas, one woman told a quirky little story about how she and her female best friend call each other "Horn" because of something to do with one of them being rude about the other being able to find a bicycle buried in a crowded storage room. After class, this woman introduced me to her friend, who had been waiting for her; I then left while they remained at school reading and writing online. When I got home and read the entries by modem, she had changed her pen name, writing the following new explanation:

> Hi my name is HOPE 7. I chose this name because I am extremely attracted to KEVIN JOHNSON of the PHOENIX SUNS!!!!!!!!!!!!!!!!!!! xxxxxxxx oooooooooo. I HOPE to marry him and have 7 children with him.

She may have feared that her first pen name might have been considered suspect by others in the class; admitting to having nicknames of "Horn" with a same-sex friend might have provoked homophobia in other students. Her new pen name is so strongly hegemonic in terms of traditional, heterosexual gender stereotypes that she might even have been parodying these stereotypes. It is also significant that the first entry was never responded to by other students, while the second received the following applause: "Hope, Hey I used to think Kevin Johnson was fine too." These changes might have provided an opportunity to discuss with students how they feel constrained in their writing, even when they are anonymous to their classmates. Discussion with the class of what types of entries provoked response or were ignored might also have been an opportunity to encourage subversion of hegemonic norms. But I didn't take advantage of this opportunity, partly because I didn't catch the possible significance of it until several weeks later, and partly because at that time, I didn't want to make the student uncomfortable. Asking her privately about the changed pen name or discussing the posts with the class while protecting her anonymity would have been an opportunity to discuss prejudice against gays and lesbians. However, given that I had several Rush Limbaugh fans in the class, and having noticed that the woman avoided mentioning her sexuality, I did not want to place her in a situation in which she had to either listen to their prejudice (even if they didn't know who she was) or feel obligated to discuss her sexuality (to either come out or to assert heterosexuality), even just with me. However, as Elizabeth Ellsworth (1989) and other poststructural feminists point out, lack of such discomfort and even conflict may lead to suppression of difference. As a white, middle-class woman, I am at times uncomfortable speaking much about race or social class myself, but I am also reluctant to ask people to contribute if they seem reticent or don't volunteer. It is wonderful to have diverse groups of people who are eager to speak of their experiences, but this rarely seems to happen. Not attempting to eradicate these silences makes me complicitous in delegitimizing difference.

Does It Matter?

Feminists place much hope in our abilities, as Bronwyn Davies (1993) says, to discover "the very mainsprings of power that have held . . . marginalised groups in place. . . . To know how oppression is achieved is the essential first step to knowing how to change it" (p. 8). But herein lies the extraordinary difficulty of liberatory pedagogy: this understanding our own positioning and our own complicity in power structures, and then attempting to envision change and to act on this vision. Encouraging development of critical literacy through attempting to teach about positioning and critiquing dominant discourses calls into question my own abilities to do these things. When I face resistance from students while also dealing with numerous institutional constraints, I recognize that my own power to effect social change through the classroom is limited. I like the way William Bigelow (1990) describes our position: "Until the economic system requires workers who are critical, cooperative, and deeply democratic, teachers' classroom efforts amount to a kind of low-intensity pedagogical war" (p. 447). More dialogue and sharing of stories between educators and between educators and students is essential to nurturing my hope in the collective power of educators to effect social change, albeit small. As students in my classes tell me their stories, I am repeatedly impressed by their persevering in school despite adverse circumstance and often immensely harried lives and by their hope that a college education will improve their lives. Their hopefulness, resilience, and courage, their trust and offers of friendship have moved me deeply and have strengthened me in my own struggles. I continue to hope that what we do in my classes may matter to some of them; I believe that doing what we can to help students achieve their goals and to urge the educational system, including my courses, to become deserving of their hopes and trust are worthy endeavors. As critical theorist David Purpel (1989) says, "I continue to have . . . faith that schools . . . can actually contribute to the creation of a more loving, more just, saner world" (x). This faith motivates my ongoing struggles to practice liberatory pedagogy.

Notes

1. This last goal is my salute to the district-mandated, mode-centered course competencies.

2. Many have decried the exploitation of adjunct faculty in higher education; however, as the disparity between the haves and have-nots among educational workers continues to increase, I want to add my voice to the controversy. A pay raise for the Maricopa County Community College District means that this fall, I will receive $1,527 for teaching a three semester-hour course, one-fourth to one-fifth of the average full-time faculty member's pay for the same course in the same district. I receive no health insurance or sick leave, have no office, work without any contract and thus can be dismissed without notice or due process, am lucky to be granted the maximum of $300 professional development funding per year, and am paid the same hourly wage as all other part-time faculty, regardless of experience, advanced degrees, or training. When I presented a version of this paper to the Conference on College Composition and Communication in Milwaukee last March, my paycheck was docked $112 for missing two days of classes, despite my having been online during class one of those days, telnetting into the classroom and thus participating in the discussion much as I would have had I been in Phoenix. Although my department chair and the few colleagues I've spoken with are congenial, sympathetic toward our plight, and supportive, I am most certainly a second-class faculty member. The prevailing attitude among

both part- and full-time faculty parallels that of other professionals toward this nation's large underclass: because many of the full-timers also paid their dues as adjuncts, we seem to assume that those of us who are any good will likewise pull ourselves up by our bootstraps and be hired full-time. But when the adjunct faculty outnumber the full-timers four to one—the most recent data I have show that adjuncts comprise 73 percent of district faculty (Webster, 1996, B5), when only a few full-time positions are filled each year, and when competition for available positions is keen, chances of being hired full-time are slim for most of us. As elsewhere in society, this bootstraps mentality among both part- and full-time faculty members encourages, at best, ineffectual and superficial reform attempts and discourages the collective action needed to force substantial reform.

3. Although I have the option of participating anonymously in our online discussions, as my students do, I do not believe this is a practical or an ethical choice. It is impractical because students recognize my I'm-an-authority-here voice and my I-hate-to-make-mistakes style unless I deliberately disguise my writing, which seems a rude parody of student prose. Given the power imbalances between us, my anonymity is unethical because students are not anonymous to me.

4. Because so many college students drop out of classes then later return, the term *stop out* is often used now instead of *drop out*.

Appendix: Metaphors of Education

Group-Assignment Instructions

First, discuss how the teachers, students, and knowledge are viewed differently in these metaphors. Second, create other metaphors that describe your group members' educational experiences, or, if you wish, modify one or more of these metaphors to fit your experiences. Third, give stories and descriptions from your experiences that explain your choices of metaphors. Last, discuss the effectiveness of the teaching and learning resulting from these different metaphors. Which metaphor(s) would you prefer to learn under? Why? Does your answer differ for different subjects or for different people? Again, give examples.

The Teacher as a Sheep Dog

Captured in this metaphor is the image of a teacher having a destination in mind for his or her flock, the class. A trajectory through the semester-long curriculum can be envisioned, and when the flock appears to depart from the path that leads to the ends sought by the teacher or the state, the teacher begins nipping at the heels of the flock to keep it from straying too much. The teacher uses past experience to guide the decision about whether or not to nip at the heels.

DAVID C. BERLINER, "If the Metaphor Fits, Why Not Wear It?"

Student as a Stone; Education as Erosion

Important changes in human behavior are not produced overnight. No single learning experience has a very profound influence upon the learner. Changes in ways of thinking, in fundamental habits, in major operating concepts, in attitudes, in abiding interest and the like develop slowly. It is only after months and years that we are able to see major educational objectives taking marked concrete shape. In some respects educational experiences produce their effects in the way water dripping upon a stone wears it away. In a day or a week or a month there is no appreciable change in the stone, but over a period of years definite erosion is noted.

RALPH W. TYLER, *Basic Principles of Curriculum and Instruction*

Education as a Race, Competition

Two men are running from a bear and one stops to change into his running shoes. His companion tells him he is foolish to think he can outrun the bear. But then his friend says, "You don't get it, John. I don't have to outrun the bear; I just have to outrun you."

This second joke feels to me to be about the discomfort of liberal professionals over an educational system which is so competitive that each person's success takes place at the expense of others. In this sense no one is really successful.

MARY C. SAVAGE, "They Shall Turn Their Mourning into Dancing"

Student Failure/Success as a Fragile Flower

Grade school failure in America is a fragile flower, no less fragile in fact than school success, and both are perfectly normal ways of growing up in America. . . . Failure is waiting every morning in every classroom in America; before children or their teachers arrive, failure is there. . . . Failure is a culturally necessary part of the American school scene. . . . We help to make failure possible by our . . . successes; similarly, those who fail in school . . . make our successes possible. . . .

School success and school failure can be understood only in terms of our willingness to turn small and generally uninteresting differences in test-defined learning into institutional facts with devastating consequences for the children differently labeled by the system. It is in this sense that every failure belongs to us all.

R. P. McDermott, "The Explanation of Minority
School Failure, Again"

Student as an Empty Bank

In the banking concept of education, knowledge is a gift bestowed by those who consider themselves knowledgeable upon those whom they consider to know nothing. . . . Education thus becomes an act of depositing, in which the students are the depositories and the teacher is the depositor. Instead of communicating, the teacher issues communiqués and makes deposits which the students patiently receive, memorize, and repeat. This is the "banking" concept of education, in which the scope of action allowed to the students extends only as far as receiving, filing, and storing the deposits. . . .

The more students work at storing the deposits entrusted to them, the less they develop the critical consciousness which would result from their intervention in the world as transformers of that world. The more completely they accept the passive role imposed on them, the more they tend simply to adapt to the world as it is and to the fragmented view of reality deposited in them. The capability of banking education to minimize or annul the students' creative power and to stimulate their credulity serves the interests of the oppressors, who care neither to have the world revealed nor to see it transformed.

Paulo Freire, *The Pedagogy of the Oppressed*

Teacher as Midwife

Midwife-teachers are the opposite of banker-teachers. While the bankers deposit knowledge in the learner's head, the midwives draw it out. They assist the students in giving birth to their own ideas, in making their own tacit knowledge explicit and elaborating it. Midwife-teachers focus not on their own knowledge (as the lecturer does) but on the students' knowledge. They contribute when needed, but it is always clear that the baby is not theirs but the student's. . . . Midwife-teachers help students deliver their words to the world, and they use their own knowledge to put the students into conversation with other voices—past and present—in the culture. . . .

Even those [students] who were most respectful of authority wished to be treated at least as containers of knowledge rather than empty receptacles. Many women expressed—some firmly, some shakily—a belief that they possessed latent knowledge. The kind of teacher they praised and the kind for which they yearned was one who would help them articulate and expand their latent knowledge: a midwife-teacher.

MARY FIELD BELENKY ET AL., *Women's Ways of Knowing*

References

Annas, P. (1985). Style as politics: A feminist approach to the teaching of writing. *College English, 47*(4), 360–371.

Belenky, M. F., Clinchy, B. M., Goldberger, N. R., & Tarule, J. M. (1986). *Women's ways of knowing: The development of self, voice, and mind.* New York: Basic Books.

Berliner, D. C. (1990). If the metaphor fits, why not wear it? The teacher as executive. *Theory Into Practice, 29*(2), 85–93.

Bigelow, W. (1990) Inside the classroom: Social vision and critical pedagogy. *Teachers College Record, 91*(3), 437–448.

Booth, W. C. (1983). "LITCOMP": Some rhetoric addressed to cryptorhetoricians about a rhetorical solution to a rhetorical problem. In W.B. Horner (Ed.), *Composition and literature: Bridging the gap* (pp. 57–80). Chicago: University of Chicago Press.

Brint, S., & Karabel, J. (1989). *The diverted dream: Community colleges and the promise of educational opportunity in America, 1900–1985.* New York: Oxford University Press.

Chase, G. (1990). Perhaps we need just to say yes. *Journal of Education, 172*(1), 29–37.

Christensen, L. M. (1994). Whose standard? Teaching standard English. In W. Bigelow, et al. (Eds.), *Rethinking our classrooms: Teaching for equity and justice* (pp. 142–145). Milwaukee: Rethinking Schools.

Clark, B. R. (1961). The "cooling-out" function in higher education. In A. H. Halsey, J. Floud, & C. A. Anderson (Eds)., *Education, economy, and society: A reader in the sociology of education* (pp. 513–523). New York: Free Press.

Cole, B. (1986). *Princess Smartypants.* New York: Putnam.

Cole, B. (1987). *Prince Cinders.* New York: Putnam.

Davies, B. (1993). *Shards of glass: Children reading and writing beyond gendered identities.* Cresskill, NJ: Hampton.

Elbow, P. (1973). *Writing without teachers.* New York: Oxford University Press.

Ellsworth, E. (1989). Why doesn't this feel empowering: Working through the repressive myths of critical pedagogy. *Harvard Educational Review, 59*(3), 297–324.

Fawcett, G. (1992). Moving the big desk. *Language Arts, 69*(3), 183–185.

Freire, P. (1991). Pedagogy of the oppressed. In N. M. Bradbury & A. Quinn (Eds.), *Audiences and intentions: A book of arguments* (pp. 105–115). New York: Macmillan.

Gilligan, C. (1982). *In a different voice: Psychological theory and woman's development.* Cambridge, MA: Harvard University Press.

Griffith, M., & Connor, A.. (1994). *Democracy's open door: The community college in America's future.* Portsmouth, NH: Boynton/Cook, 1994.

Lemke, Jay. (1990). *Talking science: Language, learning, and values.* Norwood, NJ: Ablex.

McDermott, R.P. (1987). The explanation of minority school failure, again. *Anthropology & Education Quarterly, 18*(4), 361–364.

The Merseyside Fairy Story Collective. (1986). *Snow White.* In J. Zipes (Ed.)., *Don't bet on the prince: Contemporary feminist fairy tales in North America and England.* New York: Methuen.

Purpel, D.E. (1989). *The moral and spiritual crisis in education: A curriculum for justice and compassion in education.* Westport, CN: Bergin & Garvey.

Reinking, J. A., Hart, A. W., & von der Osten, R. (1993). *Strategies for successful writing: A rhetoric, reader, and handbook.* 3rd ed. of Annotated Instructor's Edition Englewood Cliffs, NJ: Prentice-Hall.

Savage, M. C. (1990). They shall turn their mourning into dancing. Unpubl. ms. Presented to "Reading and Movements for Liberation:

they were actually a major improvement over one-shot, talk-at sessions—and many teachers found them helpful, they took place within a larger organizational context that had a powerful influence over how teachers perceived and reacted to the district-level change initiatives. Even though many of us in leadership roles tried to invite teachers into the change process by supporting their learning, many of them interpreted our attempts as more top-down demands from supervisors who had power over them. I became very frustrated with what I perceived to be teachers' ill-founded resistance to changes that I believed were in the best interests of students. It was not until I shifted my gaze from the teachers to the social and political context within which they worked, that I could begin to understand their resistance. That shift came as I became familiar with the work of critical theorists (Giroux, 1987; Simon, 1987; Giroux & McLaren, 1986; McLaren, 1989) and of educators who were making the political agenda of whole language more explicit (Shannon, 1992; Edelsky, 1991, 1994).

It became obvious to me, in ways that it had not been before, that many of our systemic schooling practices perpetuate inequities—that these practices maintain the power of dominant groups and subvert our espoused democratic principles. I was persuaded by arguments that whole language needed to have a more critical edge—that we whole language educators, whether our learners are students or teachers, need to bring issues of social justice and equity to the fore in our teaching. I realized that if I hoped to have influence over teachers' beliefs and practices, I needed to understand how they are positioned within the highly bureaucratic, hierarchical school system. I came to see the teachers' resistance to the changes I espoused, not as individual acts of people who did not want to improve their teaching, but as a rather healthy reaction to what they perceived as top-down coercion.

I had not intended to be coercive, but I could not avoid my own positioning as a supervisor within a network of hierarchical power relationships. Many of the teachers saw me as an instrument of the system—another person from outside the classroom attempting to impose change on them. Historically, as layers of administration have been added to school systems and more and more regulations have been imposed, teachers have had less and less control over their work lives. Those above them in the hierarchy control their use of time, access to resources and to professional development, and, often, their curricular goals. It was no wonder that they saw the ambitious reform effort associated with whole language as a threat, rather than as an opportunity. There was nothing in the way in which we introduced the change to teachers that suggested that they had the right to question why the change was coming and how these new ideas about literacy fit with their current beliefs. They also had no opportunity to determine how and when they would explore these new ideas.

I came to the conclusion that it was not enough to have a powerful theory of teaching and learning; I needed to become more explicitly political. As Shannon (1992) helped me to see, "All teachers are political, whether they are conscious of it or not. Their acts contribute to or challenge the status quo in literacy education, in school, and in society" (p. 2). To effect the curricular changes I believed would benefit students, I would need to make the organization itself the focus of my reform efforts by challenging traditional power relationships and ways of working. While I still believed in many of the principles of whole language, I began to think and write about what it might mean to bring critique to the fore in the classroom, the school, and the institution as a whole (Church, 1996).

During the time I was grappling with these issues, the school district in which I worked was moving rapidly to restructure in response to a number of pressures: fiscal restraints, proposed governance changes at the provincial level that shifted power from district to site, and the district's own commitment to decentralization and more community involvement in schools. As well, a number of senior staff took advantage of an early retirement package. It seemed to me that the context was sufficiently fluid and open that there might be some opportunities to take action toward the kinds of changes I thought needed to be made. When the position of superintendent of education services opened, I decided to apply and, much to my delight, was the successful candidate. For the next two years, until our school district was amalgamated with two others in the summer of 1996, I explored what it might mean to lead critically—to be a leader who made issues of equity and social justice my business and who acted wherever I could to change systemic practices that disempowered groups because of race, culture, gender, class, ability, or position in the hierarchy.

Although the district's espoused agenda was to shift more decision making to the schools, the organization was still highly bureaucratic and hierarchical. The senior team, which included the chief education officer and five superintendents, had a great deal of influence over policy, the allocation of human and material resources, and many other decisions that affected schools. Therefore, being a member of senior administration endowed me with positional power. By behaving differently, I believed I could disrupt the status quo. I could bring about systemic change, especially in the important areas for which I was responsible: programs and student services. For example, I could share power more equitably across the levels of the system and make it possible for diverse perspectives to be heard. I could allocate resources within my control to support initiatives that advanced equity and social justice. I could challenge systemic practices, such as tracking, that research has shown disadvantage poor and minority students (Oakes, 1985). I could give my active support to the implementation of board policies in the area of human rights, specifically one for race relations that we had been attempting to implement for several years and a newly adopted one for sexual harassment.

Small Successes

As I discovered almost immediately, there are powerful forces that work against a leader who decides to take a critical stance. I learned a great deal during two years of grappling with the challenges of trying to lead in this way. I discovered how firmly many of our systemic practices are entrenched despite the rhetoric of restructuring and empowerment. Before I turn to a reflection on the lessons I learned and to some thoughts about where to go next, however, I want to focus on what it was possible to accomplish in collaboration with colleagues who shared a commitment to change. Those colleagues were the dozen program and student services supervisors and consultants I was fortunate enough to have in my department and the many principals and teachers who became part of our ongoing conversations, continually challenging us to act on our beliefs. Had the school district amalgamation not occurred, I believe the following small successes might have grown into real forces for positive change. I offer them as examples of what the critical theorists (Simon, 1987) call "projects of possibility."

Rethinking Disruptive Behavior

Over the course of ten years, the school district had made significant progress in eliminating tracking and ability grouping and developing an inclusive environment for children of all ability levels. Virtually all segregated special education classes had disappeared, and all students received support within the classroom or through pullout for focused intervention. For the most part, administrators, teachers, and the community had been supportive of this move toward full inclusion; however, many schools had concerns about their capacity to cope with children and adolescents with disruptive behavior. Community mental health services, like the education system, had been pared down through several years of fiscal restraint. This diminished community support had exacerbated the schools' difficulties in accommodating students whose behavior often had a negative impact on the learning of other children and sometimes threatened the safety of both children and adults. As a result of growing concerns about these young people, there had been ongoing discussions about the possibility of creating some segregated settings in which their needs could be better addressed.

While there were many who saw alternative classes as the solution, there were also voices, including mine, suggesting that we needed to recast the problem; specifically, to explore ways in which the "regular" system might change to become more supportive of these students. A number of us had taught segregated classes in the past and, while it is more than possible to create supportive learning environments in those settings, the programs seldom "fix" the students sufficiently to allow them to return to regular programs, and nothing happens to make the schools more hospitable. In the long term, removal from the regular stream cuts off many future avenues for these students. It seemed to some of us that we should put our energy into creating more flexibility and support within the students' home schools and communities rather than into expensive alternative programs that would actually further disenfranchise the students. As well, we felt it was important to look beyond the educational system to draw upon the expertise and resources of community agencies in a more coherent way.

We asked the proponents of segregated classes to consider the following sorts of critical questions. What is happening in these students' lives that makes them so angry? Are they reacting against social inequities that are based upon class, culture, race, or gender? How have the students and their families been affected by the ongoing decline in the economy? How many of the students are living in poverty? How do our schools perpetuate inequities? How many of the students have significant learning difficulties that contribute to their disruptive behavior? What might we do to change the system to become more flexible and responsive? A teacher who works in a junior high with a large African Canadian population once said to me, "They give these kids anger management workshops, but they don't look at all the reasons why they have every right to be angry. The kids know the system is failing them." Fine (1990) argues that we need to unpack the label "at risk" and "turn our critical concern onto the very ideological and material distinctions that privilege educationally those already privileged, and disadvantage those already disadvantaged" (p. 64).

During the 1995–96 school year our district became involved in a small pilot project designed to address the needs of this population of students. District staff developed the project, which focused initially on the junior high level, in collaboration with two other school districts and a number of community agencies. Although there were two or three segregated sites established as part of the initiative, we took this opportunity to explore options other than special classes. Two supervisors in our district worked with principals and teachers to design flexible programs for students within their home schools. The possibilities included part-time attendance combined with community-based experiences, academic programs designed around the students' strengths, outdoor education and other recreational activities, and even music and art lessons for students who expressed interest. Schools drew upon the expertise of a school psychologist, a family counselor, a youth counselor and a para-professional support worker to help them and the students design and carry out programs that would meet their needs. Although one or two of the schools were skeptical at first, over time they all acknowledged that this approach had real potential for making a difference. No miracles occurred, but all of the students were more successful. Moreover, different kinds of working relationships among professionals evolved, and the schools became much more open to and capable of responding to the diverse needs of students.

The results of this pilot program were promising. Unfortunately, the amalgamation brought it to an end. On the eve of the disappearance of our district as an independent entity, we allocated some additional funds to the project schools, and they continued on their own the following year. Recognizing the benefits of reaching younger students, we invited the elementary schools that fed into these junior highs to participate as well. The schools worked together to plan further interventions, contracting with some of the professional staff who had worked in the pilot project. I kept in touch with some of the principals, who told me that the groups of schools were gradually developing ways of working together and additional creative approaches for making the system more responsive. All agreed that focusing on elementary-age students was a positive move. As I write, it is unclear whether the new amalgamated district will continue to fund these small projects, and there is much discussion about the need for alternative classes. From my conversations with those who developed school-based alternatives, I am confident that projects like that will continue, despite the lack of district support. These teachers and principals seem convinced that engagement in long-term collaborative efforts to alter disenfranchising systemic practices is the only means of creating equitable learning opportunities for all their students.

Shared Decision Making

As the district set about to restructure in ways that would vest more control with schools and their communities, many tensions arose at the senior- and middle-management levels. District-level administrators struggled with how best to fulfill their roles; some supervisors actively resisted giving up their power over schools. While those of us in programs and services had many questions about how to shift more power to the schools and still sustain our involvement with and influence over teaching and learning, there was general agreement that we had to work differently. We spent time familiarizing ourselves with the research on school reform and explored what it might mean to apply its lessons. For example, we thought about how we could create a structure that provided the appropriate combination of bottom-up and top-down influence that Fullan (1993) and others have shown is most likely to have positive results for students. We recognized that there was little or no evidence that site-based management models in which schools are left to cope on their own—with no outside resources and supports—were any more effective in transforming student learning than traditional top-down approaches had been.

As a program/services team, we decided to work at systemic change—to renegotiate our relationships with schools so that they really could make decisions about issues that were important to them, including how they used available human and material resources. During the 1980s, when budgets had been richer, the district had developed quite a large cadre of district staff who took leadership for program implementation and for managing services for students. Although there were many fewer people working in district roles by 1994, there had not been much change in the expectations for how these individuals would operate. Both the district and many schools held them responsible in much the way they had in the past. Our goal was to shift the responsibility to the schools—to bring them to the center of the organizational chart and then build a flexible system of supports around them. We knew many schools would struggle with this, having become dependent on district staff. We also knew that schools would be skeptical about whether this proposed change really meant that they would have more control or if it merely meant that they would have all of the responsibilities and no right to make important decisions.

During the two years, we made some progress toward this goal. We put time and effort into helping schools develop school-based teams which would problem solve around the needs of individual students and draw upon expertise from outside the school as needed. The district set an expectation that principals would meet regularly in a self-governing family of school groupings (the senior high and its feeder school) to work collaboratively on issues of interest and importance to them, accessing district staff as needed. We assigned system staff, such as speech pathologists and psychologists, to these families of schools and asked the principals to decide how best to use these resources. The program and services supervisors took on leadership for projects that were generated by groups of schools, for example, facilitating connections with the arts community and working with secondary school principals in their school-restructuring efforts. As much as possible, we tried to configure system resources in response to needs identified by schools, but we also saw a role for the system in gathering and disseminating information about research, provincial program changes, and other issues of relevance to schools. We envisioned that the district could become a resource for schools as they determined for themselves how best to fulfill their obligations to implement provincial programs and as they worked on their school priorities.

There is no doubt that we experienced growing pains as we attempted to make these changes. There were pressures on the supervisors to shift back into their old roles—to take responsibility and control from the schools. Parents were not always satisfied to resolve conflicts at the school level; we still received a great many calls asking district staff to intervene when parents were not happy about a decision that had been made by a principal. Some district staff from other departments complained that supervisors in our department were not doing their jobs because they turned problems back to the school. Some supervisors clearly wanted to return to the predictability and stability of their old roles. Others found ways to re-exert the power they felt they were losing. Although some principals seemed reluctant to take on the responsibilities we devolved to them, most reacted positively and were willing to live with the uncertainties as new structures, processes, and relationships evolved. The self-governing family of schools groups gradually took shape and began seeking out district support for projects they wanted to undertake.

It is not possible to predict how the district structures would have evolved had the amalgamation not occurred. As I reflect on our two-year exploration, I can see that power relationships were changing. Principals and teachers were beginning to have more voice. District staff were moving—some reluctantly—away from command and control forms of leadership. We were, however, far from transforming the hierarchical nature of our bureaucracy. We had taken only small steps toward the creation of a different kind of organization and had only begun to envision what forms a system like that might take.

Advocacy

Having a position of relative power in the organization enabled me to be an effective advocate for equity and social justice through my proactive support of district policy implementation. In particular, I became the champion of a committee responsible for implementing the sexual harassment policy which the school board had approved just before I became superintendent. Of all my efforts to bring critical issues to the center of my work, the support of this committee was the least complicated and most rewarding. I became a mentor for the committee chair, ensured that the committee had resources and released time for professional development activities, and kept the policy implementation on the district agenda. We found funds to hire an outside resource person who helped district staff bring a gender analysis to issues of sexual harassment. My active involvement in the implementation process sent an important message to the system about the importance of the policy. Inquiries that began with the policy soon broadened to include thorny issues such as gender discrimination and homophobia that previously had been rarely, if ever, discussed openly.

Creating Critical Conversations

For me, becoming critically literate has meant tackling the political issues head on in my writing. As a superintendent, I tried to use writing to create critical conversations through raising questions about systemic practices that I saw as disempowering. For example, I wrote to my colleagues in senior management about the nature of the discourse in our meetings, pointing out how alienating and counterproductive I found the constant battles for control to be. Although I was unsuccessful in drawing any of my colleagues into sustained written conversations, this informal writing did help to generate some dialogue. As well, I contributed short pieces to the newsletters of several professional organizations, in which I critiqued top-down reform efforts, proposed changes in governance that had only the appearance of giving more power to schools and communities, and the dismal record of employment equity in the public education system in Nova Scotia.

Political Lessons

In my two short years as a senior administrator, I learned many lessons about leadership. I know that I was successful in leading differently and that I was able to effect change. Yet, I also became painfully aware of the politics of organizational change. Despite the rhetoric of restructuring—the fine-sounding words like collaboration, empowerment and shared decision making—most people who had occupied formal leadership roles in the hierarchy were loathe to give up the power associated with those positions. Furthermore, males had dominated for such a long time in district administration that their ways of leading and knowing had become the norm. When I, as the only female in the senior leadership group, questioned certain of their practices, they often could not see why I saw a problem with the way they had operated successfully for years. Having now moved on from that district leadership role, I can see how formidable are the institutional barriers to the kinds of changes my colleagues and I were advocating. We had many struggles in trying to enact our rather modest agenda, for example, giving schools more control over resources, inviting more voices into decision making, and taking a proactive stance in support of human rights' policies. In light of that, bringing about the systemic changes needed to make public education truly socially just and equitable seems quite daunting. While I recognize that these systemic changes can only occur through the actions of individuals like me, I also know the high personal cost of being proactive in an environment in which one feels like an alien much of the time.

That sense of alienation was particularly strong in my interactions with my male colleagues on the senior team. It is clear that more than one factor contributed to my marginalization. Gender was an issue, but so were professional orientation and philosophy. I had taken a nontraditional path to senior administration through teaching and curriculum leadership; my colleagues collectively had many years of experience as managers in educational and private-sector settings. When I offered my perspectives on leadership, one of my male colleagues would often deliver a lecture on the fine points of management. When I tried to talk about how we were doing our work, specifically, to point out the contradictions between what we said the system was about and what we were actually doing, the others soon brought the conversation back to the real business—the more urgent, practical matters of "running the system." As Australian researcher Jill Blackmore (1995a; 1995b) has documented in her ongoing studies of gender, educational administration, and restructuring, many senior female leaders in organizations experience being simultaneously insiders and outsiders.

Blackmore interviewed seven female senior bureaucrats in the Australian Ministry of Education, all of whom had a history of voluntary and paid community work and social action before coming into government to provide leadership for policy development. These so-called "femocrats" were "part of the mainstream of everyday bureaucratic life and yet marginalised because of their concern with equity as a primary motivation for being in administration." Like me, they entered administration with the idea that they could change the system: "to make it more equitable and empowering, and all saw it as an opportunity to influence policy-making at the centre. Their ambivalence about the bureaucracy derived from the tension between their past experiences which confirmed the view that bureaucracies were largely disabling structures, and their personal experience as leaders in many organisational contexts which led them to understand that administration was about people not things" (1995a, p. 300). One of the women quoted by Blackmore could have been me talking: "Bev recalls how her attempts to promote debate or reflection meant 'a lot of people see me as oppositional, others see me as a dinosaur left over from the seventies who hasn't realised the world has changed'" (1995a, p. 302).

When the women moved inside the bureaucracy, they discovered that their beliefs about how policy should be developed, through an ongoing, recursive consultative process, and about how the day-to-day work of the organization should be carried out were at odds with the dominant, masculinist, technical-rational modes of working. Moreover, they found that there was

> an often uncritical acceptance that bureaucratic rationality
> means fragmentation and specialisation of tasks, territoriality
> and hierarchy. It assumes that policy can be divided into dis-
> crete stages and that it is a neutral task. Julie commented that
> the dominant technical-rational approach meant that "what
> was a very masculinist, patriarchal environment was seen by
> most merely as bureaucratic practice." (1995a, 303)

In reading the excerpts from these interviews, I relived many of my own feelings of marginalization in senior administration and my frustrations at my inability to articulate my critique in such a way that the institutional practices that I found so alienating would be problematized for my male colleagues.

Like so many other women who have taken on leadership roles, I found that the atmosphere became chillier and chillier, the higher up the bureaucratic ladder I climbed. It is important to understand, however, that my concerns are not primarily about what happened to me personally but about the larger questions raised by my experiences. How can those of us who believe whole systems need to be transformed in order to create socially just public education have a greater impact on the organization? Is it possible to reform the system from within? I must say I am less optimistic about that than I was before I tried to do it. I am convinced that one person in a strategic position can make a difference, but it is very lonely work and I am skeptical about the possibilities of one individual having much impact on entrenched institutional practices.

Yet, everything I read about educational reform tells me that the institutional practices I found so disempowering on a personal level are the very ones that have proven to be barriers to successful, enduring change. As Hargreaves (1997) expresses it, "If our struggle is for the needs of all children and not just for the elite few, then markets and managerialism will help us little in our quest." What we need are "openness, informality, care, attentiveness, lateral working relationships, reciprocal collaboration, candid and vibrant dialogue, and a willingness to face uncertainty together," not only within the schools which have been the focus of so much of our reform efforts but within the bureaucracies that surround them:

> The struggle for positive educational change must now move beyond the school in order to enrich what goes on within it. It must fully engage our hearts as well as our minds. And it must extend emotionally beyond the internal management of schools themselves to the high-powered politics of educational reform and restructuring above them. City halls and school district offices should not be fortresses against feelings. (p. 22)

Leading from the Edge

Despite the difficulties I encountered, I would have stayed in senior administration and kept working at effecting change. In the spring of 1996, however, the provincial government's decision to amalgamate twenty-one school districts in Nova Scotia into seven regional organizations resulted in our district being joined with two others in the area to create a school system of nearly sixty thousand students. Unfortunately, the hiring process was highly politicized, and many of us in leadership roles became caught up in the turf wars across organizations as the three school districts being amalgamated struggled for dominance in the new regional organization. Not only I, but most of the colleagues who had been part of the community working for change, found ourselves excluded from the positions for which we were most qualified and in which we had the most interest. Like many others who endured this process, I was exhausted and extremely angry by the end of the school year. I chose not to move into another administrative position at the district or school level and took a leave of absence to accept a term appointment in the faculty of education at Mount Saint Vincent

University. A major focus of that assignment has been to explore ways in which the university can partner with other members of the educational community to enhance professional development and action-research opportunities for teachers. Again I find myself at the center of an organizational-change effort through which we are trying to share expertise and resources and to create more flexibility within and across institutions.

I have a sense that working from slightly outside the school system, but still connected, creates more space within which to experiment. Being positioned at the center of the organization did nothing to decrease my feelings of marginalization; if anything, they were exacerbated. Perhaps it is from the edge that I will be able to foster the contexts within which the critical questions about disempowering institutional practices can become part of the discourse of organizational change. Leaving my administrative position has given me the time to begin a doctoral program with a focus on organizational change and leadership. My brief sojourn as an insider generated enough research questions to keep me going for a long, long time.

I have had a number of conversations with principals, teachers, and other educators both within and outside the district about what my colleagues and I were trying to accomplish and about how those efforts were brought to an abrupt halt by the amalgamation. It has been gratifying to learn that we were making a difference and that many in the system are outraged that we are not part of the leadership team in the new district. While I assumed that the treatment we experienced in the hiring was just nasty interdistrict politics, others have interpreted those experiences differently. It was widely circulated that I, in particular, was passed over for leadership "because I was too supportive of teachers." I also heard that I was considered a problem because of my politics. Many said, "If they can do this to you, imagine what might happen to us!"

Clearly, many believe that the treatment we received was punishment for trying to act on our beliefs and for speaking out. While there were certainly painful and difficult personal consequences for me and others as a result of the amalgamation hiring process, the more serious, long-term consequence may well be the silencing of those who fear that the costs of speaking out may just be too high for them. I recognize that the risks may be too great for individuals who have fewer options and resources than I have. Yet, as Michelle Fine commented at a conference several years ago, "silencing is the glue that holds the hierarchy together." Therefore, as I contemplate the bureaucracy from my position outside the system, I am more determined than ever not to be silenced and to prevent the silencing of others in whatever ways I can. I have no regrets about spending two years in senior administration and would return if the right opportunity presented itself. Now, however, I would have the advantage of a more informed critical analysis to guide me along the way. Meanwhile, there is no shortage of leadership opportunities, and there is an abundance of laughter, learning, and productive work out here on the edge.

References

Blackmore, J. (1995a). Policy as dialogue: Feminist administrators working for educational change." *Gender and Education, 7*(3), 293–313.

Blackmore, J. (1995b). Where's the level playing field? A feminist perspective on educational restructuring. Paper presented at the Annual Conference of the Australian Association of Research in Education.

Church, S. M. (1996). *The future of whole language: Reconstruction or self-destruction?* Portsmouth, NH: Heinemann.

Church, S. M. (1991). *With literacy and justice for all: Rethinking the social in language and education.* New York: Falmer.

Edelsky, C. (1994). Education for democracy. *Language Arts, 71*(4), 252–257.

Fine, M. (1990). Making controversy: Who's "At Risk?" *Journal of Urban and Cultural Studies, 1*(1), 55–68.

Fullan, M. (1993). *Change forces: Probing the depths of educational reform.* New York: Falmer.

Giroux, H. A. (1987). Critical literacy and student experience: Donald Graves' approach to literacy. *Language Arts, 64*(2), 175–181.

Giroux, H.A., & McLaren, P. (1986). Teacher education and the politics of engagement: The case for democratic schooling. *Harvard Educational Review, 56*(3), 213–238.

Hargreaves, A. (1997). Rethinking educational change: Going deeper and wider in the quest for success. In A. Hargreaves (Ed.), *Rethinking educational change with heart and mind* (pp. 1–27). Alexandria, VA: Association for Supervision and Curriculum Development.

McLaren, P. (1989). *Life in schools: An introduction to critical pedagogy in the foundations of education.* New York: Longman.

Oakes, J. (1985). *Keeping track: How schools structure inequality.* New Haven, CT: Yale University Press.

Shannon, P. (Ed.) (1992). *Becoming political: Readings and writings in the politics of literacy education.* Portsmouth, NH: Heinemann.

Simon, R. (1987). Empowerment as a pedagogy of possibility. *Language Arts, 64*(4), 370–382.

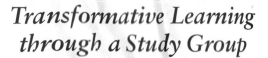

CHAPTER FIFTEEN

Transformative Learning through a Study Group

ELIZABETH R. SAAVEDRA

University of New Mexico

My journey in transformative learning began as a classroom teacher and eventually led me to the University of New Mexico as researcher and educational activist. Through the years, I have been working with groups of teachers at their school sites, learning a great deal about the process of teacher transformation through study groups. In this chapter I will be describing one of these, the Davis Teacher Study Group. But first, a bit about the beginnings of my own transformative journey.

A Bit of History

In the summer of 1980, I had just finished my fourth year as a classroom teacher, and had made a critical discovery. I found that I knew precious little of how children learn, and more specifically how they learn to read and write. I knew how to follow teachers' manuals and how to use textbooks and reading basals. I had assumed that the materials and activities I used in the classroom were based on sound ideas about learning and literacy processes, and therefore if I diligently used these materials I was sure to be an effective teacher. In other words, I had swallowed—hook, line, and sinker—the concept of "teacher-proof materials." And no wonder. In my undergraduate preservice teaching program and then in the District inservice workshops during my first four years of teaching, I had been presented with a transmission view of learning and a skills orientation toward literacy development—viewpoints I dutifully applied. But the more I worked and applied what I had been taught to do, the more I realized that my students, who were linguistically, ethnically, and socioeconomically diverse, were barely progressing in their learning and literacy development. Frustrated with the present and disillusioned with the future (i.e., with my own potential as a teacher), I came to a critical insight: Studying was going to help. I simply had to learn more about learning and literacy development. Little did I know that studying (goal-driven questioning, serious investigating, and critiquing) and study groups were going to become such constants in my professional life.

That summer I took a class entitled "The Reading Process," taught by Claudia Dybdahl, a visiting professor who had been a student of Ken and Yetta Goodman. In this class I began to examine my own history as a learner, a reader, and a writer and the schooling I had experienced as a working class Chicana. In that class it started to become clear: Certain educational opportunities had been kept out of my reach. Not just mine, but minorities' in general. Through expectations, pedagogical methods, and content, we had been denied a rigorous education. Eventually, I made the connection between opportunities denied to me as a student and opportunities I was offering (or withholding) as a teacher. I also began to question how, within a female-dominated profession, teachers are situated in a bureaucratical and paternalistic hierarchy and how they/we live a general tradition of disempowerment.

When I returned to school in the fall, I began a new position as a Chapter 1 reading teacher. I was eager to try out my new views. However, I was met with opposition by my peers, students, and parents; others were not charmed by the changes I had made. Still, I kept on studying, talking with others, and reformulating my goals, choosing as my ultimate goal working to eradicate social inequity and injustice, and helping to create an educational system that transforms, rather than reproduces and perpetuates social injustice. The loftiness of that goal felt right for me then; it inspired me. It still does.

The following year, I pulled together the first of what became a series of weekly study groups to explore whole language theory and, with my peers, to pursue some of the questions that had transformed my own thinking and sense of myself as a teacher. I did not presume to be the expert, capable of teaching my peers; instead, we met because we were unable to find experts or even support from the district to learn about whole language. What the district provided were one-shot workshops. What we hungered for was an opportunity for dialogue, reflection, support, and continuity so that we could learn about the things we were interested in and what we then felt was crucial to our own working conditions—namely, whole language.

The Davis Teacher Study Group

Ten years later, as a doctoral student at the University of Arizona, I began a teachers' study group at Davis Bilingual Learning Center in the Tucson Unified School District. For the first time, I was not only participating in a teacher study group; I was studying study groups. I was interested in transformative development—i.e., changes in basic beliefs to be brought about by pursuing one's own questions while maintaining an awareness of power relationships. Our first meeting began with a discussion of the teachers' major concerns—teaching language-minority students and how to effectively facilitate their learning. Throughout the study, two layers wove through our exploration—questions chosen by individual participants and those chosen by the collective group. As the teachers engaged in critical inquiry concerning these questions, my own questions dealt with teachers' emancipatory learning and the transformation process itself. Both of these simultaneous inquiries included an analysis of the internal and external effects of power.

At the heart of the Davis Teacher Study Group was an agenda for emancipatory learning; i.e., for making sure that the major activity was critical reflection and self-reflection for the purpose of facilitating transformations. We were trying, through self-conscious and informed critique, to free ourselves "from forces that limit our options and our control over our lives, forces that have been taken for granted or seen as beyond our control (Cranston, 1994, p. 16)."

As is common for teacher study groups, the Davis study group met weekly with a designated facilitator (a role that alternated among members), for an agreed amount of time (one and a half hours, in our case). Both outside that time and within it, we read, wrote, critiqued, reflected, dialogued, and came to new conclusions. Just as important, we created together a community for our mutual support as learners, one that could (and did) lead to significant personal and professional change.

During the two and a half years we were together, our studies went through cycles. We would begin by establishing a topic and a direction. Then, after lengthy discussion of interests and needs and how these related to the topic, we would discuss various issues and questions we had about the topic. From these questions, the entire group would decide on one or two as focal questions for the group. Additionally, each participant chose questions for individual study. Usually, we spent two or three sessions generating and negotiating topic and question choices.

Next, the Davis Teacher Study Group would determine individual and group goals and plan the directions, activities, and strategies of the investigation. We planned what articles and books we would read, by when, and by whom; what kinds of activities we would undertake (reflective journals, demonstrations, classroom observations, data collection such as students' reading or writing samples); and who we would call upon as expert consultants (often these were our own members), over what length of time. It often took a couple of sessions to work out these plans.

As we met to plan and subsequently to talk about the work we had agreed to do (the reading, classroom observations, journal writing, etc.), we worked at developing collaborative, cooperative, respectful, and nurturing interactions. We were determined not to replicate the social and power structures and ideological stances of the institutional status quo. We had established conditions and activities that helped us to avoid that replication (e.g., settings for dialogue, direct access to sources of knowledge, ownership of topics and processes, a safe space for dissonance and conflict, etc.) But the collaborative interactions were what supported us as we tried to integrate our classroom experience with our investigations and to learn at "deep" enough levels to effect transformations. On the one hand, the transformative conditions were constructed through study group interactions; on the other, they emerged from our growing professional and intellectual strength.

Though we shared our discoveries informally in each session, we also planned a more formal, deliberate presentation of what was learned in order to culminate the investigation. These formal presentations would address what was learned about the topic (including our beliefs about the topic); about students' learning and the implications for our teaching; and about ourselves as teachers, researchers, and educational activists. Each of these cycles (developing questions, planning activities for investigating the questions, presenting our learning) enhanced our professionalism and competence. And each led us toward new directions and helped us to refine new questions.

Facilitating the Process of Emancipatory Learning and Transformations: Some Conditions

As a result of studying (and participating in) the study group at Davis, I have had to rethink my work as a teacher educator—what I know and what I do—vis à vis both my students and my colleagues.

The Need for Dedicated Space

I now understand more about the need to create a specific space for collaborative, transformative learning. It is always difficult to meet with peers during the regular teaching day. Without specific space in our week being set aside for the study group, we could not have experienced the same kind of learning. We needed those study-group sessions in order to push the edges of what we knew and what we experienced. We needed the regularity of the time and at least that amount of uninterrupted time to sustain a problem-posing stance, to keep focused on the topic we had chosen and the quality of our interactions. There was always the lure of letting immediate business and what was occurring in our day-to-day lives intrude into our study group sessions. We had to challenge ourselves about how we spent our time together. That we were able to keep to our intention during the space/time we had set aside can be seen in the coherence of the topics and activities we engaged in during the two and a half years of the study group (see Figure 1).

Being able to work seriously on these topics would not have been possible without the time we had carved out and the space we had created by temporarily moving aside the demands of our daily lives in school.

Critical Questioning

I am now even more convinced of the importance of the inquiry process in transformative learning. That inquiry process was central to our personal and professional changes as well as the changes in how we worked as a group. It enabled us to explore, shift, change, and develop. It pushed us to ask questions of importance to us. It let us venture far beyond the typical learning of methodology and practice that we were accustomed to. It helped us to learn about the content we teach, the contexts in which we teach, and the reasoning and beliefs which ground both the content and contexts we were responsible for. It also helped us to learn about ourselves and each other, about the experiences that have shaped our thinking and actions, about the knowledge and expertise we have, and the ways our interactions shape our learning and teaching.

More than that, through inquiry, we grew into a collaborative and reflective collective. Learning how to learn together and to work together was a major transformation. It did not happen quickly, smoothly, or easily. We experienced dissonance and frustration as we struggled to understand what we were learning and sharing with each other. We tended to want to find ideal solutions, to try to resolve hard issues and lay them to rest once and for all. It took considerable work before we achieved mutual trust and before we were able to welcome ambiguities. But as we persisted in the inquiry process to which we had committed ourselves, we began to experience some profound and exhilarating

Davis Study Group Themes

Issues/questions about biliteracy; Davis goals/objectives

Collecting unassisted student writing samples in Spanish

Transforming deficit myths (Flores, et al.)

Involving parents of students learning Spanish as L2

Analysis of students' bilingual reading/writing; development of
    appropriate evaluations for Davis students

Teacher demonstration v. teacher intervention

Writing program components

Management of writing workshop

Getting kids to edit

Sharing student writing

Influence of reading on writing

Theme cycles introduced

Students as researchers

Writing process: from multiple drafts to publication

Children helping children

Designing instructional strategies that really address the objective

Writing conferences

Groupings in the classroom

Writing to learn

Tracking students' writing progress while at Davis

E. Saavedra works with small group of students

Daily writing time

Process writing

Cumulative writing folders

Generativeness in writing

Importance of demonstration by a more knowledgeable person

Introducing different types of writing

Using literature to help students develop their writing

Theme cycles introduced; process discussed

Communicating with other teachers (other grade levels)

Revisiting students' work: marking for reference to peer comments

continued on next page

FIGURE 1. *Topics and activities engaged in during the study-group period.*

Figure 1 continued

Planning for next year:
  biliteracy development (different disciplines)
  portfolios/assessment
  faculty-meeting study groups once a month
  facilitating development of writing in both languages
  developing ourselves as writers/teachers with literature study
  student research (documenting with audio/video)

Brainstormed study-group topics (integrating curriculum, biliteracy
  development, writing process/developing children's writing,
  literature studies, developing reading and writing in the content
  areas)

Using the study-group experience for personal development

Elizabeth as a resource in the classroom

Portfolios

Writing/reading samples from bilingual students

Miscue analysis (choose a child; set up analysis schedule; review reading selections)

Research skills; check out library for teachers

Teacher's role in theme cycle studies

Getting to the heart of the matter: a search for origins (Steven Levy)

Practicing the first step of the theme cycle (brainstorm/web)

Teaching kids to do research: what is research?

Practicing miscue analysis: Luis M [student] (silent reading/retelling)

Learning through experiencing the theme cycle process in study group

Asking students to help define research by describing what they do
  when they want to find out about something

---

changes. The examples that follow concern only two teachers, Ellen and Maria. It is important to note, however, that transformative development also occurred for the other participants.

In the first year, when the study group began, Ellen (and the other teachers) came to the study group expecting to be handed ideas, knowledge, and direction. Over time, Ellen realized that she must construct and shape her own learning—in her classroom and in the study group. In her written reflection on students becoming writers in both Spanish and English, she noted:

We started out in study group examining the process children go through in developing the ability to write for various purposes. Elizabeth began bringing us, over the next few months, articles about both the writing process and the teaching of writing . . . we commenced talking, we did discuss, and discuss, but that discussion lit a fire; it served as a catalyst for me, in that it inspired me with new knowledge, both theoretical and practical, that I was able to translate into action. I set out to try these ideas in my own classroom, to try to replicate the successes I read about, and finding that some worked better than others (of course), for a variety of reasons—which reasons I was encouraged to identify, to reflect on, to use as a basis for adaptation of classroom events to this particular group of students and to my own personal style of teaching.

At about the time of this writing, Ellen began to deliberately take a more active role in facilitating the activity of the group. It was through the inquiry process that she became conscious of her beliefs about learning. When she realized that she saw learning as a passive process, she began to make changes in how she approached her own learning and in how she facilitated her students' learning. Later, she broadened her focus to include the content (the "what" of her learning and teaching); the underlying ideological and theoretical premises of that content; the structure, goals, and methods within the institution of schooling and their effects on teachers and students (especially minority learners); and her theories, beliefs, and goals concerning all of the above.

Our inquiry process was not one of questioning for questioning's sake. We questioned with a critical eye toward systems of power, and we questioned in collaboration; i.e., we had a conceptual frame combined with an interactional context that pushed us to discover, learn, and transform. We recognized that most of our professional learning had occurred through staff development activities which had provided little more than new ideas for current practice. Almost never did staff development activities lead to substantial changes in our knowledge and beliefs.

Our study group provided a very different result. For instance, during one of the study group sessions, when Ellen was relating that her daughter had been tested on cultural knowledge as defined by E. D. Hirsch, she began to realize that what is to be taught and therefore what knowledge is privileged are "handed down" to teachers from the powers that be. "Obviously," she said, "there's been a lot of handing down for a lot of years, and here we are in the middle of the system." Ellen was changing her beliefs and ideologies about learning and teaching, but she was aware that the ideologies that govern the system stayed the same. She went on to talk about this tension as it would emerge in the community: "I'm wondering how this [the changes she was making] is all going to come out, and how it's going to be accepted by parents." She also pointed out that she wanted to talk with the principal about the paradox of administrators supporting her for her innovative teaching but also pressuring her to get high test results by focusing on specific skills. Finally, she juxtaposed her work in helping children develop into critically conscious learners with what she called "putting our print on them," preparing them to be well-trained vessels of standard knowledge. Through inquiry with the study group, Ellen became more conscious of the conflicting voices of the different positions she needed to reconcile in order to teach according to her new beliefs. She came to see more clearly that as a subordinate within a hierarchical system, she had to consider the vision, expectations, and goals of her supervisor and also of the parent community in trying to negotiate change. Indeed, a major consistent thread throughout our study group sessions was not only to reconcile the space between our ideological beliefs and our practice, but also to figure out how to navigate the space between what was best for the students and ourselves and the requirements and mandates of the institution.

Ellen was not the only one who shifted paradigms, found herself faced with new dilemmas, but faced them knowing she had come to them through traveling a considerable professional and personal distance. Maria, another participant, talked about her own shifts. She remembered how she had taken her plans and agendas and imposed them on her students, but then through her own critical inquiry realized that students had "their own minds" and experiences that they could draw from, their own abilities and knowledge that could be extended through an inquiry process. This was an important statement for Maria. Until that time, she had held back, abstaining from making definite statements about her own beliefs. In a subsequent meeting, she began to talk about how, in previous times, when she heard teachers talking negatively about students and their learning abilities, she would quietly listen. Now, however, "I can no longer sit in silence—when I hear these teachers talking about their students' shortcomings, I have to speak up. I have to ask them about their teaching and how they think about the way students learn. I can't keep quiet anymore. I won't be quiet anymore."

Acting on What We Had Learned

From the beginning of the Davis Teacher Study Group, I had understood, to some extent, the history and experiences that get teachers to devalue their own knowledge. Participating in the study group showed me how important it is for teachers who are devoting themselves to critical inquiry—inquiry that is likely to contradict accepted knowledge in the system—to learn to value their learning and to help others to see it as legitimate. Our study group's new knowledge resulted from reflection and empirical investigation, and we had to learn to trust it. And we did—by acting on it in our classrooms and by sharing it. Acting on it in our teaching led us back into further inquiry that deepened our understanding and our confidence in what we knew. Sharing (indeed, building) our new knowledge with each other led us, eventually, to want to tell others about what we were experiencing and discovering. Toward the end of the second year of the Davis study group, we returned to questions that we had raised at the very beginning, questions about teaching linguistic-minority students in ways that would draw on their strengths and knowledge and extend their intellectual abilities.

As we began to reconsider these questions in light of what we had come to know and understand, we felt compelled to encourage the other teachers at Davis to deal with these issues. Perhaps, if the other teachers couldn't come to the study group, the study group could go to the other teachers. The study group teachers approached the principal, who consented enthusiastically, and plans were made to conduct the first schoolwide study group. I asked the teachers why they felt so strongly about taking an action such as this. Maria said,

> I am learning a lot. I have changed my thinking. I am aware of how much we affect children, how our teaching affects them. The way we think about and talk about children has an effect. I can't just sit and watch this school keep on doing the things I have discovered are not good for children. I have to do something. Before, I wouldn't have. But now I have to.

Ellen added,

> We have goals concerning biliteracy, and our practice is not achieving those goals with our students, and from the research that I have read and from our discussions, and from maybe smaller pieces of . . . what other people have done in other places, I BELIEVE that we can make this goal happen, that we can work toward biliteracy. . . . There is a way. I really believe this. It's not an unfounded belief, entirely on faith. In reading about what other people have done, I've said, "Yeah, this is what we could do." We could. It's going to take some sacrifice; it is going to take a lot of learning and change. But we will do it."

In that first meeting with the staff, the discussion was lively and engaging. The focus was on ways to determine schoolwide development of bilingualism and biliteracy, and on how to examine the social and political learning contexts for linguistic-minority students. The core participants had found that their peers supported their growth and ideas. The entire staff felt that these issues were important to them as well and decided at the end of that first meeting to begin a biweekly study group composed of the entire staff.

Conclusion

The Davis Teacher Study Group was based on a major premise: If teachers are to transform learning contexts for their students, then the learning contexts for teachers must be transformed. This premise is, in turn, based on the assumption that teachers need to work together in order to develop knowledge and practice that will affirm themselves and their students. The Davis study group provided a radically different professional culture for the participants. Not only did it offer a space for participants to determine the direction of their own personal and professional development, and not only did it provide a context for creating a collaborative, collegial learning community, it also opened up a critical space. It gave us all opportunities to confront our own situatedness, as male or female, and as members of diverse racial, ethnic, cultural, and economic groups. It helped us to use a framework of relations of power to analyze (not just to complain about or to feel oppressed by) our own interactions and intersections with institutional structures—all as part of a process of transforming ourselves and our schools.

Reference

Cranston, P. (1994). *Understanding and promoting transformative learning: A guide for educators of adults.* San Francisco, CA: Jossey-Bass.

CHAPTER SIXTEEN

Literacy Education as a Site for Social Justice: What Do Our Practices Do?

BARBARA COMBER & HELEN NIXON

University of South Australia

Each of us grew up in working-class families who saw education as the way to a better future. Like many women of our class and generation who "made it" with moderate success in school, we trained for a "helping profession" and became teachers. We saw ourselves as charged with a moral mission. We were ready to "give" other children the same chances that we had had, chances we thought were related to success in reading and writing. However as classroom teachers we found "no quick fix" for our students (Allington & Walmsley, 1995). Later, as teacher educators, we met hundreds of other literacy teachers who worked to make a difference in the life chances of their students. Yet, despite good intentions and successive innovations with regard to literacy pedagogies, statewide audits indicate that children disadvantaged by poverty remain statistically more likely to perform in the lower bands of the range on mainstream literacy assessments (Education Department of South Australia, 1992). As literacy educators in the university setting, we remain committed to social justice. But what kinds of interventions can we make? In this chapter we raise questions about the relationships between school literacies and social justice; we describe a project which foregrounds literacy, diversity, and socioeconomic disadvantage; and by referring to the work of three teachers, we illustrate the complexity and the possibilities in working for social justice.

School Literacies and Social Justice?

> People know what they do; they frequently know why they
> do what they do; but what they don't know is what they do
> does. (Michel Foucault, quoted in Dreyfus & Rabinow, 1983,
> p. 187)

Language teachers often hold a social-justice agenda. We
employ discourses of liberation and hope that our work has a
positive impact on the immediate and postschool lives of students. In recent times, many of us have believed that the acquisition of literacy is best achieved through child-centred pedagogies.
The removal of teacher direction would enable the child learner
to grow naturally. Egalitarian communities of learners, including
the teacher-learner, would behave in just and democratic ways.
We have assumed that whole language classrooms were ideologically sound utopian sites, where students and teachers would
automatically become better people through literacy. We have
assumed that the power offered by school literacies would be the
same for all students and equally divided among them; that
school literacies would empower previously disadvantaged students. School graduates would be empowered, literate citizens
committed to democratic ideals. This is the story we have told
ourselves.

As whole language teachers we have, in Foucault's terms,
known what we do and why we do it, but perhaps known less
about what we do does! Our assumption that literacy offers
power and justice arises from the realisation that language use
always involves power relations. A whole language philosophy
promises power for students, yet our theory tells us little about
how power might be exercised in classrooms or in society, only
that language and literacy are pivotal. We have invited children
to join our "literacy clubs" now and promised them better
futures, without thinking about whose clubs these are and what
kinds of identities they require and who might be excluded. We
have been reluctant to consider the unanticipated effects of
school literacy practices, that certain formations of literacy,
including whole language, may maintain disadvantage, may be

normative rather than transformative, domesticating rather than liberating, alienating rather than connecting (Donald, 1993; Edelsky with Harman, 1991; Stuckey, 1991). Without an analysis of how language and literate practices work in social and political contexts for and against different groups, our philosophy is of limited use for a pedagogy for social justice.

Whole language educators have made many claims for literacy. Potentially, whole language repositions teachers as researchers and producers of local knowledge and students as active initiators of and participants in conversations and literate practices. These moves are important for a pedagogy driven by social justice agendas. However, we think it is time to further question the stories we have told ourselves about literacy and about the promises we have made for progressive pedagogies. Our questions include: What do whole language practices do? What kinds of students do they produce? What different effects might whole language practices have on different groups of students? Can we assume that removing the teacher from the centre produces democracy? Ironically, while theorists may make claims that whole language empowers disadvantaged children, the local enactment and effects of the pedagogy may be quite different. It is not so much that pedagogies do not "work," but that they "work" in ways we do not anticipate.

Studies of literacy practices and power relations in child-centred classrooms challenge claims that whole language produces justice or empowerment, either in the immediacy of the classroom or in students' life trajectories (Delpit, 1988; Luke, 1996). When classrooms are constituted as sites for individual children to find a "voice," *which* children produce *which* texts, and to *what ends,* must be the subject of ongoing scrutiny (Dyson, 1993; Gilbert, 1989; Lensmire, 1994). If literacy is socially constructed, how gender, race, class, religion, and geographic location make a difference in school literacy teaching and learning become urgent questions for language educators. Socially critical researchers emphasise that students learn to read and write particular kinds of texts that represent different kinds of worlds, different kinds of knowledge, and position readers in different ways (Baker & Freebody, 1989; Gilbert, 1990; Luke, 1993).

Recent research and theorising suggest that literacy practices are multiple, historically contingent, and culturally specific. Literate practices are not neutral or innocent; literate practices privilege and celebrate texts which maintain the disadvantage of minority groups (including women and girls, people of colour, rural people, religious groups, aged people, people with disabilities). In classrooms, teacher commentary and questioning around text interpretation and construction may reinforce dominant cultural ideologies. Choice of texts may maintain a literary canon and exclude other genres and formations of language use and literacy which are important in students' peer and family communities. Choice of pedagogical techniques, interaction patterns, and assessment tasks may maintain the advantage of students who are already practised with mainstream cultural norms. Choice of topics may limit children's inquiries to safe, apolitical studies. Whole language alone does not automatically counter such problems.

The everyday moment-by-moment choices teachers and students make, and how they talk about those choices, construct the literate practices of the classroom. Those choices and ways of talking may have little to do with democracy or social justice. Even where multiculturalism is the object of inquiry, for instance, our practices can trivialise and depoliticise the nature of study. In one elementary classroom, when children mentioned skin "colour" as one difference between them and a Hawaiian visitor, their teacher redirected them to investigate food preparation in traditional Hawaiian culture as a more appropriate topic. There is always the potential to explore topics in ways that either take children's questions seriously or that reconstruct them as neutral and safe. A review of what can be talked, read, and written about in the classroom, and what is excluded, may be a good place to begin in evaluating literacy curriculum in terms of social justice. If children are not allowed to talk about colour, how can an antiracism curriculum function? It may be that the sentiments teachers fear go underground. We do not wish to suggest that it is easy for teachers to talk with children about race, class, culture, wealth, poverty, injustice, gender, and religion, but failure to talk about such topics in schools which proclaim their democracy results in a romanticised and individualised view of difference.

To take another illustration of how whole language pedagogies and theories can unwittingly create difficulties for children, let us consider the importance which has recently been given to parents reading to children and hearing their children read— home reading. Family literacy practices have become central during the past two decades because children whose parents read to them and hear them read perform better on school reading. The aim of many projects is to ensure that parents read to children. In a national survey of early years teachers in schools serving socioeconomically disadvantaged communities in Australia, teachers reported the two most important strategies in their literacy programs were parents reading to children and parents hearing children read (Badger, Comber, & Weeks, 1993). Home reading events were considered more important than what the teacher or children did at school. It seems to us that there is a problem with such thinking; that as whole language educators who have advocated sharing books with children, we have created a problem rather than a solution. The reason why home reading events make so much difference to success in school is that school reading events are replicated upon them. So children who have more practice in such events do better; hence the rationale for getting families to do more at home of what teachers do in school. But surely there are other ways to consider the question of how children come to early literacy.

Other literacy practices go on in homes and communities which may be equally important to foster in schools and which may not disadvantage children without access to regular home reading practice (in English) with parents. Families read environmental print, the packaging on food and other commodities, the junk mail which arrives daily in mailboxes, the advertising and credits on television, the letters which arrive from relatives elsewhere. Any of the multitude of literate practices in the home and community could be models for what goes on in school. There is no developmental or biological reason why children must learn to read with storybooks, and many children who learn to read prior to schooling do so through their own writing, through access to computers, and so on.

Our point here is not to criticise literature-based reading programs, home reading, shared-book experience, or any of the wonderful activities generated from the insight about the importance of parents reading to children. We simply argue that parents reading storybooks to children is a cultural practice in some communities only. We need to ensure that it does not become a new form of "reading readiness," the absence of which is used to exclude and negatively evaluate children who come with experiences of other forms of literate practices. What is needed is an "opening out" of school literacies so that children are able to use the resources they do bring. Children may bring strong oral traditions; a knowledge of heroes and heroines of popular culture; songs, prayers, and poetry from religious and cultural communities; and the expertise of consumerism. They bring a multiplicity of language and literate practices, some of which are excluded from their school day and some of which are welcomed as "proper" and "appropriate."

When specific cultural practices such as home reading are seen as the norm, then children who have not participated in such practices can be seen as "deficient," "lacking," "without experiences," or "without proper models." Some teachers in the national survey referred to above argued that parents reading to children and hearing children read were so important that the absence of these events put children "at risk." But it is the privileging of such literate practices and their associated behaviours and knowledges at school which puts children "at risk." Clearly, this "deficit discourse" is the opposite of what whole language educators advocate when they stress the importance of family literacy practices. What this example shows, however, is that we need to check out how our recommendations are heard and taken up in local sites. Teachers' own life worlds and values mediate the uptake and enactment of pedagogical practices and curriculum theories.

It is not our intention to review the critiques of whole language in detail (see Comber, 1994; Willinsky, 1990). It is sufficient to say here that we no longer assume empowering effects for school literacy or for particular pedagogies, but we continue to explore what working for equity through literacy education might mean. What kinds of interventions towards social justice can educators make? As university educators with an up-front social justice agenda, how can we act against media onslaughts and economic cuts in order to work in positive ways with teachers in communities which experience material and educational disadvantage?

Documentaries about Literacy, Diversity, and Schooling: A Social Justice Strategy

During the past decade, cumulative research evidence and our own experience forced us to confront the possibility that our teaching, despite our career-long commitments to social justice, may contribute to silence about class, poverty, and race in the English/language arts classroom in both school and university settings. Teachers in disadvantaged schools[1] continued to tell us that mainstream approaches to literacy pedagogy did not work within their contexts, and recent graduates argued that the university did not prepare them to teach in disadvantaged schools. A recent national project found that issues of social justice were largely absent from university courses on language and literacy (Christie et al., 1991). In reviewing our teaching we recognised that our preservice and inservice courses about literacy and schooling failed to foreground educational disadvantage. How could we change our own practices so that equity issues were not ignored or treated in token ways?

We recognise that "social justice" is itself a discursive construction used to different ends by groups with different political agendas (Harvey, 1993). For us, social justice means an ongoing commitment to exploring the effects of our own institutional and discursive practices. In the interests of teachers and students in communities disadvantaged by poverty, this means resisting and changing deficit discourses which attribute blame to people who live in poverty (Kress, 1994; Polakow, 1993). A social justice commitment means disrupting images of disadvantaged students which perpetuate myths about "these kids" as literacy failures and consequently of their schools as the nurseries of potential delinquents. How could we put these principles into our university practice and at the same time produce something that might be useful for our colleagues in schools?

Rather than undertake a traditional research project, we decided to make educational documentaries about teaching literacy in disadvantaged schools.[2] Our aim was to produce polyvocal videos involving student teachers, academics, staff, parents and students from disadvantaged schools, policymakers, consultants from charitable organisations, bureaucrats, and educational researchers. We saw the production of educational documentaries as a positive intervention. By creating an easy-to-use video text about literacy and disadvantage, we might increase the possibility that social justice would be talked about in university literacy and language education classes, beginning with our own work site. In this way we could begin to work against the maintenance of "deficit" discourses. We intended to do this by making problematic the myths that surround constructs such as poverty, literacy, diversity, and disadvantage. We designed the videos to generate conversations and debates and at the same time to document some of the innovative practices of teachers in disadvantaged schools who were explicitly committed to working for social justice.

One of our first tasks was to identify schools where teachers built language and literacy curriculum around critique and social justice, where teachers and students questioned "systems of domination." Because we wanted the documentaries to work for change, we wanted to produce visions for possible action, not only critique. At the same time we did not want to make grandiose claims for the programs we documented. Finding educators in schools who shared our commitments and were prepared to make their work public, and therefore subject to potential criticism, was crucial to the project. Without school-based visionary educators working on socially critical curriculum action there would be no videos. Some of the most innovative teaching of literacy occurs in disadvantaged schools, yet some of the greatest stress and intensification of teachers' work is also present at these sites. We were conscious that we were asking a lot of these school communities. We were fortunate. A number of educators, parents, and students agreed to work with us. This meant student teachers, researchers, camera crews and producers in classrooms, staff rooms, and offices. It meant permission slips to parents and so on. It meant more work. But it also meant an opportunity to document the productive, positive work going on in disadvantaged schools. For us as producers of the documentaries, it also meant facing up to selections—which administrators, teachers, parents, student-teachers, and students in which schools would we show, involved in what kinds of language and literate practices?[3]

The documentaries are concerned with how teachers work for social justice through literacy-related projects in disadvantaged schools. There are six videos entitled: *Literacy, Poverty and Schooling; Becoming a Literacy Teacher in a Diverse Community; Teaching Literacy in Disadvantaged Schools; Communities, Literacy, and Schools; Teaching and Learning at Paralowie R-12 School;* and *Literacy Assessment in Disadvantaged Schools.*

Each video attempts to inform (e.g., we describe how material poverty is defined; numbers of people who are homeless; which groups are considered to be "disadvantaged"); to explain theories (e.g., we explain deficit, difference, and structural inequality theories of educational disadvantage; whole language, genre, and critical literacy); to problematise (e.g., we provide differing views on poverty and on the importance of literacy); to generate conversations (e.g., the voice-over and the images together pose challenging questions); and to work against deficit views of disadvantaged communities. We attempt to take viewers into disadvantaged school communities, to disrupt easy assumptions about what might or should be, and to offer some ways forward.

In the remainder of this chapter we try to reproduce in prose some "vivid portrayals of classroom scenes" from the documentaries to illustrate the struggles and possibilities facing teachers who make social justice central in their curriculum. We focus on the work of our colleagues in the project, teachers and school administrators who were aware that schooling sometimes reproduces educational disadvantage, and who made questions of equity central in their day-to-day work with parents and children. We begin with Barbara Fox's Aboriginal studies class, where students were writing an essay about Aboriginal deaths in police custody; we move next to Nigel Howard's community studies class, where students were producing a brochure about cooperative learning; and finally we focus on Jennifer O'Brien's classroom, where students were analysing gender representation in a picture book.

Barbara Fox: Foregrounding Issues of Race

Barbara Fox, a young Aboriginal woman with majors in Aboriginal studies and Australian history in her undergraduate degree, began her working life with the state's Catholic education system as a project officer for Aboriginal studies. In this position, she worked with others writing, implementing, and trialing the Aboriginal studies syllabus developed for the elementary and junior high school years by the state education department. In the year that our video project began, Barbara was undertaking a one-year postgraduate teacher education course to become a secondary teacher of Aboriginal studies and social science. This was her first step towards achieving her personal and professional goal— to work as a teacher for social justice and equity, with and for Aboriginal people.

For her first practicum as a student teacher, Barbara chose to work at Paralowie R-12 School. This school is located in a low socioeconomic area to the north of Adelaide, the capital city of the state of South Australia, and has more than one thousand students ages 5 years to 18 years. More than half of the school community lives on or beneath the poverty line, and more than half of the students' families receive government assistance for their children's schooling. Twenty-five percent of the students are from non-English-speaking backgrounds (Italian, Greek, Vietnamese, Cambodian, Polish, Spanish) and, important for Barbara, there were more than forty enrolled Aboriginal students (a high proportion for our city). The school had a reputation as a leader in Aboriginal education. In the practicum, Barbara taught Aboriginal studies as a senior school academic subject and worked as a volunteer in the after-school Nunga Homework Centre set up by Aboriginal parents to support Aboriginal students with their studies. The centre is staffed by Aboriginal parent tutors and teacher volunteers. Barbara agreed to being filmed during her practicum and again the following year when she was no longer a student teacher but an employee of the education department as a teacher at Paralowie R-12 School. This allowed us a unique opportunity to record and discuss with Barbara aspects of her development as a teacher working for equity, which we believed would be useful in teacher education classes about literacy teaching and disadvantage.

For this practicum, Barbara's Aboriginal studies lessons were planned with the (white, male, Anglo) classroom teacher, within the framework of a state-accredited tertiary-entrance syllabus. She could be flexible with the topic and pedagogy, but the syllabus required Barbara to help the students research and produce a formal essay which would count for their final assessment. Although young and inexperienced, her commitment to social justice meant that she went straight for a topic that "mattered"— Aboriginal deaths in police custody, thus foregrounding an overtly political and contentious issue within Australian society in general, and an issue of deep personal and political meaning for Aboriginal people in particular. She tackled this topic with a diverse class. Her students included a mix of sixteen- and seventeen-year-old white, Anglo and Aboriginal students who had come through the school in a traditional way, and several mature-aged Aboriginal students who were returning to schooling after many years' absence. These older Aboriginal students were also parents of students at the school, and the class included a father, mother, and daughter from one large family in the community, as well as one of her own middle-aged male relatives who had been closely involved with the school as a parent and tutor for more than six years.

Barbara's curriculum had critique at its centre and made use of typical whole language practices (e.g., drawing on the students' experience, interest, and knowledge; providing students with choices; positioning herself as a facilitator and resource to be consulted rather than an expert or transmitter of information). Barbara provided her students with a range of literacy experiences to draw upon in producing their essays, including viewing and discussing a documentary video on Aboriginal deaths in police custody, and reading and analysing a range of texts: newspaper clippings, transcripts from inquests, investigations into police brutality, and other public documents (e.g., government statistics about the proportions of various sectors of the Australian population arrested and convicted of crimes).

Barbara's situation illustrates what can happen when certain kinds of critique are made the centre of a curriculum and whole language pedagogies are used in a diverse school community. As teacher educators we cannot simply argue from a theoretical position that teachers should "take risks" in the interests of working for a socially just community. We also need to explore the possible real-world consequences of taking certain kinds of risks and using certain pedagogies. In the video project we use instances of what did happen to pose questions and to encourage different ways of understanding what such practices might do. Let's take the example of Barbara's Aboriginal studies class. First, we could ask how Barbara was positioned as a teacher in this class. Ideally, we could say, she was a role model for Aboriginal students; a successful Aboriginal woman training for a profession. But this is not the whole picture. We must also consider that Barbara's race, age, and gender put her in a complex personal and professional situation within this context—and that the personal and the professional are not easily separated. As a teacher in this class, Barbara was in a position of authority. Yet she was also a young, Aboriginal woman teaching male relatives and elders with whom, in other contexts, a very different set of social and power relations existed. It is possible that such a situation generates uncertainty and tension for all participants and affects student learning.

Second, we could ask how Barbara was using the content to work for equity in this class. Ideally, we could say Barbara was working in the interests of democracy by choosing a topic about structural inequality and injustice—Aboriginal deaths in police custody. But once again, this answer may be incomplete. The diversity of the class meant that Barbara could assume no consensus among her students, either before or after the topic was "taught." On the contrary, the topic of black deaths in police custody may have many meanings for that range of students. For some students it could be just another social science topic. Others may be angered by being placed in a situation in which a young, Aboriginal woman teaches them, as white Anglo Australians, about subject matter that includes strong indictments of the dominant culture to which they belong. For still other students, some of whom have direct knowledge of the experiences of imprisoned friends and relatives, the topic may be highly charged, emotionally and politically. We cannot pretend that classrooms like this will always be comfortable. There may be real and perhaps unimagined consequences—for instance, students in conflict with each other and the teacher, or students in distress. Dealing with unpredictable outcomes may not be easy. What Barbara attempted was ambitious. She was not playing it safe. She was putting on her classroom agenda a subject which many experienced teachers might baulk at, and which many students might resist. We do not necessarily know what real-world consequences ensue for teachers' teaching and students' learning when particular pedagogies are used in diverse classrooms.

In her first year as a registered teacher at the Paralowie R-12 School, Barbara continued to put critique at the centre of her curriculum. The outcomes were not entirely what she had predicted. She found, for example, that putting racism on the agenda in social science classes did not necessarily make the students more tolerant or rational about the issues. This was true even when she put her own and her students' experiences at the centre of classroom learning. Barbara describes incidents from her classroom:

> When they are actually working with each other, it doesn't matter what cultural background they've got, or where they are from. They seem to have these blinkers about who the "other" people are, until somebody actually mentions an issue like "immigration" or "the Aborigine problem." . . . Yeah, it's really strange, even dealing with the immigration issue. The kids are saying, "No, no. We really can't have 'them' coming in and taking over," and all this sort of stuff. And yet their best friend, if they are an Anglo-Saxon type person, is a Vietnamese person. "Oh, it's all right for *them*. He's my *friend*. He can stay."

Despite repeated placements of antiracist work at the centre of her curriculum, Barbara found that her students did not easily see a contradiction between their positive personal experiences of "the other" and their unquestioning alliance with institutionalised racist values about, say, immigration or Aboriginal land rights. This is not to say that no gains were made, but it illustrates that the outcomes of what we do, even in a curriculum we think is working for social justice, cannot be taken for granted.

Barbara was continually reminded that her own experiences as an Aboriginal person and teacher did not necessarily explain, or prepare her for, the ways in which her students and her classroom "worked." She had come into the school as a confident young woman, experienced in teaching to and about Aboriginal people and their culture. She knew the complexities of her Aboriginal students' lives. What was going on "behind the scenes" was not a mystery to her. She hoped that their shared culture would enable her to help Aboriginal students succeed in the school curriculum. But this is not how it happened. Long after the students had left school for the year, she kept hearing things about her students' lives and wondering whether, if she had known them earlier, she could have done something differently, done something else to make a difference for these students. For a teacher committed to equity, such doubts are deeply felt, both personally and professionally.

Like many beginning teachers in her first year of teaching, Barbara was concerned to establish her "identity" in the school. Yet what exactly constitutes the identity of a young, black, female teacher in a school? How do the various facets of that identity conflict or work together? For the video, Barbara explains that in her day-to-day work in the school, she found herself being positioned in certain ways because of her racial identity. She felt that colleagues and students held certain expectations of her as an Aboriginal person and teacher, expecting that her racial identity "explained" her actions:

> You know, they think, "Oh, she's Aboriginal, she's got some things that she's got to deal with, and that's why she's involved in it." . . . And that wasn't the initial idea at all. Like I was saying before, I was hoping to develop myself as a teacher, not go on this Aboriginal search.

Barbara is not accusing her colleagues of racism. She knows they work very hard for equity in their school, often at great personal and professional cost. What Barbara was beginning to articulate was that her racialised identity was both integral to, and yet somehow separate from, the struggle she was experiencing in her project to become a "good teacher." When used as a label, *Aboriginality* was not always as informative as first appeared, sometimes masking other facets of identity that need to be foregrounded.

Barbara's experiences illustrate that constantly placing equity issues at the centre of the curriculum can have unanticipated effects. In the video Barbara speculates that at her school a kind of antidote effect built up around the discussion of Aboriginal issues in the curriculum: i.e., students' "knew the problem"; it had been discussed before; it had been dealt with. Students' attitudes seemed to be that once it had been "covered," they should get on with learning about "mainstream" Australian history, politics, and culture. Barbara describes an incident from one of her classes:

> I think at Paralowie the Aboriginal community is starting to be an "it's them again"–type thing, which is sad in a way, because my year-11s, they said to me "Why don't we get some *real* Australian history?" And I asked them what they meant by that . . . and they said, "Enough of this Aborigines stuff. Give us some *real* Australian history." And I thought, "Oh, *this* is very interesting." So I gave them some *real* Australian history, as they put it, and I talked about the Foundation Act of South Australia and then, lo and behold, there we are negotiating with the Aborigines and I said, "Oh, I'm sorry I mentioned them, but they're *there*" [laughs].

What Barbara Fox's experiences show is that it is possible to build a curriculum around a critique of racism and to do this in ways which avoid teacher-centredness. It is possible to question systemic sources of inequity that disadvantage indigenous and minority racial groups. But it is not always comfortable, not always safe, and does not inevitably lead to more equitable, democratic classrooms. Our video project attempts to describe and problematise equity projects such as Barbara's by posing sometimes difficult questions about equity interventions and assumed "liberatory" pedagogies. Barbara did not anticipate what she or her students experienced and came to know as a result of tackling the difficult topic Aboriginal deaths in police custody. For example, whole language pedagogy suggests that a teacher should encourage the use of personal knowledge and experience in classroom work. But who and what might be jeopardised by doing this when working with "substance that matters" such as black deaths in custody? How might the answer to this question be different for an all-black class or a mixed-race class; with a white or a black teacher? Do teachers know what emotional distress might arise from using such content and such pedagogy? In what ways is such a classroom "safe," as we would want critical whole language classrooms to be? Who is safe, and from what, when personal discourses about such topics are present? Are absent? These are difficult questions, but questions which we must address if we are to explore what it is that our classroom practices do.

Nigel Howard: Teaching for Social Action

Nigel Howard is a male colleague of Barbara Fox's at Paralowie R-12 School. A secondary teacher of some fifteen years' experience, Nigel's professional commitment has been to work with students whose lives have often been lived "at the margins" of traditional schools: children with physical and intellectual disabilities, children with behaviour difficulties, and adolescents who do not readily engage with what has been offered them by traditional schooling practices. Nigel has also been a curriculum developer in the state education department. His work there has been to broaden the curriculum offerings for senior secondary students so as to make senior schooling more relevant to them, thereby increasing the retention rate of students at risk of failing and leaving school early, and increasing the chances that the full range of students can achieve personal and publicly accredited success.

Attendance and retention of students are key social justice and equity issues because research has shown that the longer students stay at school, the better chance they have of gaining employment. For this reason, Paralowie R-12 School, located in an area where there is more than 70 percent youth unemployment, counts among its greatest successes the fact that its retention rate of students beyond the age of fifteen years, the age of compulsion, has risen during the past five years from 36 to 90 percent. Nigel believes that this success has been due to two essential factors. First, at a schoolwide, structural level, there is an ongoing commitment to provide resources and programs with flexible pathways for completing senior school education and with a variety of choices for training for a range of possible futures. Second, at the classroom level, the students' lives are central to the curriculum, and the pedagogy is student-centred. Teachers know the community and their students, and the curriculum and pedagogies reflect this knowledge. Nigel argues that:

> There's a real effort to make this stuff fit the kids. At this
> school the kids are saying, "We would rather be here than out
> on the street or at other schools," and that's related to what's
> happening in the classroom.

Nigel maintains that the students are voting with their feet. Whereas in the past, many postcompulsory students at Paralowie R-12 School left school for the streets, significant numbers now attend school. Nigel attributes this difference to more attractive programs being offered by the school. By being connected to students' worlds, the curriculum and pedagogy work for equity, providing the possibility of better futures for a range of students who were previously alienated and marginalised by systemic practices.

Teachers at Paralowie R-12 School know how their students and local poor community are structurally positioned within society in ways that maintain disadvantage. They take an active role in lobbying state and federal governments for better resources for their school. They work through the state credentialing agency to have their curricula accredited for university entrance and other forms of further education and training. This is the work Nigel does at Paralowie R-12 School as the coordinator of work-related pathways. For our video project, we filmed Nigel working with a group of year-11 students who had a history of failure to attend and failure to achieve at school. These were students designated in their earlier years at school as students "at risk"—at risk of leaving school early, of not achieving a high school certificate, of not gaining employment. The introduction of a community studies curriculum at the school meant that at the ages of fifteen and sixteen years, these "at-risk" students were offered the opportunity to stay on at school in a state certificate-accredited course and spend a significant proportion of their time working with Nigel in a range of nontraditional ways. The community studies curriculum attempts to connect school and community, school knowledge and real-world knowledge, skills valued at school and skills valued in workplaces. On video Nigel explains the rationale behind his curriculum:

> We had a large number of kids who in the best of all possible worlds would be out there testing out their knowledge in very real ways, and so we wanted to produce that back in the school . . . the question was, "How can we get them to use those skills in real ways?"

How can a school curriculum replicate real-world situations? What are the possibilities and the constraints? How can a school pedagogy help students learn in ways that are potentially useful for gaining employment or for taking social action in the community? What risks do teachers take in attempting such work? These are questions we explored with Nigel in our videos. Nigel explains how one community studies project to produce a brochure came about and what it involved:

> In this project we had a group of students who were asked by the National Schools Network in the area to publicise some of the collaborative learning activities that were going on in the primary schools. One of the aims I had for these students was to get them to look at their own learning by talking to teachers about what they were doing in the classroom about collaborative learning, interviewing students, photographing groups, and putting together a picture of what people are trying to do in primary schools. An important outcome of this project is that it has a real product . . . that's the brochure and the poster that's got to be done now . . . to actually publicise what happened.

A key feature of Nigel's curriculum is that it is grounded in real-world activities and learning experiences. For example, Nigel's students acted as researchers and publishers to carry out a commissioned, funded project. They were commissioned to research and produce brochures to be used in the public domain to advertise the nature of the learning programs in neighbouring elementary schools. They had to plan and rehearse their research and interview questions; learn and adopt procedures for making contact and visiting local school principals and teachers; assume responsibility for booking, borrowing, and returning expensive audio and camera equipment; and visit schools and interview young students and their teachers. Once back at their own school, with Nigel's assistance and support, the students drew on their photographs and interview audiotapes to plan, write copy for, and illustrate a brochure and poster for the schools that had engaged them to do the project.

In carrying out this project as part of the curriculum, Nigel's students learned competencies valued in the world of work, such as the negotiation of roles in group work and collaborative action. These are also the skills necessary for successful social action both inside and outside school. While helping students gain access to paid work is central to the senior school curriculum at Paralowie, an important additional objective of Nigel's curriculum is to develop in students the desire and ability to be active participants in their communities. For Nigel, one indicator that this objective is being achieved is students taking action for change. Nigel describes one instance of this happening:

> Today we had a group come up to us and say, "This is the problem; this is what we intend to do about it; what do we have to do to get someone to listen to us?"

Although Nigel was not at liberty to discuss the nature of the "problem," he explained that a group of students saw a real-world issue of concern to them that needed to be addressed and wanted something to be done about it. More than that, they decided what they thought needed to be done and took responsibility for initiating that action themselves. They knew that they had to make someone with the power to effect that change listen to them. The students approached Nigel and the school's administration as equals, requesting guidance about how best to establish communication with the appropriate people. Nigel quotes this example because it demonstrates students achieving his objective for a curriculum based on social justice. Here were students taking action to effect change about a "matter of substance" to them in their lives. Teachers who work for democracy in this way are teaching more than language arts. For them, putting critique at the centre of what they do is not merely including topics often left out of the curriculum. It is not merely planning particular kinds of "language activities." It is teaching in a way that results in action for change in the real world.

Nigel is very clear about how his curriculum is based on social justice principles. On video he explains:

> The program addresses disadvantage because it works on what the students are doing now. It's not a program that is beginning to say "Learn these things so that in the future you can get a job, and learn these things so that in the future you can have some power." . . . It addresses disadvantage in that it's about working in socially just ways for now, with the understanding that, if we can keep that going, it's saying you will be part of the future and you will be an actor in your own future.

Nigel's project is a radical one. His approach requires teachers to step back from direct control. It requires shifting real power, and the responsibility that goes with it, from the teacher to the students. And for Nigel, if it is to be real power, it has to be effective in the present, not in the future. His project is not about teaching students skills in the abstract so that they might later apply them; e.g., so they might later approach local businesses or politicians when they want something done. For Nigel, teaching for social justice is about constructing a curriculum which provides opportunity, incentive, and support for students to do such real-world things right away, while they are still enrolled in school. He argues that if they do it "now," they experience power "now," and so they know that they can exercise this power for the rest of their lives. They can be "actors in their own future," active participants in their living communities, both now and in the future.

In working for social justice, Nigel begins from what the students know and can do. He helps students plan to use language and action to make a difference in their community. This may require thinking differently about literacy. Students may do more talking or audio- and videotape recording than writing. Teaching and learning objectives might be achieved using a variety of forms of English, or languages other than English. To implement programs like community studies requires innovative approaches to resourcing and timetabling. For example, the subject has to be timetabled in large blocks of time, challenging the way senior schools are traditionally structured. Students need the freedom and responsibility, often withheld by the school, to leave the school grounds to do community research. The tension between the "safety" of the school and the "unknown" elements outside presents difficulties for both the teacher planner and the student learner. Teachers may have to work hard to change school structures and procedures so that they have the time required to set up possibilities for student-community access. They may also find it hard to take the necessary risks in sending students away from the school.

Implementing a student-centred pedagogy in a context like this can be very hard for teachers. Standing back and allowing students to make their own mistakes and "learn by doing" can go against teachers' deepest impulses to lead and show, to take over and "rescue." The student learner may also find this kind of program difficult to accommodate. For example, students who have little history of success and little social confidence may suffer anxiety at being apparently cut off from traditional types of teacher direction and close teacher supervision. Nigel describes how student expectations might require courage and resistance from teachers:

> But also sometimes you're battling against students' expectations of what school is; that rather than saying "If you fail this essay, I'll give you a bad mark, and isn't that terrible," there's a lot more at risk. "If this project doesn't succeed, then you haven't done what you set out to do . . . and you can actually see that there are going to be payoffs and conse-

quences." And so, one of the difficulties is resisting students actually pulling the project back into schoolwork.

For Nigel's students, becoming an active participant in the community does not always feel safe. Students who have a history of being excluded and marginalised by dominant practices do not easily become independent "actors in their future." Nigel's community studies program encourages and gives credit to students for meeting challenges and overcoming obstacles, for taking risks and moving away from known, comfortable school practices. For Nigel, this is what makes the program powerful for students in transition to postschool lives.

Nigel's goal is to teach in ways that produce students who challenge the commonsense view that they somehow have to "accept their lot" as failures. Nigel aims to help students "at the extreme end of disadvantage and poverty" to change the relationships they have with the school and the community. But Nigel knows that this is not easy, and there is no formula for achieving that goal. The answer does not lie in exemplary programs or curriculum models. Schools and individual teachers must own the inequalities that exist, and must find their own ways to address them in local contexts. This requires commitment by individuals as well as whole-school support. In Nigel's view, teachers working for equity goals make complex ethical and pedagogical decisions, lesson by lesson, day by day, as they "proceed tentatively toward social justice" (Howard, 1995).

Jennifer O'Brien: Critical Readers from the Start

Jennifer O'Brien is an experienced teacher who has worked for a number of years as a teacher/librarian and also in a professional development role in literacy education in her school district. In these roles Jennifer worked with students and teachers to research student-centred literacy pedagogies, while continuing to take seriously teachers' responsibilities for making explicit how all students could be successful. In Jennifer's view it was important to examine how teachers helped students select, read, and use different kinds of texts. In her graduate studies Jennifer pursued feminist and poststructuralist theories about textual practices which suggested that texts are constructed, not vehicles of unquestionable "truths"; texts are not neutral and have specific and differential effects; texts represent people in ways which are gendered, raced, and classed; and texts can be deconstructed and critically interrogated.

Jennifer decided to explore with children in their first years of schooling the poststructuralist contention that texts are constructed objects which could have been constructed differently. Her starting point was investigating the representation of gender in texts. Her explicit standpoint was to disrupt the oftentimes-limited gendered identities produced in texts for children, where, as Jennifer puts it, girls are constructed as "pretty and compliant" and boys as "cheeky and naughty." What Jennifer tried to do was to give her students access to critical and feminist discourses so that other positions were made available for them in the classroom (O'Brien, 1994).[4] Together with her students, she began to research ways of changing what could be said in her classroom about boys and girls, men and women, mothers and fathers and as we will see below, "aunts."

While critical literacy has sometimes been seen as the province of high school, college, and adult education, Jennifer took on the challenge made by socially critical researchers that "children at the earliest stages . . . contest, debate, and argue with texts" (see Luke in Jongsma, 1991). She explains what she intended:

> My response to these challenges has been to alter fundamentally the interactions between my students, their classroom texts, and me. . . . I use critically framed conversations, questions, and tasks to put into practice two key decisions: first, to challenge the taken-for-granted nature of the construction of children's texts; and second, to ask students to think about the constructions of reality authorised by the text and to consider different possibilities for constructing reality. (Comber & O'Brien, 1993, p. 3)

These are important insights for young readers to grasp, and they are not necessarily obvious in classroom discussions, which sometimes give the impression that the characters in books are "real" or represent "people like that" in the real world. In Jennifer's classroom, the author and illustrator were referred to as people who make decisions to portray things, people, and events in certain ways. During the period of her research, she asked children to consider questions including the following: What do writers say about boys, girls, mothers, and fathers in the books you read? What do mothers/fathers/girls/boys do in this story? Who had the power in this story? What do adults think that children like to read about? If you only knew about mothers from reading this book, what would you know about what mothers do? What doesn't the writer tell you about this person? What does the writer tell me that I already know? What do I know that the writer doesn't tell me?

Jennifer's research project involved her consciously changing the ways in which she spoke about texts and changing the invitations she made to children to speak about texts. The preceding questions are examples of those which she found provoked different kinds of discussions. She did not begin with a set of new or politically correct critical questions; rather, with the children's help, she explored ways of generating new kinds of conversations which would allow them to argue with texts, to interrogate the apparently "natural" gendered identities that appeared daily in their storybooks, factual texts, and the media and everyday texts in the community. It was common to hear Jenny interrupt herself with comments like, "No that's not a good question," and then rephrase what she wanted to say. Hence, she continually demonstrated to children a critical reflexivity about her own discursive practices.

These are very different kinds of questions than were being discussed in other classrooms we had observed, where children were asked about their favourite characters, their favourite pages, and why the characters acted in the ways they did. Classroom conversations about shared texts frequently treat the characters as real, the plots as natural, as the ways things are. The rationalities and visions of the authors and illustrators are often seen as natural and as beyond question. The role of the children in these classrooms is to notice what the teacher notices and to match the teacher's interpretation of the book (Baker, 1991). In Jennifer's classroom there was the potential for children to engage in critical text analysis from the beginning of schooling. Our aim in the video was to capture Jennifer and the children in conversation around texts, in order that we could show students and teachers other possibilities for talk around texts in the early literacy classroom which deliberately foregrounded social justice issues. As an introduction, we asked Jennifer to explain what critical literacy meant in her classroom:

> Critical literacy, to me, is an important part of showing children a way of looking at the world so that they don't simply accept things as they are presented to them. For example, they don't just take for granted the presentation in their storybooks of themselves as being perhaps cute, perhaps dependent, if they are boys being cheeky and naughty, or if they are girls, as pretty and compliant; that in their writing, for example they will start to think first; instead of just taking on board the usual ways of thinking about women or of thinking about girls or of thinking about children and writing those things down, they'll think first, "Can I change it? Can I take a different position on these things? Can I look at the world differently?"

Jennifer's position was that simply by following children's interests and inquiries, no redistribution of power or social justice outcomes are guaranteed. Children's interests and inquiries are no more "disinterested" or "natural" or "innocent" than those of the communities in which they are constructed. In Jennifer's view, teacher direction can be proactive. Critical literacies don't necessarily emerge unless teachers work with children to construct spaces where such conversations can be safely had.

In the video we show several brief classroom episodes of Jennifer's teaching, selected because they demonstrate how she frames tasks and conversations in order to have children work on the ways that texts are constructed, the ways in which authors and illustrators choose to represent particular kinds of characters. The focus of this work denaturalises the text and encourages children to ask questions about the way texts are constructed. Below, we outline one classroom episode in which Jennifer leads the children in posing critical questions. One of the children in Jennifer's class had commented that writers often

represent aunts as "mean" in stories. This observation is interesting in itself. In Jennifer's classroom, the decisions writers
made—such as how to represent aunts—were the object of
study, and the child readers were positioned to notice what writers often do across texts.

Shortly after the student's comment about "aunts being
mean in stories," Jennifer spotted *Beware of the Aunts* (Thompson, 1991), on the new book shelf in the library. She realised that
here was a chance to test out the student's hypothesis. Jennifer
begins by having the children study the cover and think about
other books which include aunts, and then focuses on the blurb
where we are told that the writer and the illustrator "gently poke
fun at the foibles of aunts," but that "there is one time of the year
when you cannot do without them." Jennifer asks the children to
predict a time when the writer will say children cannot do without their aunts:

> JENNIFER: What will Pat Thompson, who wrote this book, decide
> to put in the book? Have a think. Do you need to talk to
> someone near you about it?
>
> STUDENT: Or close my eyes and think about it?
>
> JENNIFER: Or close your eyes . . .

Here Jennifer breaks up the usual pattern of question-answer
sequences which often go on around texts by encouraging children to share ideas with each other or to just think. The children
quickly tap into the logic of the book and begin to offer suggestions: "On your birthday," "At Christmas," "At Easter." The
children realise that the author's joke is that however odd aunts
may be, they are still good for present giving. Jennifer scribes the
children's suggestions as a list. Next, she asks them to work in
pairs to draw and label pictures of the kinds of aunts the writer
and illustrator might portray in this book. When they have done
this, Jennifer begins reading the story, inviting children to interrupt her when they come across an aunt they had predicted
would be in the book. Jennifer does not get far before groups of
children start to call out, "Fat aunt," "I drew a fat aunt," "You
saw I drew a fat aunt." The children's predictions were accurate.

Here was another text which positioned aunts as people to be made fun of; the first character being an aunt who cannot stop eating.

Prediction is not new to whole language teachers. What is different about the way it is done in Jennifer's classroom is that she does not have the children predict narrative as though this is the way things are. Predictions in this classroom are about the ways authors commonly represent different kinds of people; in this case, Jennifer directs children's attention to the construction of gendered identities.

Later, Jennifer explained that there were a number of things she wanted students to learn from this lesson:

> [W]riters very, very frequently draw on ideas about the world, about women, about children, about men, that are already there; as if the ideas are ready-made and they just pick them up and slot them in and use them. So these ideas about aunts being figures of fun, being mean, all these sorts of things that we come across, I wanted to show the children that there was a distinct possibility that, that sort of view of the world would come through, but I also wanted to put the question to them: "Does the writer of this book, whose name is Pat Thompson, does she alter things in any way? Does she decide to treat aunts differently?"

Because Jennifer makes her agenda explicit by openly exploring how limited gender identities are portrayed in many children's books, it should not be assumed that the children neatly fall in line and reproduce her point of view. To the contrary, Jennifer's transcripts are full of instances of contestation, debate, and resistance. A few days after the lesson described above Jennifer returns to the discussion of *Beware of the Aunts:*

JENNIFER: OK, and what did Pat Thompson seem to be saying about the one who loved sewing? Alison?

ALLISON: She likes making her own clothes.

JENNIFER: OK, and is this a successful thing she does? Or is Pat Thompson making that out to be a good thing or a bad thing?

STUDENTS: A good thing.

JENNIFER: In what way?

ZOE: It's a good thing that she's recycling things like the bedspread.

JENNIFER: Is that what Pat Thompson's saying or what you're saying?

ZOE: It's what I'm saying. She once made something out of a bedspread, and she must have had a hole right in the middle of it which was big enough for her head so she must have made a dress out of it.

JENNIFER: OK, fine. You're saying it's a good thing. Do you think Pat Thompson is saying it's a good thing or a bad thing?

STUDENTS: Good.

ZOE: It's good that she's recycling.

JENNIFER: OK, what about this other comment here [reading the text], "I'm afraid she sometimes makes us things." Is that a good thing or a bad thing about an aunt?

STUDENTS: Good!

JENNIFER: Have a good look at the picture.

ALISON: Bad!

JENNIFER: What makes you say that, Allison?

ALLISON: Because the sleeves are too long and they don't look right on them.

In the preceding transcript, we can see that Zoe takes up a strong position as reader, drawing on her knowledge of recycling, in order to read the aunt's sewing as positive, in spite of the text and the illustrations. Other children are convinced by Zoe and also see the aunt's sewing as positive. What follows then is a close analysis of the text and pictures, with Jennifer drawing children's attention to what is in the text itself, including the print and the pictures. Jennifer listens and continually redirects their attention to what the author and illustrator have produced. Each of the children's contributions is taken seriously, which means not simply accepting each comment, but asking children to expand on their opinions and justify them by making reference to the text itself.

Some whole language teachers may find this interaction teacher-directed. Jennifer does indeed direct children—for example, to look closely at what is going on in the text. She deliberately challenges texts which maintain limited and negative views of who women are and who they can or should be. She does not do this by closing down what children can say or by subtly imposing her interpretations. She *teaches* children ways of reading which allow them to see texts differently. How much respect for the child reader would have been demonstrated if Jennifer had simply accepted Zoe's reading and moved on to the next question? In this instance, Jennifer's questioning indicates that children's responses to texts are indeed important, too important to simply accept as one more idea. It is in closely examining children's responses to texts and analysing how texts work that literacy educators can lead children to question dominant inequitable representations in the worlds of print.

This does not mean that children stop having fun, or that they are simply trained in politically correct responses. On the contrary, it means producing students who argue and debate, who at five and six can sustain arguments not just across a lesson, but across days and weeks, who develop understandings about inter-textuality so that they detect patterns in their reading, who read and reread from different positions. We can reconceptualise teacher direction as an ethical practice where the teacher inserts her voice to ensure the space for difference, contest, and justice. In Jennifer's classroom the children, along with their teacher, were engaged in new forms of inquiry about texts and their effects.

Jennifer's critical literacy curriculum was not restricted to analysing children's storybooks. As she explains in the video, she considers any text "fair game" and uses newspaper clippings, junk mail, encyclopedias, nonfiction books, books tied to movie promotions—texts that children might encounter in and out of school. More recently, Jennifer has documented her analysis with young children of the representation of women in catalogues advertising gifts for Mother's Day (Luke, O'Brien, & Comber, 1994). In this work, Jennifer and her students explored gender, race, and class and involved parents and caregivers in their inquiries. Jennifer and other teachers in South Australian schools have begun to analyse everyday texts: cereal boxes; corn-chip packets; tea-bag boxes; the texts on toy catalogues and on the associated television advertising (Comber & Simpson, 1995). These everyday texts and texts of popular culture may form important ways of establishing what Anne Dyson calls a "permeable curriculum" (Dyson, 1993), in which children might bring to the official school world text and story resources they use and play with in their peer and home worlds.

Jennifer's work has been an important catalyst for change amongst early literacy educators in the local and national educational community. Jennifer demonstrated what might be done with very young children and made public her work with and on theory. She generously offered her work to other teachers, not as an exemplary model, but as work-in-progress and as evidence of what children can do given the space and tools. The effects of Jennifer's work are impossible to anticipate; however, we do know that other teachers are following her lead in exploring other ways of talking about texts while making gender, race, and class subjects that can be talked about from the earliest days of schooling. What is needed are forums where teachers can safely discuss issues about difference and social justice (See Dyson, 1995). We hope that our educational documentaries about teaching literacy in disadvantaged schools provide material to generate and support such discussions.

Confronting the Silence and Seeing Things Differently

As literacy educators, we can no longer take for granted that access to reading and writing automatically works for social justice. Brave teachers, such as Barbara, Nigel, and Jennifer, who are prepared to put themselves on the line on video in the public arena so that others may learn, are crucial in the educational community. Their practices generate possibilities for other ways of doing school, for other kinds of school literacies. Each of these teachers begins not with a set of "good literacy practices," but with a theorised analysis of how power works in society and the ways in which textual practices and schooling are implicated in the maintenance of inequalities. In making decisions about what to do in their classrooms, they are informed by their commitment to working against injustice, now, by giving students the space to question the way things are and to take action within the spaces of schooling and community.

We take the view that as language and literacy teachers in a world increasingly mediated by texts, we have a responsibility to foreground relations of power and social inequities. In the production of our educational documentaries, made in collaboration with Barbara, Nigel, Jennifer, and others, we attempt to produce open-ended texts. We attempt to create for our teacher-preparation students a range of ways of seeing literacy, poverty, education, and disadvantage. One view we explicitly present is the framing of the "poverty problem" as systemic, and state-constructed and legitimated through a politics of unequal distribution of entitlements (Polakow, 1993). We attempt to counter the silence that has surrounded this view in educational sites. We acknowledge that teacher-training institutions as well as schools can play a part in the formation or the contestation of deficit images of children, their race, class, family, and culture. As Polakow (1993) argues:

> Teachers do not live above their culture; they too are participants in the pervasive poverty discourse that conceals economic and educational inequalities, state-induced destitution. (p. 146)

We hope we are collaborators with classroom-based literacy teachers in

> [c]onfronting the silence, naming the classroom world with different forms of talk, shifting our ways of seeing, opening up spaces for possibility that can shift the tenuous ground on which young children of poverty stand. (Polakow 1993, p. 147)

We conclude with a story about one teacher enacting this kind of "shifting the ground" to create new ways of seeing. Anne Haas Dyson (1993, pp. 41–43) describes a lesson she observed in an elementary, multiracial classroom where the teacher, Louise, had invited in parents to talk about their jobs. On this occasion, a father, who was white, spoke about his work as a scientist. Afterwards the teacher asked the children who would like to be scientists. Four children raised their hands. The teacher asked these children to go to the middle of the room. Then the teacher pointed out a problem: four white boys in the middle of the room. The teacher went on to ask a series of questions about who was there and who wasn't and how the group of future scientists could be changed. Gradually, other children went to the middle of the room—girls, boys of colour, girls of colour—with the teacher helping the children analyse how the group in the middle was changing and why that was important. Eventually the teacher asked the children again to go to the middle of the room if they might like to be scientists and all but the scientist's daughter went to the centre of the room. She wanted to be a vet!

This story is important as it shows the way in which a teacher who has a social analysis and who is committed to equity can use situations as they arise in the school day. This language activity is about who people are and who they might be; the teacher sees the possibility for a wider lesson about identity and futures and demonstrated to children a way of analysing life situations: Who is in the centre and who isn't? We do not see choices in regard to pedagogy as limited to the binary oppositions of teacher-centred and child-centred. Relatedly, we don't see power as owned by the teacher or students, but as constantly negotiated and exercised in different ways in different contexts. We do not see that the absence of teacher-direction necessarily results in democratic power redistribution amongst children, nor that teacher direction excludes the possibilities of democratic classrooms. Making justice our project involves teachers exercising power in positive ways to challenge untested and inequitable hegemonic assumptions at work in classroom cultures.

As teacher educators we believe it is important that the work done by teachers like Louise, Barbara, Nigel, and Jennifer is made central to discussions of teaching for social justice. They make literacy lessons the sites for social justice. They challenge accepted notions of what literacy might be and what it can do for students. The video documentaries involved an alliance between university and school-based educators and their communities. From this collaborative strength we were able to begin to explore the dilemmas which confront teachers as they work for social justice. We were also able to portray school communities actively working for change. But none of this is simple. We document no easy answers. Our strongest hope for our project is that it prevents a complacent silence and generates conversations among educators who see schools as potential sites of transformation, as places where democracy is learnt and practised.

Notes

1. Australian schools are designated as "disadvantaged" if they satisfy the criteria for federal government equity funding under the Disadvantaged Schools Program (DSP).

2. In 1993 and 1994, we were members of a team awarded national grants to improve the quality of university teaching in teacher education about teaching literacy in disadvantaged schools. With Susan Hill, Lynne Badger and Lyn Wilkinson, we have produced two sets of three videos under the titles *Literacy, Diversity and Schooling* (Comber et al., 1994) and *Literacy Learning and Social Justice* (Hill et al., 1996).

3. For an exploration of the ethical and practical dilemmas in implementing the project, see Nixon and Comber (1995).

4. The authors were involved in this project as co-supervisors.

References

Allington, R. L., & Walmsley, S. A. (Eds.). (1995). *No quick fix: Rethinking literacy programs in America's elementary schools.* New York: Teachers College Press.

Badger, L., Comber, B., & Weeks, B. (1993). *Literacy and language practices in the early years in disadvantaged schools: A report on the National Survey.* Canberra, ACT, Australia: Department of Employment, Education, and Training.

Baker, C. (1991). Literacy practices and social relations in classroom reading events." In C. D. Baker & A. Luke (Eds.), *Towards a critical sociology of reading pedagogy: Papers of the XII World Congress on Reading.* Amsterdam: John Benjamin's.

Baker, C. D., & Freebody, P. (1989). *Children's first schoolbooks: Introductions to the culture of literacy.* Oxford, UK: Blackwell.

Christie, F., Devlin, B., Freebody, P., Luke, A., Martin, J. R., Thread-gold, T., & Walton, C. (1991). *Teaching English literacy: A project of national significance on the preservice preparation of teachers for teaching English literacy.* Canberra, ACT, Australia: Department of Employment, Education, and Training.

Comber, B. (1994). Critical literacy: An introduction to Australian debates and perspectives. *Journal of Curriculum Studies, 26*(6), 655–668.

Comber, B., & O'Brien, J. (1993). Critical literacy: Classroom explorations. *Critical Pedagogy Networker, 6*(1/2), 1–11.

Comber, B., & Simpson, A. (1995). Reading cereal boxes: Analysing everyday texts. In *Texts: The heart of the English curriculum.* Broadsheet ser. 1, no. 1, Adelaide, South Australia: Department of Education and Children's Services.

Comber, B., Nixon, H., Hill, S., & Badger, L. (1994). *Literacy, diversity and Schooling.* Three videos and user's guide. Melbourne, Victoria, SE Australia: Eleanor Curtain.

Delpit, L. (1988). The silenced dialogue: Power and pedagogy in educating other people's children." *Harvard Educational Review, 58*(3), 280–298.

Donald, J. (1993). Literacy and the limits of democracy." In B. Green (Ed.), *The insistence of the letter: Literacy studies and curriculum theorizing* (pp. 120–136). London: Falmer.

Dreyfus, H., & Rabinow, P. (1983). *Michel Foucault: Beyond structuralism and hermeneutics.* 2nd ed. Chicago: University of Chicago Press.

Dyson, A. H. (1993). *Social worlds of children learning to write in an urban primary school.* New York: Teachers College Press.

Dyson, A. H. (1995). (Ed.). What difference does difference make? Teacher perspectives on diversity, literacy, and the urban primary school. *English Education, 27*(2), 77–139.

Edelsky, C., with Harman, S. (1991). Risks and possibilities of whole language literacy: Alienation and connection. In C. Edelsky, *With literacy and justice for all: Rethinking the social in language and education* (pp. 127–140). New York: Falmer.

Education Department of South Australia. (1992). *Writing-reading assessment program (WRAP): Final report.* Adelaide, South Australia: Education Department of South Australia.

Gilbert, P. (1989). Student text as pedagogical text. In S. DeCastell, A. Luke, & C. Luke (Eds.), *Language, authority, and criticism: Readings on the school textbook* (pp. 195–202). London: Falmer.

Gilbert, P. (1990). Authorizing disadvantage: Authorship and creativity in the language classroom. In F. Christie (Ed.), *Literacy for a changing world* (pp. 54–78). Victoria, SE Australia: Australian Council of Educational Research.

Harvey, D. (1993). Class relations, social justice and the politics of difference. In M. Keith, & S. Pile (Eds.), *Place and the politics of identity* (pp. 41–66). London: Routledge.

Hill, S., Nixon, H., Comber, B., Badger, L., & Wilkinson, L. (1996). *Literacy learning and social justice.* Three videos and user's guide. Melbourne, Victoria, SE Australia: Eleanor Curtain. Howard, N. (1995). What does it mean to teach in an unjust society? Paper presented at the Centre for Studies in Educational Leadership, Underdale, University of South Australia.

Jongsma, K.S. (1991). Critical literacy (questions and answers). *The Reading Teacher, 44*(7), 518–519.

Kress, G. (1994). Text and grammar as explanation. In U. H. Meinhof, & K. Richardson (Eds.), *Text, discourse, and context: Representations of poverty in Britain* (pp. 24–46). London: Longman.

Lensmire, T. (1994, December). Writing for critical democracy: Student voice and teacher practice in the writing workshop. Paper presented at the National Reading Conference, San Diego, CA.

Luke, A. (1993). Stories of social regulation: The micropolitics of classroom narrative. In B. Green (Ed.), *The insistence of the letter: Literacy studies and curriculum theorizing* (pp. 137–153). London: Falmer.

Luke, A. (1996). When literacy might not make a difference: Textual practice and cultural capital. In C. D. Baker, J. Cook-Gumperz, & A. Luke (Eds.), *Literacy and Power.* Oxford: Blackwell.

Luke, A., O'Brien, J., & Comber, B. (1994). Making community texts objects of study. *The Australian Journal of Language and Literacy, 17*(2), 139–149.

Nixon, H., & Comber, B. (1995). Making documentaries and teaching about disadvantage: Ethical issues and practical dilemmas. *Australian Educational Researcher, 22*(2), 63–84.

O'Brien, J. (1994, July). It's written in our head: The possibilities and contradictions of a feminist poststructuralist discourse in a junior primary classroom. Unpubl. master's thesis, University of South Australia.

Polakow, V. (1993). *Lives on the edge: Single mothers and their children in the other America.* Chicago: University of Chicago Press.

Stuckey, J.E. (1991). *The violence of literacy.* Portsmouth, NH: Boynton/Cook.

Thompson, P. (1991). *Beware of the aunts.* London: Macmillan.

Willinsky, J. (1990). *The new literacy: Redefining reading and writing in the schools.* New York: Routledge.

INDEX

Critical stance, taking,
286–89
Critical text analysis, 339–40
Critical whole language, 5,
19–24
general characteristics of,
24–33
activist, 29–30
grounding of, in student's
lives, 25–26
lack of exercises, 24–25
offering of classroom as safe
place, 26–27
pro-justice, 29
taking of critical stance,
27–29
long-term projects in, 22–23
why, what, and how of, 7–33
Cry Freedom, 105
Cultural conversations, 166–67
Cultural critique, 167–79
Cultural hostility, reality of,
196–204
Cultural identity, 217
Cultural obviousness, 276
Culture
language embedding in, 213
probing, in literature-discussion
groups, 163–89
Curriculum. *See also* Education;
Learning; Schools
centering of planning of, on
authority cycle, 56–57
conversation in development
of, 74–75
critical literacy across, 103–6
critical pro-justice, 27, 32
grounding of, in student's lives,
25–26
hidden, 243–45, 250, 251–52
improving, 135–37
permeable, 345
placement of equity at centre
of, 330
planning for spontaneous,
117–22

student negotiation of, 4
transformation of, 77–95
wholeness of, 129–31

Davies, Bronwyn, 258
Davis Teacher Study Group,
303–15
Decision making, shared, 292–95
Dedicated space, need for, 307–8
Democracy, 4, 9–14, 192–93
participatory, 191
Descriptive writing, 269–70
Dialects, 270, 271
Discussion panel, 236–37
Distance, 182
Drama, student-created, 96–113

Ebonics, 218, 220
Economic class, 191–207
and expectations, 253
Economics
focusing of classroom
discussion on, 194,
195–96
relationship between politics
and, 12–13
using questions to guide
development of
classroom, 122–29
Education. *See also* Learning;
Schools
business-inspired innovations
in, 14
call for radical decentralization
in, 14
critical whole language, 5
earning profits from privatized,
13–14
literacy, as site for social
justice, 316–48
manufactured crisis of
public, 13
metaphors of, 259, 269,
280–83

EDITOR

Carole Edelsky is professor at Arizona State University. She is the author of *With Literacy and Justice for All* and *Writing in a Bilingual Program* and a co-author of *Whole Language: What's the Difference*. She taught fourth grade in Denver and in Cincinnati, seemingly a lifetime ago. She wishes she had known then what she's learned since about the connections among language, literacy, education, and politics.

CONTRIBUTORS

James Albright has taught elementary and secondary school English language arts for the Halifax Regional School Board for twenty-three years. He has recently completed doctoral studies, at The Pennsylvania State University, with a dissertation entitled *Rewriting English and the Problem of Normativity: A Bourdieuian Analysis*. He is currently teaching at Teachers College, Columbia University, in New York.

Bess Altwerger is professor of elementary education at Towson University in Baltimore, Maryland. Throughout her career, she has worked collaboratively with classroom teachers to develop a practical theory of literacy development. Her research on the "theme cycle" and critical literature studies has focused on the potential for creating meaning-centered, critical and democratic classroom communities. Bess has been very active in bringing a social justice perspective to professional organizations such as NCTE and WLU and is currently a facilitator of an NCTE Reading Initiative site. Bess resides in Columbia, Maryland, with her husband and two children. Her greatest hope is that we as educators help to create a more equitable, democratic and peaceful world for all of our children to enjoy in the future.

Bill Bigelow teaches at Franklin High School in Portland, Oregon. From 1979 until 1994, he taught at Jefferson High School. He has written and co-edited several curricula and books on teaching and learning, including *Strangers in Their Own Country: A Curriculum on South Africa; The Power in Our Hands: A Curriculum on the History of Work and Workers in the United States; Rethinking Columbus: The Next 500 Years; and Rethinking Our Classrooms: Teaching for Equity and Justice*. He is an editor of the education reform journal, *Rethinking Schools*.

Marie Elaine Boozer is the full-time parent of Bonnie Elizabeth and a lecturer in the Literacy Education and Diversity Settings program at Ohio State University in Columbus, Ohio. She is also completing a doctorate in language education at Indiana University and is a free-lance educational consultant.

Bill Brummett teaches third and fourth grades at Geneseo Central School in Geneseo, New York. He is currently interested in involving students and parents as collaborators in curricular decisions and learning experiences.

Beverly Busching is a professor in the Department of Instruction and Teacher Education at the University of South Carolina, and the director of the Midlands Writing Project. She has collaborated for many years with Betty Slesinger, inquiring into the humanities as the center of a language arts program.

Linda Christensen taught language arts for more than twenty years at Jefferson High School in Portland, Oregon, until the school was reconstituted. She is a member of the *Rethinking Schools* editorial board, director of the Portland Writing Project, and currently works as language arts coordinator for the Portland Public Schools.

Susan M. Church has fulfilled a number of different teaching and administrative roles in public education. She has published widely in educational journals and is the author of *The Future of Whole Language: Reconstruction or Self-Destruction?* She recently returned to the Halifax Regional School Board as assistant superintendent of schools after working as a teacher educator at Mount Saint Vincent University for several years. She also has been engaged in doctoral studies through the University of South Australia.

Barbara Comber is director of the Language and Literacy Research Centre at the University of South Australia, where she teaches in Masters of Education and Ph.D. courses. She also directs a teacher-researcher network, exploring responsive and critical literacies in diverse communities. Her research interests include teachers' work, social justice, critical literacies, public education, school-based collaborative research, tertiary pedagogies and literacies, and the development of multimedia research and educational artifacts and sites. She is currently editing two books: *Negotiating Critical Literacies in Classrooms* (with Anne Simpson) and *Inquiry into What? Empowering Today's Young People, Tomorrow's Citizens Using Whole Language* (with Sibel Boran). Her Ph.D. thesis was entitled *The Discursive Construction of Literacy in a Disadvantaged School* and employed ethnographic and poststructuralist discourse analytic methods.

Cecilia M. Espinosa was born in Ecuador, South America. She team taught with Karen Moore at William T. Machan Elementary School for seven years. She is now the Title VII coordinator at William T. Machan.

Rebeca García-González was a bilingual teacher for eight years in the San Francisco Mission District before finishing graduate school. She is currently assistant professor in the Department of Teacher Education at the University of San Francisco, where she teaches courses in bilingual education. She also works with the parents and teachers of Latino students as a mentor, coach, and consultant.

Rebecca Jarvis teaches basic writing and directs the writing lab at Eastern Arizona College, a rural community college in Thatcher, Arizona. She is also completing a doctorate in curriculum studies at Arizona State. When she wrote this article, she was teaching composition as an adjunct at Glendale Community College, near Phoenix.

Cynthia Lewis is assistant professor in the Literacy, Language, and Culture program at the University of Iowa, where she teaches courses in children's literature and literacy education. Her research focuses on the sociopolitical dimensions of literary response, and her articles have appeared in such journals as *Research in the Teaching of English* and *Language Arts*.

Lisa Burley Maras recently began doctoral studies in language and literacy education at Pennsylvania State University after teaching for several years. She most recently taught courses in language arts and reading at colleges in the Buffalo, New York area. Previously, she taught at the elementary level. Her primary interest is in working to make classrooms, at all levels, more critical and just places.

Pilar Mejía was the principal of César Chávez Elementary School in San Francisco's Mission District. She is now principal on special assignment for the San Francisco Unified School District, where she recently served as coordinator of the Latino Education Summit, Latino Honor Roll Celebration, and the Latino Family Conference. Her career in education began when she started a parent-run "free school" in the early 1970s.

Karen J. Moore was a bilingual teacher at William T. Machan Elementary School in Phoenix, Arizona for seven years. She taught a multiage primary class and team taught with Cecilia Espinosa from the beginning of her career at Machan. She is now the collaborative teacher for the Title VII Project at William T. Machan.

Helen Nixon, a former high school English teacher, is now senior lecturer at the Language and Literacy Research Centre in the School of Education at the University of South Australia. She has recently completed her doctoral thesis and has published on the topic of university-school collaborations in researching literacy education and educational disadvantage.

Winnie J. Porter is a Spanish bilingual teacher in a first- and second-grade multiage class at César Chávez Elementary School in San Francisco. She became a bilingual teacher because of her own negative experiences as an immigrant child learning English.

Elizabeth R. Saavedra, assistant professor in the Division of Educational Leadership and Organizational Learning at the University of New Mexico, has worked throughout her career with teachers on the process of transformative learning that takes place in teacher study groups and ongoing inquiry. Currently her work focuses on two research projects. The first is an examination of how the study group process leads teachers to reconceptualize their roles and responsibilities, and shifts practices to enhance the transformation of their classrooms and schools by rooting them in community goals, needs, and expectations. The second is a historical and genealogical study on the constitution of bilingual/ESL education in New Mexico as a discourse, as a practice, and as policy, from territorial times to the present.

Ramón A. Serrano is associate professor at St. Cloud State University, St. Cloud, Minnesota. He currently teaches reading and language arts methods courses and heads the Institute of Critical Pedagogy and Children's Rights forum. Having been a gang member during his youth, he is interested in how schools contribute to the formation of gangs and how schools can change this cycle by showing that they truly care.

Sue Settle is an elementary teacher and learner with the Halifax Regional School Board in Nova Scotia, Canada. Her research interests include critical literacies and social justice causes.

Paul Skilton-Sylvester earned a Ph.D. in education at the University of Pennsylvania, doing an ethnographic study of organizational change in an inner city school and a Fortune 500 company. He is now teaching third grade and studying a skyscraper with his class.

Betty Slesinger retired from teaching at Irmo Middle School Campus R in Columbia, South Carolina. She and Beverly Busching have been longtime educational research collaborators in humanities and language arts.

Maria Sweeney has taught grades 2–4 in New Jersey public schools for thirteen years. She previously published articles on teaching social justice issues using a child-centered whole language approach in *Democracy and Education* and *Radical Teacher*. She has led inservice workshops and courses on teaching for social justice and also on using a reading/writing approach for literacy instruction. She lives in northern New Jersey with her husband and son.

Vivian Vasquez is assistant professor of reading and language arts at American University in Washington, D.C. Her research interests include exploring critical literacy in practice, looking specifically at how to negotiate spaces within curriculum to address issues of social justice and equity which are raised by the social and cultural lives of the students. She is also interested in looking at how language and literacy education in teacher-education programs contributes to social justice. Formerly, she was a preschool and elementary teacher for fourteen years.

This book was typeset in Sabon.
The typeface used on the cover
is ITC Officina Sans.
The book was printed by
Versa Press, Inc., on 50-lb. Opaque.